The
Connectir
to Your Story

Kenneth Onstot

LUCAS PARK BOOKS

ST. LOUIS, MISSOURI

ISBN: 978-1-60350-005-0

Published by Lucas Park Books
www.lucasparkbooks.com

Contents

Introduction

In a class introducing people to the Bible, I sometimes hand out a list of 12 Bible stories and ask class members to number them in the order in which they take place. The events are

_____ Adam and Eve eat the forbidden fruit.

_____ Jesus is born in Bethlehem.

_____ The Babylonians destroy Jerusalem and take the people of Israel into exile.

_____ Moses parts the Red Sea and leads the Israelites out of slavery.

_____ Noah builds the ark.

_____ Jesus is crucified and rises from the dead.

_____ Abraham almost sacrifices his son Isaac.

_____ Joshua wins the battle of Jericho.

_____ Joseph is sold into slavery in Egypt.

_____ David slays Goliath.

_____ The church grows and spreads across the Mediterranean.

_____ Daniel survives in the lions' den.

Before proceeding, try your hand at putting these 12 events in order. The correct order is found in Appendix A.

I have discovered that most people are familiar with many if not all of the stories on the list. This is true even for those who have little background in a church. Thanks to Christmas, everyone has heard the story of Jesus' birth in a stable in Bethlehem. Thanks to movies like *The Ten Commandments* or *Prince of Egypt*, most people in our culture are

1

acquainted with the story of how Moses led the people of Israel out from slavery in Egypt. Thanks to musicals like *Joseph and the Amazing Technicolor Dream Coat*, many people know the story of how Joseph was sold by his brothers as a slave and became one of the chief rulers in Egypt. Thanks to bathtub toys, many children grow up with some knowledge of Noah and the ark. These and other Bible stories like David and Goliath and Daniel in the lions' den are still popular fare in children's books, church school lessons, and children's animated videos.

But very few people in the class, even those who had attended churches for years, could put all of these events in the proper sequence. While people in our culture still know many Bible stories, they have little concept of how these stories fit together into a larger story. Hence they approach the Bible with a sense of disorientation.

This is aggravated by the style of preaching practiced in many churches. In liturgical churches pastors preach each week from the lectionary—selected passages from the Old or New Testament. The focus is on individual texts, not on large segments of the Bible covering entire books or sections. In other churches the sermons focus on specific topics related to Christian living: marriage, parenting, finances, forgiveness, witnessing, or other practical issues. In these sermons brief Bible texts are often quoted as illustrations or authorizations for the points being made, but the broad sweep of the Bible story is lost.

These styles of preaching have three effects: 1) Even when people know many Bible stories or verses, they have no idea how these stories or verses fit together into a larger whole. 2) People miss some of the issues and dynamics at work in the individual stories because they do not know the larger plot into which these stories fit. 3) People do not see how they personally fit into the Biblical story. They may appreciate the "lessons for living" in the Bible, but they fail to see that the Bible invites us to be part of something bigger: a massive, worldwide, generations-long movement by God to restore a broken creation.

On this last point I am reminded of a story told by William Willimon. He met a man in his church who had served in the army during World War II, participating in the D-day invasion of Normandy. The man told of harrowing experiences of danger and deprivation, but then he said, "Still, I look back on those four years as the very best years of my life. For once in my life I really had the feeling that I was part of something bigger than myself. I was on the move. We had a mission."[1]

When the Bible is seen only as a collection of isolated stories which illustrate general religious truths, we miss seeing the larger drama in which we have a part. The Bible not only teaches us how to live but why. It reminds us that we are part of something bigger than ourselves. We have a mission.

This book focuses on the overarching plot of the Bible. The plot of a story is more than a list of the events that took place. It is a description of how the events are connected in ways that move toward a climax. E. M. Forster gives this example: "'The king died and then the queen died' is a story. 'The king died and then the queen died of grief' is a plot."[2] The difference between the two is in the way the events are meaningfully linked. A plot has patterns of connections between events that unfold in a certain direction toward a particular end.

This is also true of the Bible. The seemingly isolated events and stories in the Bible are connected in a larger movement toward a particular end. Along the way there are unexpected twists and turns, setbacks and recoveries, developments of character, and foreshadowing of future events, but the story keeps moving in a certain direction. This movement or flow of the story gives us a glimpse of how God works, not just in individual lives but in the whole sweep of human history.

There are several traditional elements of a plot:[3]

1. Exposition—the background information that sets up the plot
2. Crisis—a peak in the tension of the story needing resolution

3. Climax—the decisive turning point in resolving the tension
4. Resolution or denouement—the final stage of tying together loose ends and showing how the climax resolves the crisis.

The Bible's plot has these elements. The creation of the universe could be considered the exposition of the story. The crisis is human sin. The climax is Jesus' life, death, and resurrection. The story of Revelation could be considered the denouement. But this does not begin to capture the many subtleties in how this plot develops. Within the Bible's plot there are a number of recurring *plot-patterns*. These patterns are not just literary devices; they are theological expressions of how God works in our lives and world. Some of these recurring patterns are

1. Promise, threat, and deliverance
2. The ripple effect of sin
3. God's tendency to choose unexpected people
4. The narrowing of God's focus in order later to expand it (exclusiveness for the sake of inclusiveness)
5. A covenant relationship between God and people where both are bound by certain commitments
6. The sovereignty of God displayed through ironic use of human actions and decisions
7. Concern for the real world of environment, economics, politics, and family life.
8. Foreshadowing of later twists in the plot
9. Living for a promise not fulfilled in one's lifetime
10. The fulfillment of God's promises through a person rejected by God's people

This is not an exhaustive list, but it illustrates the dynamics of the Bible's plot—patterns that we see more plainly when looking at the broad sweep of scripture, and not just at individual stories.

Many writers have described the movement or flow of the Bible in terms of a progression:

1. A progression from law to gospel

2. A progression from promise to fulfillment
3. A progression of covenants: Noah, Abraham, Moses, David, and Jesus
4. A progression from bondage to liberation
5. A progression of dispensations (different rules and expectations for how God will relate to people at different times)

There is validity in all of these patterns. But the plot of a story is seldom a simple progression. There are unexpected twists and turns, as well as set backs and surprises, and these are as important to understanding God's work in our lives as the simple progression from law to gospel or promise to fulfillment. This presentation of the Bible's plot leans heavily on the progression from promise to fulfillment, but the subtleties of the plot incorporate many other dynamics as well: irony, foreshadowing, conflict, threat, reversal, and resolution—elements of the plot that tell us much about how God works in human history.

This is different than an historical-critical approach to the Bible. The historical-critical approach analyzes the Bible in terms of when the text was written, who might have written it, its purpose or setting in the community's life, and whether the story is "historical"—meaning whether it actually happened in the way described. These are important issues, but they are not the focus of this book. I am less concerned about who wrote a particular story than in how it fits into the plot of the Bible as a whole. The approach of this book is "canonical" in the sense that it focuses on the Bible in its final form, not on issues of authorship, sources, or historical verifiability.

In his book *The Eclipse of the Biblical Narrative* Hans Frei notes that beginning in the 18th century Bible commentators lost sight of the Bible story as a narrative and began to focus on two other issues: 1) History—whether the story as depicted in the Bible actually happened, or 2) Theology—whether the story illustrates a timeless moral or religious truth that can be stated as an abstract principle without the need for a story.[4]

An example of the first approach is the debate about whether there could have been a fish in the Mediterranean Sea big enough to swallow Jonah and whether Jonah could have survived in such a fish for three days. An example of the second approach is looking for a timeless "lesson" to be learned from the story of Jonah, like "You can't run from God" or "God loves even our enemies."

Both of these approaches treat the story of Jonah as an isolated event. They fail to appreciate that the story of Jonah is part of a larger plot. We will not understand the purpose of God sending Jonah to Nineveh unless we understand the strategy God has been pursuing since the days of Abraham. In the story of Jonah, God's actions and Jonah's actions weave together in ironic and complex ways toward God's ultimate purpose, a purpose that God has been pursuing since the early chapters of the Bible and which is fulfilled in the book of Revelation.

It is revealing that many people have heard of Jonah and the whale, but they could not tell you why God wanted Jonah to go to Nineveh or why Jonah did not want to go. Such questions are much more important to understanding the story than the question of how someone might survive in a fish for three days.

The inability to see the true significance of Jonah stems from a failure to understand the big picture. The dynamics in the story of Jonah are a microcosm of the whole story of Israel. Israel was chosen by God for a mission. Like Jonah they proved unfaithful to that mission, and as a result they were "cast out." But God rescued them, just as God rescued faithless Jonah, and in the end the mission of Israel in the world succeeded, just like the mission of Jonah, but in a totally unexpected way.

Large portions of the Bible are not narratives and therefore do not have what we normally call a "plot." One third of the book of Exodus contains architectural plans for the tabernacle. Most of the books of Leviticus and Deuteronomy contain laws governing the life and worship of the people. Psalms, the longest book of the Bible, is a collection of hymns. Proverbs is a collection of wise sayings. The last half of the Old Testament is a collection of messages from various prophets. About one-third of the New Testament is letters written to specific churches. None of these parts of the Bible have what you would call a plot. Yet they are all in one way or another connected to a plot. It is not by accident that the laws of Exodus, Leviticus, Numbers, and Deuteronomy are given to the people of Israel in the middle of their journey to the Promised Land. The giving of God's law to the people of Israel at this particular moment in the story is itself part of the plot. I will explain more about that in chapter 3. Even some of the psalms have brief introductions tying them to elements of the story that have been told up to that point. The same is true for the writings of the prophets. This will be covered in chapters 5 and 6. The letters in the New Testament are part of a story which begins in Acts and culminates in the book of Revelation (see chapters 8 and 9). Even the non-narrative parts of the Bible have new meaning when viewed as part of a larger story.

When we view the Bible in terms of a plot, we not only discover how the Bible fits together, we discover new dimensions to the individual stories. At one level the story of Abraham offering to sacrifice his son Isaac is a heartrending test of Abraham's faith. But when viewed in terms of the Bible's larger plot it is also a test of God. I will explain this in chapter 2.

In the pages that follow I will not try to cover every Bible story or even every book of the Bible. Nor will I try to explain every issue or solve every problem of Biblical interpretation. (Some questions of interpretation are dealt with in the endnotes.) The goal is to keep the big picture in view. I will try to cover enough stories to give you a feel for the entire Bible. But the goal is to show you the whole puzzle in a short book, so that when you come across the individual pieces, you will know where and how they fit.

At the end of each chapter I will offer suggested sections of the Bible to read and questions for reflection. I recommend reading the suggested sections of the Bible *after* reading the chapter of this book.

One final point: I do not claim that this book represents

the only way to view or describe the Bible's plot. The very fact that we have four gospels proves there are multiple ways to tell the story of Jesus' life, each helping us see it from a different angle. In the Old Testament books of I and II Chronicles, the story of David and the kings of Israel is retold from a different perspective than in the books of II Samuel and I and II Kings. Even within individual books of the Old Testament, a single story may be recounted multiple times from different angles (probably from different sources) to show us different aspects of its meaning. I suspect that the Bible's plot could also be described in different ways, giving us different angles on its meaning.

This short book does not begin to tell you everything you need to know about the Bible. It is only a short introduction. But I hope it gives you a helpful way of looking at the Bible that accomplishes three goals:

1. To show how individual stories of the Bible fit into a larger story.
2. To show how the meaning of individual stories is shaped and changed by the larger story.
3. To show how we today fit into that story.

The Bible is not just the story of people who lived long ago. It is our story. The plot of the Bible is still unfolding, and we are invited to be part of it.

1

The Good Life and What Went Wrong

In a *Calvin and Hobbes* comic strip, the young boy Calvin lies in bed with his pet tiger Hobbes and says, "I wonder why man was put on earth. What's our purpose? Why are we here?" Hobbes smiles and says, "Tiger Food." After that Calvin can not go to sleep.[1]

Why are we are here? The Bible's answer to that question will set the stage for the rest of the plot. But first we must look at the Bible's picture of creation.

Creation as an Unfolding Plot

Much time and energy has been spent defending the Bible against science, including tortured attempts to justify a literal interpretation of Genesis 1—that the world was created in six days, not the billions of years claimed by geologists. School boards debate whether the species that inhabit the world today were created individually out of nothing or whether they evolved from a common primitive organism.

But this misses the point of the story. The reference to "days" in Genesis 1 must be considered symbolic. How else do you explain that the sun and moon were created on the *fourth day*? What meaning does a "day" have if the sun has not yet been created? Instead of arguing whether the world could have been formed in seven days, it would be better to ask: Why is the story told this way? There are many parallels between the Bible's description of creation and the description of creation in other ancient writings, but no other ancient writing arranges the creation into a series of seven days. Why does the Bible?

Nothing in nature corresponds to a week. A day corresponds to the time it takes the earth to rotate once on its axis. A year is the time it takes the earth to make one complete revolution around the sun. A month is approximately the time it takes for the moon to revolve around the earth. But there is no precedent in nature for a week. If you ever thank God it's Friday, thank the Jews. They gave us the idea.

Why does Genesis describe creation as happening over seven "days"? By describing it this way, Genesis makes creation part of a plot—an unfolding drama of God's work in the world. As described in Genesis, creation is not a random series of collisions between molecules; it is a work of God moving toward a definite culmination. That culmination is the seventh day, which later became the Sabbath—the day of rest and worship (see Genesis 2:1-3).[2]

Into this unfolding drama God put human beings. Here we reach the first answer to Calvin's question. Why were people put on this earth? To celebrate the Sabbath—to worship God and rest in the joy of God's creation. The Westminster Shorter Catechism says we are here "to glorify God and enjoy God forever." The goal of creation is the Sabbath—the life of glorifying God and enjoying together the goodness of God's gifts. From the very beginning, creation is an unfolding plot headed toward that goal.

This goal is still not realized. Genesis does not mention an evening and morning of the seventh day. The Sabbath is not yet complete, as the writer of Hebrews points out later: "So then, a Sabbath rest still remains for the people of God" (Hebrews 4:9; all Bible quotations are from the New Revised Standard Version, unless otherwise noted). God's rest on the seventh day of creation foreshadows the rest that God will give the whole creation when all things are made new. But that is getting ahead of the story.

Genesis also tells us that people have a special purpose in the creation. We are made in the image of God. The Hebrew word *selem* refers to an image that a foreign ruler might set up in a conquered territory. To say that people are created in the image *(selem)* of God means they are meant to represent God to the rest of creation. This is the sense in which humans have "dominion" over the other animals.[3] We are God's authorized ambassadors to the world. Why were people put on earth? To demonstrate in person God's care for creation.

Genesis, chapter 2, elaborates this point. In many ways Genesis 2 reads like a second retelling of creation. Beginning in the second half of verse 4 it describes the story of creation again, this time beginning with the creation of people and following this with the creation of plants and animals. Even though Genesis 2 may have come originally from a different source than Genesis 1, in combination with Genesis 1 it serves to develop the plot.

What does it mean when chapter 1 says that human beings are given dominion over parts of creation? It means, as chapter 2 explains, that people are caretakers for the creation. "The Lord God took the man and put him in the garden of Eden to till it and keep it" (Genesis 2:15). In verses 19-20 the relationship between the man and the animals is not exploitive or destructive. They are like pets. The man gives them names. Genesis 2 describes a harmony between people and the rest of creation that cannot justify the rape of nature in the name of dominion. Those who exploit nature in destructive ways for greedy and self-centered purposes are not acting in the image of God.

Neither are men who dominate women in exploitive ways. The last section of Genesis 2 concerns the relationship of men and women, particularly in marriage. At this point many people have used the Bible to justify the husband's domination of his wife on the grounds that the woman was made to be a "helper" to the man. (The word helper is a translation of the Hebrew word *ezer*.) But notice two things.

First, the idea of a helper does not imply a subordinate. The Hebrew word *ezer* is used of God in Deuteronomy 33:7 and Psalm 20:2. God may be a "helper" to people, but God is certainly not considered subordinate. Secondly, there is an interesting twist at the end of the story. In Genesis 2:24 the Bible says, "Therefore a man leaves his father and his mother and clings to his wife, and they become one flesh." If the woman were created only for the sake of the man, we would expect that verse to read differently. We would expect it to say, "For this reason the *woman* shall leave her father and mother and cling to her husband." Instead it says that the *man* shall leave his father and mother and cling to his wife. At a wedding ceremony it should be the groom who is given away to the bride! The wording of verse 24 introduces an intentional balance to the story. Just as the woman is created to be a helper for the man, so now the man is called to leave his family in order to be joined to the woman. As chapter 1 says, both are created in the image of God. Both are meant to be God's representatives as caretakers of creation.

You will not find this explained in a science text. Genesis does not need to be defended from science. Its own message needs to be proclaimed, especially in a world where science combined with greed could destroy the rest of creation.

In his book *Foolishness to the Greeks*, Lesslie Newbegin makes this observation:

> A machine is a collection of components that can be analyzed chemically into their elements and physically into the molecular and atomic particles that constitute them. Yet the most exhaustive chemical and physical analysis would not enable me to understand the machine unless I understood the purpose for which it was designed.[4]

Genesis 1-2 is a picture of the purpose for which the world and its human beings were designed. It tells us:

1. Life was initiated by God. God "said" and it happened. This does not exclude natural processes. But it means

that we are created *intentionally*. Life is not an accident, a meaningless collision of chemicals that happened to diversify in amazing ways. We were put here by Someone for a reason.

2. Life has a goal. Creation is an unfolding drama moving toward a goal portrayed in the weekly celebration of the Sabbath: glorifying God and enjoying God's blessings.

3. People have a specific purpose in this drama: to be representatives of God to the creation and to be overseers of the creation for God's good purposes.

Understanding these three points will help the Bible's plot make sense.

What Went Wrong?

By the end of Genesis chapter 2, the world is not only good, it is almost perfect. The man and woman are delighted with each other. They have a harmonious relationship with other living creatures. They have productive, fulfilling work and plenty of food. We are even told that there is a Tree of Life in the midst of the garden. We discover later that the humans might have been able to eat of this tree and live forever. But by the end of chapter 3 they have lost it all. What happened?

Genesis 3:1 says, "Now the serpent was more crafty than any other wild animal that the Lord God had made. He said to the woman, 'Did God say, You shall not eat from any tree in the garden?'" Notice that the first temptation did not come from some otherworldly being with a pitchfork. It came from one of God's own creatures. Admittedly a talking snake is a symbolic figure, but at this point the snake is not identified as Satan or any other spiritual power that might rival God. The snake is one of the wild animals that God made, albeit a talking one.

Temptation happens when we begin to think that we know better than God. The serpent begins by questioning God's reasonableness: "Did God say, 'You shall not eat from any tree in the garden'?" What then are the poor humans supposed to eat? The woman quickly comes to God's defense: "We may eat of the fruit of the trees in the garden; but God said, 'You shall not eat of the fruit of the tree that is in the middle of the garden, nor shall you touch it, or you shall die.'" In the very act of defending God, the woman has discovered that she has the power to judge God—to decide for herself whether or not God is being fair! This opens the door for the serpent. Verses 4-5: "But the serpent said to the woman, 'You will not die; for God knows that when you eat of it your eyes will be opened, and you will be like God, knowing good and evil.'"

At its root all sin is a desire to put ourselves in the place of God. Even when people replace God with an idol, they are replacing God with something they themselves have made. If humans have the power to create gods, then humans are the real God.

The idea of "knowing good and evil" is parallel to this. The difficulty here is that knowing good and evil would seem like a good thing. Shouldn't we all know the difference between good and evil? But when the Bible uses the word "know," it often means more than intellectual knowledge. For example, Genesis 4 begins with the words, "Now the man knew his wife Eve, and she conceived and bore Cain...." You get the impression that "knowing" Eve in a Biblical sense involves more than knowing her name. In the temptation story, to know good and evil does not mean simply to understand the difference between right and wrong. It means to have power over right and wrong. It means to decide the difference between good and bad, right and wrong. That power rightfully belongs to God, but people have wanted to claim it for themselves since the beginning of time.[5]

After the woman eats the fruit and gives some to her husband, we come to one of the first ironies in the Bible's plot. Genesis 3:7 says, "Then the eyes of both were opened, and they knew that they were naked; and they sewed fig leaves together and made loincloths for themselves." Are we really to think that the man and woman did not know they were naked until they ate the forbidden fruit? Of course not. The end of the previous chapter says, "And the man and his wife were both naked, and were not ashamed." The new element that sin brings into the world is shame.

Here is the irony: the man and woman eat the forbidden fruit in order to become like God, and they end up ashamed of being human. When people try to put themselves in the place of God, they end up becoming less than human. Think of all the notorious dictators in the history of the world who have tried to exercise god-like power over people. Think of the effect that slavery had on slave owners or that spousal abuse has on the abusers. People who try to exercise god-like power over others become inhuman. They become not more, but less than the people God created them to be. For a New Testament commentary on this idea read Romans 1:18-32.

The Reverberations of Rebellion

Now we come to a recurring plot pattern of the Bible: the ripple effect of sin. Eating a piece of fruit seems so innocuous. Sure it violates God's command, but what is the big deal? But sin has a ripple effect, like a rock thrown into a pond. First it affects the human beings' relationship to God. They hide from God in the garden. Then it affects their relationship to each other. When God confronts the man about what he has done, the man responds with a classic attempt to shift the blame: "The woman whom you gave to be with me, she gave me fruit from the tree, and I ate" (Genesis 3:12). In effect the man is saying to God, "It is all her fault, and yours." The woman does the same thing. She says to God, "The serpent tricked me, and I ate" (Genesis 3:13).

Sin leads to shame, and shame leads to blame, but the ripple effect of sin is not over. In Genesis 3:15 the Lord says to the serpent, "I will put enmity between you and the woman, and between your offspring and hers; he will strike your head and you will strike his heel." Some see in this verse a reference to the future battle between Satan and Jesus. But there is another more immediate implication of verse 15. In its immediate context verse 15 means that the harmonious relationship between humans and animals has been broken. No longer will humans and animals be able to come together in a peaceful kingdom. Later in the Bible we will read about hopes to restore this harmonious relationship (Isaiah 11:6-9), but for now it has been torn asunder. Humans and snakes are at war.

So are humans with each other. In verse 16 God says to the woman, "I will greatly increase your pangs in childbearing; in pain you shall bring forth children, yet your desire shall be for your husband, and he shall rule over you." The idea that husbands would rule over their wives was not how God created it to be. It was the result of sin. Male domination is another symptom of a fallen creation. So is the pain of having children—a pain, by the way, that does not end at childbirth.

Even our jobs are affected by sin. In verses 17-19 God says to the man, "...cursed is the ground because of you; in toil you shall eat of it all the days of your life; thorns and thistles it shall bring forth for you...By the sweat of your face you shall eat bread until you return to the ground, for out of it you were taken; you are dust, and to dust you shall return."

Here we encounter another recurring plot-pattern of the Bible: the threat to God's promises and God's people, in this case through famine. The world was created to provide plenty of food for people. But because of sin's ripple effect on the creation, work is not always productive. Even people who work may go hungry, sometimes because of poor soil, sometimes from lack of rain, and sometimes because of exploitive abuse of their labor.

Work was not meant to be a curse. The human was created to till the garden of Eden and keep it (Genesis 2:15). There was food for the picking. Presumably the humans could have eaten from the Tree of Life (which was not forbidden!) and lived forever. But all that was lost when they decided it was not enough to be humans loved by God. They wanted to be gods themselves.

The next three chapters of Genesis continue the ripple effect of sin. In chapter 4 Cain murders his brother Abel. Cain is angry because the Lord "had regard for Abel and his offering, but for Cain and his offering he had no regard"

(Genesis 4:4-5). Why did God have regard for Abel and his sacrifice and not for Cain? We are not told. Many reasons have been suggested, but they are all speculation. We see here the first example of yet another plot pattern in the Bible: God chooses and shows favor to particular people for reasons that are not explained.[6] We will see this again in the cases of Abraham, Isaac, Jacob, Joseph, Moses, David, Solomon, and even Jesus' twelve disciples.

A variation of this pattern is God's tendency to choose the younger brother over the older. In the ancient near east the oldest son was assumed to be the "chosen one"—the one who would inherit the majority of the father's property and legacy. But throughout the Bible, God shows a special preference for the younger brother. Abel was younger than Cain. Isaac was younger than Ishmael. Jacob was younger (just barely) than Esau. Joseph was younger than most of his brothers, and David was the youngest. Even Solomon, who succeeded David, was not his oldest. Why does God seem to choose the younger brother? We are not told. But perhaps it emphasizes that the choice belongs to God, not to us or to our culture.

Yet even in choosing to accept Abel's sacrifice, God does not intend to exclude Cain. The Lord says to Cain, "If you do well, will you not be accepted?" This also sets the stage for a recurring plot pattern of the Bible: the narrowing of God's focus in order later to expand it. When God chooses certain people over others, it is not in order to exclude others but eventually to bring God's blessing to them. Unfortunately, Cain does not believe that promise and kills his brother out of resentment, resulting in his banishment from God's presence.

The ripple effect of sin reaches a crisis in Genesis 6:5-6: "The Lord saw that the wickedness of humankind was great in the earth, and that every inclination of the thoughts of their hearts was only evil continually. And the Lord was sorry that he had made humankind on the earth, and it grieved him to his heart." The world was created good, but it has become a place of greed, violence, suffering, and heartbreak.

Noah

At this point God decides to start over. Of course the idea of flooding the world sounds horrible. But at this point the situation in the world is already horrible. Genesis 6:11 says, "Now the earth was corrupt in God's sight, and the earth was filled with violence." The flood is a radical attempt to deal with this situation. In Genesis 1:6-7 God created the world by making a dome called the sky that separated the waters below the earth from the waters above the earth. The world was created when God held back the waters from flooding it. Now God lets go. "In the six hundredth year of Noah's life, in the second month, on the seventeenth day of the month, on that day all the fountains of the great deep burst forth, and the windows of the heavens were opened" (Genesis 7:11). In effect the flood is a return to the state of the earth before God pushed back the waters to let the dry land appear. It is an attempt to start creation over.

And it might have worked, except for one thing: God decided to save Noah and his family. Of course if God had not saved Noah, his family, and at least one pair of each kind of animal, the world would have been empty of human or animal life. It would not have been the world God wanted. But the decision to preserve Noah and his family did not get rid of sin. For as soon as Noah and his family got off the ark, sin came back into the world.

Most retellings of Noah and the ark end with the rainbow where God makes a covenant with Noah and promises never again to destroy the world in a flood (Genesis 9:8-17). The idea of a covenant between God and people is another recurring plot pattern in the Bible. I will say more about this when we come to the covenant between God and Abraham. But the story of Noah does not end with the rainbow. In Genesis 9:21 Noah gets drunk and shames himself and his family by lying uncovered in his tent. One of his sons sees his nakedness but does nothing about it. His brothers, however, go to extraordinary lengths to cover their father without looking at his nakedness (Genesis 9:23).

To understand this story we have to remember one of the laws in Leviticus that would later govern family relationships among the people of Israel. Leviticus 18:6-7 says, "None of you shall approach anyone near of kin to uncover nakedness: I am the Lord. You shall not uncover the nakedness of your father, which is the nakedness of your mother; she is your mother, you shall not uncover her nakedness."

At the very least this law demands respect for parents by not exposing them to the shame of nakedness. The phrase "uncovering nakedness" may also refer to inappropriate sexual contact. At minimum Noah disgraced himself by getting drunk and lying naked in his tent. His son Ham further disgraced him by looking at him and then doing nothing about it. In fact by telling his brothers about it he may have been mocking his father. There is also the possibility that Ham did something even worse, as in some kind of inappropriate sexual contact.[7]

The result is that Noah finally wakes up, discovers what his son has done, and curses his grandson Canaan. One might ask why Ham's son Canaan was cursed instead of Ham. This again goes back to the ripple effect of sin. When Ham behaves shamefully toward his father, such actions tend to be picked up and carried on in future generations. (Consider how often children of alcoholics become alcoholics, or people that were abused as children become abusers.) The point is that sin and the subsequent cursing of relationships is back! The flood did not get rid of the problem. Like a virus that was not completely destroyed, sin is ready to infect a new generation of people.

Babel

The epidemic of sin again reaches world wide proportions in the tower of Babel (Genesis 11:1-9). The story begins with a new technological innovation: bricks and mortar. Up to that point people could only build great monuments by stacking stones on top of each other. But bricks and mortar allowed people to build much greater monuments. So in verse 4 the people said, "Come, let us build ourselves a city, and a tower with its top in the heavens, and let us make a name for ourselves." What does it mean to build a tower with its top in the heavens? At one level it means simply to build a tall tower that reaches high into the sky. But at a deeper level it is another manifestation of the desire to be God. To build a tower up to the heavens is to show that we puny human beings can be like God.

The city's name is Babel, which in Hebrew is the same as the name translated "Babylon." This foreshadows a later development in the plot. A time will come when the Babylonian emperor tries to become like God, creating a worldwide empire and subjugating all the nations of the world including Israel. Isaiah, a later book of the Bible, describes the Babylonian emperor in words reminiscent of the tower of Babel: "You said in your heart, 'I will ascend to heaven; I will raise my throne above the stars of God;...I will ascend to the tops of the clouds, I will make myself like the Most High'" (Isaiah 14:13-14). That is what the people of Babel were trying to do. The tower of Babel represents the Babylonian empire and all future empires that try to amass wealth and power by forcibly uniting people of different languages and nationalities under one ruler. In history we see examples of this in the Greeks under Alexander the Great, the Romans under the Caesars, Napoleon and Hitler in Europe, and Lenin's vision for worldwide communism.

God refuses to let this happen. God knows that any human empire trying to take the place of God will become supremely inhuman. So God confuses the languages of the people and scatters them across the face of the earth. This thwarts the attempt to create a world empire dominated by one language, but it also destroys the harmony of relationships God intended for creation.

Later in the story we will see God's action to bring people together again across language barriers (Acts 2:1-12). But in that story God will not make all languages the same. God will help people communicate his love across different languages.

At the end of Genesis 11 the world is a mess. God created the world good and provided for a harmony of relationships between people and nature. The goal of creation was the Sabbath—a time to glorify and enjoy God forever. But this wonderful creation has been damaged by people who want to be God. What is God to do? God tried wiping out the creation and starting over. But things were as bad after Noah as they were before. How will God get rid of sin without getting rid of people? The plot thickens.

Suggested Readings for Chapter 1

Genesis 1-11. At this point don't worry about the genealogies—the chapters tracing the ancestry of various ethnic groups in the ancient world. Instead notice how the problems of sin escalate to a worldwide scale.

Questions for Reflection

1. How would you answer Calvin's question: Why are you here?
2. In what ways do people today try to put themselves in the place of God? What effect does that have on their lives and the lives of others?
3. In what ways does sin "ripple" across nations and generations? How might an act of wrongdoing or injustice in one place or generation cause acts of wrongdoing or injustice in other places or in future generations?
4. If you were God in the time of Noah, how would you have tried to straighten out the world?

2

One Family for
All Families

Up to this point the plot of the Bible has encompassed
the whole world. In the garden of Eden, Adam and
Eve represented all humanity. In the story of Noah and the
flood, the whole world was involved. The tower of Babel
begins with the whole world speaking one language and
ends with the confusion of languages and the scattering of
people across the face of the earth. Interspersed with these
stories are genealogies: lists of families and their descendants that describe the origins of all the nations that will
later figure in the Bible's story.

But now the plot takes a significant turn. At the beginning of chapter 12 the nations of the world recede into the
background, and the spotlight turns to one man: a descendant of Noah named Abram.

The Promise

Considering how important he is, we are told surprisingly little about Abram. His name means "Exalted Father,"
which is ironic since at this point he has no children. At the
end of Genesis 11 we are told that his wife is barren.

Genesis 12, verses 1-3, are, arguably, the three most important verses in the Old Testament:

> Now the Lord said to Abram, "Go from your country and your kindred and your father's house to the land that I will show you. I will make of you a great nation, and I will bless you, and make your name great, so that you will be a blessing. I will bless those who bless you, and the one who curses you I will curse; and in you all the families of the earth shall be blessed."

In these verses God makes three sweeping promises to Abram:

1. To give Abram a land. At this point Abram is what the Bible calls a "sojourner"—a nomad going from country to country herding his flock and trying to make a living. Abram is not told where this Promised Land might be. He is told simply to set out on a journey to a place that God will show him.
2. To make Abram a great nation. The first requirement in becoming a great nation is to have descendants, which Abram did not have. How these non-existent descendants with no land will become a great nation is yet to be explained.
3. Through Abram to bring blessing to all the families of the earth.

Let me comment on this last promise. There is some disagreement about how to translate the end of Genesis 12:3. Some translations read: "by you all the families of the earth will bless themselves" (see the footnote in the New Revised Standard Version). This could be taken to mean that Abram will not bring blessing to other people so much as he will be blessed in a way that other families envy. Other families will say to one another, "May you be blessed like Abram."

Even though there is some ambiguity in how to translate Genesis 12:3, the effect of both translations is essentially the same. Old Testament scholar Claus Westerman argues that even the translation "all the families of the earth are to bless themselves in you" implies that Abram (later named Abraham) and his family will bring blessing to other families of the earth. He writes, "Where one blesses oneself with the name of Abraham, blessing is actually bestowed and received. When the name of Abraham is spoken in a prayer of blessing, the blessing of Abraham streams forth; it knows no bounds and reaches all the families of the earth."[1]

Another Old Testament scholar, Gerhard Von Rad, takes a different approach but arrives at a similar conclusion. He writes, "Abraham is assigned the role of a mediator of blessing in God's saving plan, for 'all the families of the earth.' The extent of the promise now becomes equal to that of the unhappy international world, an idea that occurs more than once in the Old Testament."[2] In other words, no matter how one translates Genesis 12:3, the ultimate goal is the same. God intends to reverse the effect of the curses that descended on the world as a result of sin. (Recall Genesis 3:14-19 and the many tragic events that followed.) Through Abram and his descendants God intends to replace curse with blessing and to do this for all the families of the earth.

I have discussed this issue at some length because it affects the entire plot of the Bible. We have reached a turning point. For the remainder of the Old Testament, the other nations of the world fade into the background, and our primary focus is on one man and his descendants. Other nations are not absent from the story, but they are viewed solely in terms of their relationship to Abram and his descendants who are the key to God's blessing for the world.

If you doubt the importance of this promise, note how it is repeated to each new generation of Abram's children: Genesis 22:16-18 (to Abraham and Isaac), Genesis 26:2-5 (to Isaac), and Genesis 28:13-14 (to Jacob). Throughout the Bible people are reminded of this promise. (Read ahead in Isaiah 2:2-4 and Isaiah 49:6.) This promise is also quoted in the New Testament: Acts 3:25 and Galatians 3:8. It would not be exaggerating to say that the rest of the Bible is the story of what happens to this promise, including the many things that threaten it and the surprising ways in which it is rescued and fulfilled.

Why is Abram chosen to be the bearer of this promise? We are not told. But this illustrates another recurring pattern in the Bible. God often chooses the least likely people to carry out the most important parts of the plot. The only reason I can discern why God chooses Abram is that God likes to do things the hard way. Why else would God promise land to a migrant? Why else would God promise descendants to one who was childless? Why else would God bring blessing to other nations through a family that needed help from other nations just to survive? The Bible shows us repeatedly that the power to fulfill God's purpose lies in God and not in us.

Note the prominent role of *land* in this promise. The promise of land illustrates another pattern in the Bible's plot: God's concern for the real world of environment, economics, and politics. Later when God rescues the people of Israel from slavery in Egypt, God brings them back to a land of their own. Many of the laws given to the people of Israel are meant to insure that everyone will have a place in this land. A return to the land after the exile is a major theme of the prophets. A safe productive land on which to dwell is very much part of God's concern, a concern that does not apply only to the people of Israel.[3]

This brings us to another recurring pattern in the Bible's plot: the narrowing of God's focus in order later to expand it. For the next 1000+ years and the next 900+ pages of the Bible, the plot will follow Abram and his descendants almost exclusively. It may seem unfair that God would lavish so much attention on one person or one nation, but the Bible never loses sight of the goal. Through this one man and his descendants, God intends to bring blessing to all the families of the earth. How this works is the plot we will follow through the remainder of the Bible.

Threats to the Promise

Almost every story that follows affects one or more of God's three promises to Abram. First there is a famine in the land to which God brings Abram and Sarai. Some Promised Land! Abram and Sarai are forced to flee to Egypt to get food (Genesis 12:10-20). Here the Bible foreshadows an event that will recur several more times in the book of Genesis: a famine that threatens the ability of Abraham's family to survive in the Promised Land.

This time, however, Abram almost throws away his chance of having descendants. Fearful that he might be killed so that Pharaoh could marry his beautiful wife, Abram says that Sarai is his sister. This is incredibly stupid. Hearing that Sarai is not Abram's wife, Pharaoh immediately takes her into his harem. At this point God afflicts Pharaoh with plagues to show that he is doing something wrong. This foreshadows an event that we will read about in the next book of the Bible: God producing plagues against the Egyptians to persuade them to release God's chosen people. The irony is that Pharaoh is more "God fearing" than Abram realizes. When Pharaoh finds out that Sarai is Abram's wife, he immediately restores her to Abram and demands to know why Abram tried to deceive him. Here is the first of many cases where people outside God's chosen family respond more faithfully to God than those inside the chosen family.

The biggest problem with God's promise to Abram is the lack of a child. As in the case of the famine in chapter 12, Abram tries to take matters into his own hands and ends up creating a mess. He follows Sarai's suggestion to have children by her slave Hagar (a kind of ancient surrogate womb, Genesis 16). This works. Hagar has a son by Abram, named Ishmael. But this is not what God had in mind for the promise. In Genesis 17 God repeats the promise of many descendants to Abram, only this time God insists that the promise will be fulfilled through Sarai. As if to emphasize the point, God changes both of their names. Abram's name is changed to Abraham, and Sarai's to Sarah. Why does God choose Sarah instead of Hagar to be the mother of the promised child? We don't know. God often chooses people for reasons we are not told. But the goal is to bring blessing to all the families of the earth, so God promises blessing to Hagar's child as well (Genesis 17:20).

In Genesis 17 God's promise to Abraham is made part of a covenant. "I will establish my covenant between me and

you, and your offspring after you throughout their generations, for an everlasting covenant, to be God to you and to
your offspring after you" (Genesis 17:7). As the creator of
the universe God need not be bound to us at all. We have no
inherent claim on God's loyalty. But God binds himself to
Abraham in a covenant, just as earlier God made a covenant
with Noah. Both covenants begin with God's promises and
are declared to be "everlasting covenants." Both covenants
are accompanied by signs. In Noah's case the sign is a rainbow. In Abraham's case the sign is circumcision (Genesis
17:10).

The making of covenants is another recurring pattern in
the Bible's plot. The word covenant defines the two major
sections of the Bible. The Latin word for covenant is testa-
mentum from which we get the word testament. The Old
Testament portrays the old covenants that God made with
Noah, Abraham, Moses, and David. The New Testament
describes the new covenant that God established through
Jesus Christ. All covenants involve promises from God
accompanied by a sign or seal of the promise. Most covenants also require something from us: a sign of our acceptance of God's promise and our willingness to live by that
promise. The problem comes when human beings fail to
keep their side of the covenant. How will God keep an everlasting covenant with people who chronically break it? That
is a recurring issue in the Bible's plot.

Meanwhile Abraham still does not have a child by Sarah,
and Sarah has trouble believing it will ever happen. After all,
she is now 90 years old. She has long since passed through
menopause (Genesis 18:11). When the promise of having a
child is repeated to Abraham in chapter 18, Sarah overhears
and laughs. But the next year when Sarah has a child, Abraham names him Isaac, which means "He laughs." God has
the last laugh.

The Sacrifice

In Genesis 22 we come to a disturbing story. Verse 1-2:

After these things God tested Abraham. He said to
him, "Abraham!" And he said, "Here I am." He said,

"Take your son, your only son Isaac, whom you love, and go to the land of Moriah, and offer him there as a burnt offering on one of the mountains that I shall show you."

One attempt to explain this story claims that Abraham thought of sacrificing his son because child sacrifice was practiced by other religions of his time. Abraham thought that if other people were willing to sacrifice children for their gods, he should be willing to do at least that much for his God. According to this interpretation, the story shows that God does not want human sacrifice, only the sacrifice of animals.

But the idea for this sacrifice comes not from Abraham but from God. And here is the truly shocking part of the story: not only does God ask Abraham to kill his only beloved son, God endangers the promise to Abraham in the process. God's entire plan to bring blessing to the world hinges on the descendants of Abraham and Sarah. But Abraham and Sarah have no other descendant than Isaac. What is God thinking? If Abraham sacrifices Isaac, what will happen to the promise?

The story that follows is an amazing narration. We are told that Abraham gets up early and packs. He cuts the wood for the burnt offering and loads it. He takes the knife he will use for the sacrifice, then sets out with Isaac and two of his servants to the land of Moriah. It takes three days to get there. When they get in sight of the mountain, Abraham tells his servants to wait while he and Isaac go on ahead to worship. On the way Isaac suddenly asks, "Father, the fire and the wood are here, but where is the lamb for the burnt offering?" Isaac does not know what is about to happen! Abraham says, "God himself will provide the lamb for the burnt offering, my son." Then they journey on together.

The story is told at an excruciatingly slow pace. Each step of the way we agonize over what will happen. Will Abraham go through with it? Will God stop it? When? How long will God let this test go on?

They arrive at the site, and the story slows down even

more. Step by laborious step Abraham builds the altar, lays out the wood, binds his son Isaac, lays him on top of the altar, on top of the wood. Every detail stretches out the story, building the tension and anguish. Then Abraham takes his knife and raises it to kill his son.

Let me stop here a moment. In this whole story there has not been the slightest indication that Abraham will back down. Every step Abraham takes shows that he intends to obey God's command. Abraham may not have trusted God earlier in the story, but he certainly does now. The question is this: What is God going to do? When will God step in? What will happen if God lets Abraham go through with it?

We are told this is a test of Abraham, but it is also a test of God. Will God preserve the chosen people and fulfill the promises given to them even when God is the one putting them at risk?

In the coming chapters we will encounter times when the Israelites, the descendants of Abraham, felt like Isaac on that altar—that God was about to let them die and give up on the promises made to Abraham. They felt that way in Egypt when they were slaves of Pharaoh. They felt that way at the time of the judges when they were periodically harassed by foreign powers. They felt that way when they were conquered by the Assyrians and Babylonians, and their homes and temple were destroyed, and many of their people were killed or sent into exile. The disciples also felt that way when they watched God's own son sacrificed on a cross. Perhaps you have felt that way in your own life. How could God let this happen? Is God throwing in the towel on God's own promises?

At the last moment God intervenes. "But the angel of the Lord called to him from heaven, and said, 'Abraham, Abraham!' And he said, 'Here I am.' He said, 'Do not lay your hand on the boy or do anything to him, for now I know that you fear God, since you have not withheld your son, your only son, from me'" (Genesis 22:11-12). And Abraham saw a ram caught in some bushes and took the ram to offer as a sacrifice instead of his son Isaac. Then Abraham gave a name to the place. Abraham has a sense of humor with names. He called the place "Yahweh yireh" which means "the Lord will provide."

The Descendants

As the story continues, Sarah dies and is buried in a plot of land purchased from the Hittites (Genesis 23). Later Abraham is buried in the same plot. This is the only piece of the Promised Land that Abraham ever owns: a family burial plot! Here we are introduced to another recurring pattern in the Bible: God's people live for a promise that they do not see fulfilled in their own lifetime.

Isaac faces his own challenges in the Promised Land. He becomes a farmer and prospers, but his expanding possessions and herds make the Philistines who live in that land nervous. They try to get rid of him by filling up his wells with dirt. But he moves on from there and digs more wells, and God continues to bless him (Genesis 26:12-22). Note the implication of this story. There is room in the Promised Land for Israel and for other people! We will come back to that point later.

A bigger challenge for Isaac is his children. His wife Rebekah has twins: Esau and Jacob. They fight each other even from the womb. Esau turns out to be a blue-collar kind of guy—a hunter, a man of the field. Jacob is more white-collar, or perhaps domestic—a quiet man living in tents. The conflict is made worse by parental favoritism. Genesis 25:28 says, "Isaac loved Esau, because he was fond of game; but Rebekah loved Jacob."

This sets up the great deception in Genesis 27. Isaac is old and blind. He tells his favorite son Esau to hunt game, prepare a meal, and bring it to him, "so that I may bless you before I die." This blessing is tied to the promise to Abraham. When Isaac finally gives the blessing he says, "Let peoples serve you and nations bow down to you. Be lord over your brothers, and may your mother's sons bow down to you. Cursed be everyone who curses you, and blessed be everyone who blesses you!" (Genesis 27:29). Note the similarity of these words to the promise God made to Abraham. Isaac intends to make Esau the inheritor of God's promise

to Abraham, which in that culture seems logical since Esau
is the first born—just ahead of his twin brother.

But Rebekah has plans of her own. She persuades Jacob
to dress up in Esau's clothes and to put hair on his bare
skin, so he will feel hairy like Esau. In this way Jacob hopes
to trick his father into giving him the blessing that Isaac
intends to give Esau.

Can a person steal a blessing? Apparently so. Fooled
by the ruse, Isaac blesses Jacob with the blessing he had
intended for Esau, making Jacob instead of Esau the "lord"
over his brothers and inheritor of the promise. Later when
Esau shows up and Isaac discovers what has happened, he is
powerless to reverse what he has done (Genesis 27:35-37).

Here is yet another plot pattern that we will see throughout the Bible—what I call the sovereign irony of God. Back
when Esau and Jacob were still in the womb, God said that
"the elder [Esau] would serve the younger [Jacob]." Apparently God chose Jacob to be the bearer of the promise even
before they were born. Why did God choose Jacob? We don't
know. Jacob certainly does not impress us with his integrity.
God's choice of Jacob is pure grace—an undeserved favor.
But here is the irony. Isaac does not intend to carry out God's
choice. Isaac wants Esau to be the inheritor of the promise.
But through a nefarious deception engineered by Rebekah,
Isaac carries out God's choice without intending to. God
uses human actions, even wrongful actions, in ironic ways
to fulfill God's purpose.

Of course when Esau finds out what has happened, he
vows to kill Jacob, and Jacob has to flee for his life. Jacob
becomes the inheritor of the Promised Land, but he cannot
live in it. He must live in exile in the land of his mother's
family. This foreshadows what happens to Jacob's family
later in Genesis and even later during the time of the Babylonian exile. But before he leaves the Promised Land Jacob
has a dream of a ladder reaching up to heaven with angels
ascending and descending on it (Genesis 28:10-22). This is
the basis for the song: "We Are Climbing Jacob's Ladder."
The most important part of the dream is that God repeats to
Jacob the promise God made to Abraham:

I am the Lord, the God of Abraham your father and
the God of Isaac; the land on which you lie I will
give to you and to your offspring; and your offspring shall be like the dust of the earth, and you
shall spread abroad to the west and to the east and
to the north and to the south; and all the families
of the earth shall be blessed in you and in your offspring (Genesis 28:13-14).

As in the case of Abraham, God promises to give Jacob
many descendants who will live in the Promised Land and
bring blessing to all the families of the earth. But at this
point Jacob is fleeing the Promised Land to live as an exile
with his uncle Laban. Jacob agrees to work for Laban seven
years for the right to marry his daughter Rachel. After seven
years Laban finally agrees to the marriage, but on the day of
the wedding when the veiled bride comes down the aisle,
Laban substitutes his older daughter Leah, and Jacob ends
up marrying the wrong person (Genesis 29:1-30). Sort of a
nice touch, don't you think, considering what Jacob did to
Isaac? Even when we are chosen by grace, the ripple effect
of deception has ways of catching up to us.

In the end Jacob marries both Leah and Rachel and has
twelve sons and a daughter. For the first time in the story it
appears that the promise of many descendants to Abraham
might finally be fulfilled. But Jacob is still far from the Promised Land, and God wants him to go back. In Genesis 31:3
the Lord says to Jacob, "Return to the land of your ancestors
and to your kindred, and I will be with you." The kindred,
of course, include Esau. In order to return to the Promised
Land and claim the blessing promised to Abraham, Jacob
must make peace with Esau. Once again we see that God is
concerned not just with the chosen people, but with all the
families of the earth.

Jacob is nervous about this meeting with Esau, especially when he hears that Esau is coming to him with four
hundred men. But God meets Jacob that night and gives
him a new name. We have seen before the importance of
names. The new name given to Jacob is Israel, which means

"strives with God"—a good name for the people of Israel during most of their history.

In hopes of buying Esau's favor, Jacob sends wave after wave of gifts: 220 goats, 220 sheep, 30 camels, 40 cows, 10 bulls, and 30 donkeys. This is major appeasement. But Esau brushes aside all these gifts. Genesis 33:4 says, "But Esau ran to meet him, and embraced him, and fell on his neck and kissed him, and they wept." Apparently Esau has learned more about grace than Jacob. The non-chosen one shows more understanding of God than the chosen one.[4]

I wonder if this whole story does not have implications for the current situation in the Middle East. The people of Israel (Jacob) cannot inherit the "Promised Land" unless they are reconciled with their neighbors in the land.

Saved by the Rejected Brother

Jacob's name was changed to Israel, and Jacob's twelve sons became the ancestors of the twelve tribes of Israel. At this point Abraham has many descendants, but those descendants still do not get along with each other.

Enter Joseph, one of Jacob's twelve sons, born to his favorite wife Rachel. At best Joseph was a spoiled brat. Genesis 37:3 says, "Now Israel loved Joseph more than any other of his children, because he was the son of his old age; and he made him a long robe with sleeves." (The Greek version of the Old Testament calls this long robe "a coat of many colors.") Here again we see the kind of parental favoritism that produces problems between siblings in a family.

Joseph makes matters worse. It is bad enough that he stays home while his brothers are herding the flocks. (Remember how Jacob preferred to stay in the tents while Esau was out in the fields.) But when Joseph is sent to see how his brothers are doing, he brings back a bad report (Genesis 37:2). He tattles! Then he has the gall to tell his brothers that he had a dream about them: He said to them, "Listen to this dream that I dreamed. There we were, binding sheaves in the field. Suddenly my sheaf rose and stood upright; then your sheaves gathered around it, and bowed down to my sheaf" (Genesis 37:6-7).

His brothers are outraged. They say to him, "Are you indeed to reign over us? Are you indeed to have dominion over us?" Even if Joseph had the dream, he would have done better to keep his mouth shut.

With the special treatment, the tattling, and the bragging, Joseph has completely alienated his brothers. When he shows up one day to check on them, they decide to kill him. Then one of the brothers named Judah, says, "No, let's not kill him. Let's sell him as a slave. We can get rid of him, make a little money, and not have his murder on our hands." So they sell Joseph as a slave to a passing caravan headed for Egypt. They tell his father he was killed by animals and show his torn and bloodied coat as proof.

At this point (Genesis, chapter 38) the Bible's plot leaves Joseph in Egypt and turns its attention to Judah. We learn that Judah marries a Canaanite woman, something Abraham and Isaac did not want their offspring to do (see Genesis 24:3 and Genesis 28:1). They fear that marrying into a Canaanite family will tempt their descendants to worship the Canaanite gods and forget the promises of the Lord. Not only does Judah marry a Canaanite woman, but he chooses a wife for his own son from among the Canaanites—a woman named Tamar.

What follows is not the kind of story you likely heard in Sunday School. Tamar's husband Er dies before they have children. Judah tells his second son Onan to marry Tamar and produce a child with her in behalf of his brother. This is necessary so that Tamar will have children who can inherit the family property and take care of Tamar in her old age. Children were the social security of ancient times. This practice is later established as a law for the people of Israel in Deuteronomy 25:5-10. But Onan does not want to raise a child that will not be considered his own (again see Deuteronomy 25:6). The situation becomes sexually exploitive when Onan agrees to have sex with Tamar, but intentionally spills his semen on the ground so as not to produce a child. This is one of the rare instances in this part of Genesis where the Lord's reaction is specifically mentioned. Displeased with Onan, God puts him to death (Genesis 38:10). After this, Judah is reluctant to give any more of his children in marriage to Tamar, so Tamar is left widowed and childless. Tamar then takes matters into her own hands. Knowing that Judah's wife has died, she disguises herself as a prostitute and stands where Judah might see her and proposition her. He does, and Tamar conceives a child, which forces Judah himself to take responsibility for raising children for Tamar. Supermarket tabloids would love this story.

You might wonder why this sordid affair is even mentioned in the Bible. It turns out that the children born to Tamar out of her illicit relationship with Judah play a crucial role in the Bible's plot, something no one would have expected when they were born.[5]

Now back to Joseph. In Egypt Joseph is sold as a slave to an Egyptian officer named Potiphar. Suddenly Joseph proves that he can work. He also shows good supervision skills. So Potiphar puts him in charge of his whole household. But Joseph runs afoul of Potiphar's wife, who wants to seduce him. When Joseph refuses her advances, she accuses him of attempted rape, and Joseph is sent to prison (Genesis 39).

In all of this Joseph never bemoans his fate. He faithfully and wisely serves wherever he finds himself, and in so doing becomes a blessing to his Egyptian masters. In this way he fulfills part of God's promise to Abraham, even in captivity. While in prison Joseph interprets the dream of Pharaoh's chief cupbearer, and when the dream is fulfilled exactly as Joseph predicted, the cupbearer is impressed (Genesis 40).

Joseph foreshadows a later descendant of Abraham who will find himself in a somewhat similar situation. (You can look ahead at this point to the first two chapters of Daniel, which take place over 500 years later in Israel's history.) Daniel was a captive of the Babylonians, taken into exile when the nation of Israel was conquered in the last days of the Israelite monarchy. Daniel also proved to be a wise and trustworthy servant who interpreted dreams and brought blessing to his masters. Joseph and Daniel show that it is possible to bring God's blessing even to those who enslave you. We will encounter this theme again.

Unfortunately Pharaoh's cupbearer forgets about Joseph, and Joseph continues to languish in prison, until one day Pharaoh has a dream. He dreams about seven cows ugly and lean that swallow up seven cows that are sleek and fat. Pharaoh asks his court officials what the dream means, but they cannot tell him. Then the cupbearer remembers Joseph. He sends for Joseph, and Joseph explains that Pharaoh's dream is about a coming famine. After seven good years of abundant crops, represented by the seven fat cows, there will be seven years of bad crops, represented by the lean cows.

Not only does Joseph interpret the dream, he comes up with a plan to deal with the situation. He proposes the first government farm program. The government will collect one-fifth of the grain harvested during the good years and store it. Then when the bad years come, the excess grain can be sold back to the people to help them survive the famine. Pharaoh considers this a brilliant idea and puts Joseph in charge of the program, which means that when the famine strikes, Joseph is the one handing out food.

The famine is not confined to Egypt; it affects the whole region. (You will remember how Abraham had problems with a famine and had to go to Egypt to get food.) Jacob sends his sons to Egypt to get food, and to whom must they bow to get it? Joseph! The brothers do not recognize Joseph, but Joseph recognizes them. After a complicated bit of testing to see if the brothers will stick up for the youngest brother Benjamin (who has become Jacob's new favorite), Joseph reveals himself to his brothers, and far from seeking revenge, he provides for the whole family, inviting them to come to Egypt and live under his protection for the remaining time of the famine.

I have told this story at length, because it captures many patterns in the Bible's plot. Here is a case where God uses a descendant of Abraham to bless all the families of the earth. Joseph's actions also preserve his own family through a crisis that threatened to terminate the promises of God to Abraham. But this time a new twist is added to the plot: God's chosen people are saved by the very person they rejected. This too will become a recurring pattern.

The story of Joseph is an especially good illustration of the sovereignty of God displayed through ironic use of human actions. Did God sell Joseph into slavery? No, his brothers did. Did God cause Joseph to be thrown into prison unfairly? No, Potiphar's wife did. Did God arrange a chance for Joseph to interpret Pharaoh's dream? No, the cupbearer did. And yet, the whole thing seems to have been part of God's plan all along. The dream of Joseph that his brothers would bow down to him, a dream that seemed so outrageous at the time, was fulfilled in a way that no one expected. And the promises of God to Abraham's descendants were saved in the process. That is the sovereign irony of God.

One final note. There is displayed in all of these stories the Bible's concern for the real world of environment, economics, and politics. In the stories of Abraham, Isaac, and Jacob, God is concerned about land and food, wells and water rights, family relationships and even government programs. Joseph proposes a political solution to an economic problem, and it works. The Bible is not averse to the idea of governmental solutions to human problems.

But there is also a warning in the story. As the seven years of famine drag on, people run out of money with which to buy grain from the government. Finally, they sell their livestock to buy food, but that lasts only so long. The next year they come to Joseph and say, "Shall we die before your eyes, both we and our land? Buy us and our land in exchange for food. We with our land will become slaves to Pharaoh; just give us seed, so that we may live and not die, and that the land may not become desolate" (Genesis 47:19).

Joseph did a good thing in providing a way for government to help the people through a famine. But when government uses its power to enslave people, a catastrophe is waiting to happen. We will see just such a catastrophe take place in the next book of the Bible. Joseph may have saved his family, but his government policies set up the conditions for slavery in Egypt, and that will come back to haunt his own kindred.

Suggested Readings for Chapter 2

Genesis 12-50. You will encounter many details in these chapters that don't make sense to us because of our unfamiliarity with the culture of that time. Study Bibles or Bible commentaries may help you with some of these details. But with the background and perspective of this chapter, Genesis will come alive for you with all the tension, intrigue, and irony of its intergenerational story.

Questions for Reflection

1. What barriers has God had to overcome in your life to make you a blessing to others?
2. Why is the Bible so concerned about land? What role does land have in bringing God's blessing to people?
3. How have the promises of God been passed on to you? How have you tried to pass them on to others?
4. When in your life or in the lives of others has God taken something bad and turned it into something good?

3

From Family to Nation

An elementary school principal in Spokane, Washington, tells the story of two little girls who were hauled into his office for bloodying a large, notoriously mean 4th grader. The principal could not figure out how these two little girls managed to beat up such a big kid. So he said to them, "What did you do?" The girls said, "We were just trying to build a snow fort." "So?" the principal asked. "Well," the girls said, "he kept running and jumping on it and knocking it down." "So?" the principal asked again. "So," the girls said, "we decided to build it over the bike racks."[1]

One of the major plot patterns of the Bible is the ripple effect of sin. Wrongdoing, injustice, and cruelty are never isolated acts. They set in motion ripples of consequences that often come back to haunt the perpetrators. This is seen dramatically in the story of the Exodus.

The Exodus

"Now a new king arose over Egypt, who did not know Joseph" (Exodus 1:8). With those ominous words, a new chapter begins in the story of Abraham's descendants. The new king was afraid of the Israelites. He liked having them around for cheap labor, but he was nervous about the impact that their numbers might have on Egyptian power and privilege. It is somewhat like the uneasy relationship Americans have with immigrants from Mexico.

The king of Egypt did not have the option of putting more patrols on his borders. The Israelite immigrants were already inside the country and had grown to large numbers. So he came up with a different plan for controlling this immigrant population: "Every boy that is born to the Hebrews [the Egyptian name for the Israelites] you shall throw into the Nile, but you shall let every girl live" (Exodus 1:22). The idea was to keep a ready supply of cheap labor through female slaves, but to prevent any armed resistance that might be undertaken by men.[2]

Notice the irony in what happens. Because of Pharaoh's edict, an Israelite couple hides their baby boy until they can no longer conceal him. Then his mother puts him in a papyrus basket that she has made waterproof with pitch, and places it among the reeds on the river bank. We are not told why she did this, but she is obviously hoping that something good will happen to the boy, because she sends his older sister to watch from a distance. Then who should come along but Pharaoh's own daughter? She recognizes that the baby is a Hebrew, but she falls in love with the child and decides to adopt him. Then, since the child is only three months old, she realizes that she needs someone to nurse him. The sister casually strolls up to Pharaoh's daughter and asks, "Shall I go and get a nurse from the Hebrew women to nurse the child for you?" Pharaoh's daughter says, "Yes." So the girl gets the baby's mother, and Pharaoh's daughter pays her to nurse the child.

After this, the child is raised in Pharaoh's house and given training to become a leader of the Egyptians. But he ends up becoming a leader of the Israelites. And in the end he leads the Israelites out of Egypt, which is the very thing Pharaoh's original edict was designed to prevent. That is the sovereign irony of God.

The child's name was Moses. Moses was not immediately welcomed as a leader of the Israelites. In his first attempt at liberation he kills an Egyptian task master who was beating one of the Hebrews. Then Moses tries to stop a fight between two Hebrew slaves. One of them responds, "Who made you a ruler and judge over us? Do you mean to kill me as you killed the Egyptian?" Moses is shocked to be rejected by his own people, and frightened at what might happen when the Egyptians find out what he has done. So he flees into the wilderness for safety (Exodus 2:11-15). As in the case of Joseph, the person who saves Israel is initially rejected by them.

But God appears to Moses in a burning bush and tells him to go back and lead the people of Israel out of slavery. Moses goes, but not before raising an impressive number of reasons why God should send someone else:

- Who am I that I should be the one to go? (Exodus 3:11)
- What if I don't know enough about you to explain who you are to the Israelites? (Exodus 3:13)
- What if they don't listen to me or believe me? (Exodus 4:1)
- I am not a good speaker and never have been (Exodus 4:10)
- Lord, please send someone else! (Exodus 4:13)

Why was Moses chosen? He wonders that himself. But he was, and God promises to be with him, and that is all Moses needs to know.

Of course Pharaoh will not let go of his cheap labor supply without a fight. So Moses pronounces God's judgment on Egypt in a series of plagues. In a sense the plagues are another example of the ripple effect of sin (Exodus 7:14-12:32). Pharaoh ordered all the Hebrew baby boys drowned in the Nile River. So what is the first plague? The waters of the Nile turn to blood. This is not an arbitrary plague. The punishment flows out of the crime, like the injuries resulting from jumping on a snow fort built over bike racks. The second plague is a swarm of frogs that inundate the land. When the Nile turns to blood, the frogs are driven out of the river and cover the land. The third plague is an infestation of gnats, and the fourth is a plague of flies. When the frogs are driven on to the land and die, the gnats and flies swarm around them. Next are the plagues of cattle disease and boils. The gnats and flies spread disease. There is a kind of logic to the plagues, at least the first six. The effect of sin ripples out beyond the human world and affects the whole creation. One only has to remember the effect of war and greed on the environment to understand what this means.

This is not to say that the plagues are merely natural occurrences. Some of the plagues fall only on the Egyptians and not on the Israelites. The plagues are clearly God's judgment on the Egyptians. But the plagues are also an example of the ripple effect of sin on the creation, an effect we will see again as the Bible's plot unfolds.[3]

The last plague is the death of the Egyptian first born male children, which is the final ironic twist in Pharaoh's attempt to kill the Hebrew male children. In preparation for that final plague, the Israelites are instructed to sacrifice a lamb and put its blood on the doorposts of their houses. Then they must gather everyone into their houses for a meal of roast lamb, unleavened bread, and bitter herbs. During the night when the plague comes upon the Egyptian homes, the plague will "pass over" the homes with the blood on the doorposts, sparing the Israelites. In the future this experience is remembered by the Israelites in their celebration of the Passover (Exodus 12).

This foreshadows a later event in the Bible's plot. John's gospel tells us that Jesus was sentenced to death at the very moment when the Passover lambs were sacrificed (John 19:14-16). In the New Testament Jesus becomes the Passover lamb who saves us.

After the Passover Pharaoh gives up and allows the Israelites to leave. They go as quickly as they can, but Pharaoh changes his mind yet again and chases them. When the Israelites find themselves trapped against the Red Sea, God parts the waters of the Red Sea so that the Israelites can escape. But when the Egyptians try to follow, the water closes over them (Exodus 14). The Israelites are free.

Before we leave this story, let me say a word about the "hardening" of Pharaoh's heart. On several occasions the

Bible says Pharaoh hardened his heart against the Israelites (Exodus 8:15, 8:32, and 9:34). This usually happened after a plague had subsided and life had returned to normal. When the crisis passed, Pharaoh became reluctant to give up his cheap labor force. The surprise, however, is the number of times the Bible says God hardened Pharaoh's heart (Exodus 4:21, 7:3, 9:12, 10:1, 10:20, 10:27, 11:10, and 14:4, 8). At other times we are told Pharaoh's heart is hardened, without telling us who did it. But in all but one of these cases we are told Pharaoh's heart was hardened "as the Lord had said"—that it happened as God had planned (Exodus 7:13, 7:22, 8:19, 9:7, and 9:35).

Did Pharaoh harden his own heart against God, or did God harden it? The Bible insists both are true. The Bible's plot unfolds in such a way that God's sovereign will is woven into human actions so that free human beings end up fulfilling God's will even when they did not intend to.

How were God's purposes fulfilled in the hardening of Pharaoh's heart? God explains this in Exodus 7:3-5:

> But I will harden Pharaoh's heart, and I will mul-
> tiply my signs and wonders in the land of Egypt.
> When Pharaoh does not listen to you, I will lay my
> hand upon Egypt and bring my people out of the
> land of Egypt by great acts of judgment. The Egyp-
> tians will know that I am the Lord, when I stretch
> out my hand against Egypt and bring the Israelites
> out from among them.

Notice what this says. God hardened Pharaoh's heart not only so that Israel would know the Lord but so that the *Egyptians* would know the Lord. Remember the promise to Abraham. God plans to work through Abraham and his descendants to bring God's blessing to all nations. The blessing of God begins with the knowledge of God. By hardening his heart against God, Pharaoh actually spreads the knowledge of God among his own people. As a result, some of the Egyptians believe in God and experienced God's blessing even during the plagues. In Exodus 9, after God announces the plague of hail, verse 20 says, "Those officials of Pharaoh who feared the word of the Lord hurried their slaves and livestock off to a secure place." Some of the Egyptians as well as the Israelites were spared from the plague of hail because they believed in the Lord. God's purpose was worked out even when Pharaoh thought he was resisting it. Here again we see the sovereign irony of God.

Later in the story the apostle Paul will see the same pattern of hardening happen to his own people of Israel, but it will work for the same purpose: that the Gentiles might come to know the Lord (see Romans 11:25).

Through the Wilderness

The Israelites escaped from slavery in Egypt only to find themselves facing a new problem: journeying through the desert with no water (Exodus 15:22-24). There is a pattern here. Just when things are going well for the descendants of Abraham, a new crisis arises. Moses saves the people of Israel from dying in Egypt, but now they are threatened by death in the wilderness.

At this point God saves them again by providing clean, safe drinking water (Exodus 15:25). But God also uses this occasion to introduce Israel's responsibility to the relationship. God says,

> If you will listen carefully to the voice of the Lord
> your God, and do what is right in his sight, and give
> heed to his commandments and keep all his statutes,
> I will not bring upon you any of the diseases that I
> brought upon the Egyptians; for I am the Lord who
> heals you (Exodus 15:26).

At the very moment of Israel's liberation from slavery, God reminds them that they are bound by God's commandments. The commandments are the key to experiencing God's blessing.

The next story (Exodus 16) illustrates this. Israel faces yet another threat to its existence: no food. God responds by providing quail and a bread-like substance called manna. At the same time God establishes commandments for the reception of these gifts. First, God tells them to gather only what they need for each day. They shall not try to gather more than they need and hoard it for their future security. This does two things: It teaches the Israelites to trust God daily for their bread, and it teaches them that if they share rather than hoard, there will be enough for everyone.

When they obeyed God's instructions, it worked. Exodus 16:17-18 says, "The Israelites did so, some gathering more, some less. But when they measured it with an omer, those who gathered much had nothing over, and those who gathered little had no shortage; they gathered as much as each of them needed." However when some tried to gather more than they needed for each day and store it up, the manna bred worms and grew foul. When the people of Israel kept God's commandments, there was blessing for everyone. When they did not, their work was cursed. Recall God's words to Adam in the garden of Eden (Genesis 3:17-18).

In gathering manna, God gives the people of Israel special instructions for the sixth day. On the sixth day, they are allowed to gather enough food for two days, so that on the seventh day, the Sabbath, they can rest and worship. If you remember, the goal of creation was the Sabbath—the day when we can worship God and enjoy God's blessings forever. Each weekly Sabbath is meant to be a mini-experience of that goal. When we set aside one day of our week to remember God and give thanks for God's blessings, we celebrate the ultimate goal for which we live and work: that the whole creation may glorify God and enjoy God forever.

But some of the people disobeyed. They went out on the Sabbath to gather more, hoping to get ahead. It is not unlike our consumer-driven society where people work harder and harder to get more stuff, even though they already have enough. The tragedy is that people who work so relentlessly are never fulfilled. Like the Israelites they try to gather manna on the Sabbath but do not find any. There is a connection between keeping God's commandments and experiencing God's blessing.

Mt. Sinai

At this point there is a major break in the story. In Exodus 19, the people of Israel arrive at Mt. Sinai. In terms of distance they are about half way on their journey from Egypt to the Promised Land. However, they do not leave Mt. Sinai until Numbers 10:11, over two years later. In between there is half of the book of Exodus, all of the book of Leviticus, and the first nine chapters of the book of Numbers—a portion of the Bible filled with detailed commandments, instructions, and census lists. How does this fit into the Bible's plot?

Essentially this long stretch of time at Mt. Sinai was Israel's preparation to fulfill its purpose as a nation. At the beginning of this long stay, God says to the people of Israel:

> You have seen what I did to the Egyptians, how I bore you on eagles' wings and brought you to myself. Now therefore, if you obey my voice and keep my covenant, you shall be my treasured possession out of all the peoples. Indeed the whole earth is mine, but you shall be for me a priestly kingdom and a holy nation (Exodus 19:4-6).

Just as God called Abraham, Sarah, and their family, now God calls an entire nation to be his chosen people. They have been blessed in order to become a blessing. But they need training to live out this calling. Mt. Sinai is boot camp for the people of God.

First, the people of Israel need rules for living. Exodus 19 is followed by the Ten Commandments in Exodus 20. The Ten Commandments are the constitution that will allow Israel to experience God's blessing in the Promised Land. When Moses repeats the Ten Commandments and other instructions in the book of Deuteronomy as the Israelites are standing on the border of the Promised Land, he says,

> If you heed these ordinances, by diligently observing them, the Lord your God will maintain with you the covenant loyalty that he swore to your ancestors; he will love you, bless you, and multiply you; he will bless the fruit of your womb and the fruit of the ground, your grain and your wine and your oil, the increase of your cattle and the issue of your flock, in the land that he swore to your ancestors to give you (Deuteronomy 7:12-13).

Moses even suggests that Israel's obedience to the commandments will be a blessing to the other nations. "You must observe [these commandments] diligently, for this will show your wisdom and discernment to the peoples, who, when they hear all these statutes will say, 'Surely this great nation is a wise and discerning people!'" (Deuteronomy 4:6).

If you look closely, many of the seemingly random instructions that follow in chapter 21-23 are applications of the Ten Commandments to specific cases, somewhat like the Supreme Court interpreting the Constitution. For example, the sixth commandment says "You shall not murder." But what if there is an injury that does not result in death? What is the victim's right to justice in that situation? For the answer see Exodus 21:18-19. Or what if someone's ox causes a death? What does justice require in that situation? See Exodus 21:28-32. How does bearing false witness relate to spreading a vicious rumor? See Exodus 23:1. Does remembering the Sabbath day mean giving rest even to your slaves and foreign guest workers? See Exodus 23:12.

Some of these cases will sound odd to us. They apply to a much different culture than ours. But they illustrate one of the recurring patterns in the Bible's plot. God is concerned for the real world of family, property, business, human rights, and justice.

At the end of these "case studies," God establishes a covenant with Moses and the people (Exodus 24). Covenants often signal a new stage in the Bible's plot. Earlier we read about God's covenant with Noah, a promise never again to solve the world's problems with a flood. The sign of the covenant on God's side was a rainbow. The sign of Noah's acceptance of the covenant was a sacrifice. Then we read about God's covenant with Abraham. Isaac was the sign of the covenant on God's side. Circumcision was the sign of Abraham's acceptance of the covenant, as well as a sacrifice Abraham offered to God.

Now we come to God's covenant with Moses. In this covenant God binds himself to a nation: the people of Israel. The sign of this covenant on God's side was deliverance from slavery and giving of the law. The sign of Israel's acceptance was a commitment to obey the law and the offering of a sacrifice. There was also a covenant meal (Exodus 24:9-11). This foreshadows something we will see later in the New Testament: God will establish a new covenant through a meal and a sacrifice. (Note Jesus' words at the last supper: Luke 22:14-20.)

In Exodus, chapters 25-31, Moses goes alone up Mt. Sinai to receive God's commandments written on stone. But he also receives instructions—excruciatingly detailed instructions—for constructing a tabernacle: a mobile center for worshiping God in the wilderness. Within this tabernacle is placed a box containing the commandments given by God to Moses. This box is called the ark of the covenant. What does all this have to do with the plot?

In Egypt God sent Moses to Pharaoh with this message: "Let my people go *so that they may worship me*" (Exodus 8:1; my emphasis). This is repeated several more times over the course of the plagues. God did not set the Israelites free so they could live for themselves and do whatever they wanted. God set them free to glorify and enjoy God. (Remember the seventh day goal of creation.) Worship is the goal for which we were created and for which the people of Israel were saved. So instructions about worship and the construction of a space for worship are quite relevant to the plot at this point in the story.

Unfortunately, the Israelites thought they were free to make their own gods and follow their own desires (Exodus 32). Even as Moses came down from the mountain with the Ten Commandments, the Israelites broke them: worshiping other gods, making graven images, lying about it when Moses questioned them, and possibly even committing adultery ("rose up to revel", Exodus 32:6).[4] In anger Moses smashed the tablets bearing the commandments at the bottom of the mountain, signifying that the covenant was broken.

But God made new tablets of stone for the Ten Commandments, and God also made a new covenant with the people (Exodus 34). The covenant laws were restated, and the people began building the tabernacle.

Here is where the lengthy and seemingly redundant description of the tabernacle's construction becomes important. When building the tabernacle, the people obey God's instructions to the letter. They scrupulously follow every detail. And when the tabernacle is finished, we are told, "Then the cloud covered the tent of meeting, and the glory of the Lord filled the tabernacle" (Exodus 40:34). For the rest of their journey through the wilderness, the tabernacle and ark of the covenant will be visible reminders to the people of Israel that God goes with them into their future. Later, the temple in Jerusalem will serve a similar purpose.

Continuing the Journey

In Numbers 10 the people finally leave Mt. Sinai, and continue their journey to the Promised Land. Again the people of Israel encounter situations that could prevent them from reaching their goal. But this time the obstacles are of their own making.

- They complain to God about the food, and threaten to go back to Egypt where they had meat and cakes. Never mind that they also had slavery and death (Numbers 11).
- They complain about Moses' leadership. His own brother and sister undermine him (Numbers 12). Notice again that the Israelites are saved by someone they reject.
- They approach the Promised Land and send spies to look it over. The spies report that it "flows with milk and honey," but they are afraid to enter it because the people in the land seem so powerful. They have forgotten what God did to the Egyptians (Numbers 13).

At this point God declares that the entire adult generation of the people of Israel will have to die before he brings them into the Promised Land (all except Joshua and Caleb, the two spies who wanted to enter the Promised Land). So the people are condemned to wander another 40 years in the wilderness until the entire adult generation has died and a new generation has taken over.

During those 40 years the same problems recur.

- The people break the commandments (Numbers 15).
- There is a revolt against Moses (Numbers 16).
- The people complain again about the water, and Moses gets in trouble with God because of it (Numbers 20).
- The people again complain about the food, and there is an infestation of snakes (Number 21).
- Some of the Israelites have sex with Moabite women and start worshiping the Moabite gods (Numbers 25).

After all this, it is incredible that the Israelites made it to the Promised Land. God is nothing if not persistent.

The Mountaintop

Before the Israelites enter the Promised Land, Moses delivers one final sermon. It is 33 chapters long: the book of Deuteronomy, which means "second law." Moses reminds the Israelites of all that has happened to that point: the deliverance from Egypt, the grumbling in the wilderness, the Ten Commandments and other laws, the rebellion, and the faithfulness of God to bring them as far as they have come. It is a magnificent sermon, even if a little long.

But it is Moses' last sermon, for he will not be allowed to enter the promise land. One of the most poignant scenes in the Bible is the last chapter of Deuteronomy. Moses goes to the top of Mt. Nebo, which is east of the Jordan River just outside the border of the Promised Land, and looks down at the land he will not be allowed to enter. After all the struggles against Pharaoh in Egypt, after escaping through the Red Sea, after two years of training the people at Mt. Sinai, after 40 years of leading them through the wilderness, after battling two large armies just to get to the border of the Promised Land, now Moses can only look at it from afar. It was for Joshua, his successor, to lead the people into it.

Remember Abraham. All he ever owned in the Promised Land was his family burial plot. He heard the promise and was faithful to it, but he never saw it fulfilled in his lifetime. Remember Joseph. He died in the land of Egypt. He lived to see the day when the descendants of Abraham were numerous, but he did not see the day when they lived in peace and freedom in their own land. Now Moses looks at the Promised Land from afar. He worked for decades to bring the people of Israel into that land, but he did not get to see it happen in his lifetime. As the New Testament says later,

> All these died in faith without having received the promises, but from a distance they saw and greeted them. They confessed that they were strangers and foreigners on the earth.... But as it is, they desire a better country, that is, a heavenly one. Therefore God is not ashamed to be called their God; indeed, he has prepared a city for them (Hebrews 11:13, 16).

Over 3,000 years later Martin Luther King, Jr. addressed a rally of 2000 people in Memphis, Tennessee. Alluding to the story of Moses, he said,

> Well, I don't know what will happen now. We've got some difficult days ahead. But it doesn't really matter...because I've been to the mountaintop.... I've seen the Promised Land. I may not get there with you. But I want you to know tonight, that we, as a people will get to the promise land. And so I'm happy tonight. I'm not worried about anything. I'm not fearing any man. Mine eyes have seen the glory of the coming of the Lord.

The next day he was assassinated. Here is another part of the Bible's plot in which we today still participate.

Conquest

The land promised to the people of Israel was already inhabited. Several nations and tribal groups lived around the Jordan River and on the land between the Jordan River and the Mediterranean Sea. What were God's plans for them?

It is striking to note that God planned for Israel to co-exist with some of the other people groups in the land. Deuteronomy 2 is particularly clear on this point. In verses 4-5 the Lord says,

You are about to pass through the territory of your kindred, the descendants of Esau, who live in Seir [another name for the land of Edom]. They will be afraid of you, so, be very careful not to engage in battle with them, for I will not give you even so much as a foot's length of their land, since I have given Mount Seir to Esau as a possession.

Remember how Jacob was forced to make peace with his brother Esau, before he could return to the Promised Land. The same applies to their descendants. This peace did not always last, but coexisting in peace is what God intended for them.

A similar point is made about the people of Moab. In Deuteronomy 2:9 God says, "Do not harass Moab or engage them in battle, for I will not give you any of its land as a possession, since I have given Ar [another name for the land of Moab] as a possession to the descendants of Lot." In Genesis, Abraham and Lot agreed to coexist in peace, sharing the land (Genesis 13). Now their descendants must do the same.

But there are some people whom God gives Israel permission to dispossess. In Deuteronomy 2:31 the Lord says to the people of Israel, "See, I have begun to give Sihon and his land over to you. Begin now to take possession of his land."

It is hard to reconcile this part of the plot with God's promise to bring blessing to all the families of the earth through Abraham's descendants. Some of the battles that follow in the book of Joshua are horrible. Entire towns are destroyed along with all their men, women, and children (Joshua 6:21, 8:24-26; most of Joshua, chapters 10-11). These stories cause some people to reject the God of the Bible.

The only explanation the Bible gives for these actions is fear that the people of the land will corrupt the people of Israel and tempt them to abandon the Lord. In Exodus 34:12-16 God says to the people of Israel:

Take care not to make a covenant with the inhabitants of the land to which you are going, or it will become a snare among you. You shall tear down their altars, break their pillars, and cut down their sacred poles (for you shall worship no other god, because the Lord, whose name is Jealous, is a jealous God). You shall not make a covenant with the inhabitants of the land, for when they prostitute themselves to their gods, someone among them will invite you, and you will eat of the sacrifice. And you will take wives from among their daughters for your sons, and their daughters who prostitute themselves to their gods will make your sons also prostitute themselves to their gods.

It is like a quarantine to prevent infection. The people of Israel had to be isolated from those infected with the worship of other gods—gods like Molech (who was worshiped with child sacrifice) and Astarte (who was worshiped by rituals of sacred prostitution). To have any hope of bringing blessing to the other nations of the earth, Israel had to be different than those other nations. Israel had to be holy—set apart for the Lord.

Still, it is disturbing to think that God would try to deal with sin by killing people. It did not work in the time of Noah; nor did it work here. Throughout their history the people of Israel are seduced into following false gods, eventually to their ruin. So what was accomplished by all this carnage, except to create animosity that continues to this day?

The Bible does not answer this question. But that is why the Bible should be read as a whole. Joshua is not the last word on God's plan to bring blessing to the world. Obviously it is crucial to the plot that the people of Israel be preserved, and to be preserved they needed a land in which to live. (The 20th century has demonstrated this.) But the slaughter of enemies is not how God will finally save the world or even the people of Israel. There is a radical new twist to the plot that still lies ahead.

Rahab

Even in the book of Joshua there are signs that God is working to bring blessing to people of other nations. One of the best examples is Rahab.

The first city that Joshua must conquer in the Promised Land is Jericho. To see what he is up against, Joshua sends spies into Jericho to assess its defenses. As it turns out, Joshua did not need to send spies. In the end the people of Israel blow trumpets around Jericho and "the walls come a'tumblin down." Who needs spies for that? But a small, yet significant, development in the plot happens because Joshua sends spies.

They meet Rahab. Rahab runs a house of prostitution, which is why the spies figure that no one will ask questions if they spend the night.[5] Rahab is the ultimate outsider: a Canaanite woman who is a prostitute. If this isn't the kind of person the Israelites should destroy in order to avoid "infection," then who is? But Rahab says to the spies,

> I know that the Lord has given you the land, and that dread of you has fallen on us, and that all the inhabitants of the land melt in fear before you....The Lord your God is indeed God in heaven above and on earth below. Now then, since I have dealt kindly with you, swear to me by the Lord that you will deal kindly with my family (Joshua 2:9-12).

Rahab demonstrates a more profound faith in God than the spies. The spies are there to see if they might be able to defeat the city of Jericho. But Rahab already knows they will defeat Jericho, because she believes in God's power. So Rahab casts her lot with the God of Israel, and as a result she and her family are saved. Later, the saving of Rahab will have implications for the Bible's plot that Joshua and the spies did not foresee.

Jericho

It turns out Rahab was right. God gives the city of Jericho into the hands of Israel, but in a way that no one would expect. God says to Joshua,

> You shall march around the city, all the warriors circling the city once. Thus you shall do for six days, with seven priests bearing seven trumpets of rams' horns before the ark. On the seventh day you

shall march around the city seven times, the priests blowing the trumpets. When they make a long blast with the ram's horn, as soon as you hear the sound of the trumpet, then all the people shall shout with a great shout; and the wall of the city will fall down flat, and all the people shall charge straight ahead (Joshua 6:3-5).

No battering rams, no siege works, not even the clever ruse of a Trojan horse. The people of Israel take Jericho with an act of worship![6] The charge is led by priests. The weapons in their hands are trumpets. The walls fall from the reverberations of praise. (For another example of a battle won by praise, see II Chronicles 20:13-30.) Even the seven days of marching are significant. Remember that the goal of the seven days of creation was the day of rest—the day when people could glorify God and enjoy God forever. That was also the goal that God ultimately wanted from the conquest. After most of the battles are over, we read in Joshua 11:23: "And the land had rest from war." God's goal is that we might all have rest from war. But at this point in the story, the time of rest does not last.

Suggested Readings for Chapter 3

Exodus 1-24, 32-34; Numbers 11-14, 20-21, Deuteronomy 1-12, 34; Joshua 1-11, 23-24. In suggesting that you read these particular chapters, I have skipped many of the detailed commandments and instructions, as well as the census numbers and division of the land among the twelve tribes. There are other fascinating stories to read in this section, such as the mysterious story of Balaam and his donkey (Numbers 22-24). Unfortunately in a short introduction to the Bible, we cannot cover everything.

Questions for Reflection

1. Where have you seen the wrong actions of people come back to haunt them?
2. In the journey of your life when have you felt like complaining to God, as the people of Israel did in the

wilderness? How did God respond?

3. God gave land to the descendants of Abraham so they could become a blessing to others. What has God given you so that you could become a blessing to others?

4. When is violence justified, and when does it show a lack of faith?

4

The Politics of the Promise

In the 1993 movie *Groundhog Day*, Bill Murray plays an arrogant, self-absorbed weather man named Phil Conners. On February 2nd he is sent to Punxsutawny, Pennsylvania, to cover the appearance of their famous ground hog. Phil despises this assignment. He tells his producer, "Some day people are going to see me interviewing a ground hog and think I don't have a future." He does not realize how true those words will become. During his day in Punxsutawny, Phil meets various people whom he treats with disdain, as if they were on the same cultural and intellectual level as the groundhog. That night a blizzard hits town, and Phil is forced to spend the night. The next morning he wakes up and discovers that it is still February 2nd. The same radio host is saying the same words as his alarm clock goes off. He encounters all the same people in exactly the same situations. The next morning he wakes up and it happens again. When Phil changes his actions, it changes the way people respond to him, but no matter what he does, the next morning at 6:00 a.m. he wakes up in the same hotel bed where he starts Groundhog Day over again.

The Judges

Like the movie *Groundhog Day* the book of Judges seems caught in an endless cycle. The pattern may be summarized as follows:

Step 1. The people of Israel turn their back on God.

Step 2. God gives them into the hand of their enemies: Syrians (3:8), Moabites (3:12), Canaanites (4:2), Midianites (6:1), Ammonites (10:7), and Philistines (13:1).

Step 3. The Israelites cry to the Lord for help.

Step 4. God raises up a judge to deliver them: Othniel (3:9), Ehud (3:15), Deborah (4:4), Gideon (6:11-14), Jephthah (11:1ff), and Samson (13:2ff). Note: The judges in the Bible are more like rulers than what we normally call judges.

Then the judge dies and the steps are repeated.

The players change, but the pattern persists. After each cycle the people of Israel are no better off than they were before. In fact the situation deteriorates from cycle to cycle. After the success of Gideon in delivering Israel from the Midianites, Gideon creates an idol for the people to worship (Judges 8:24-27), something expressly forbidden by the Ten Commandments (Exodus 20:4-6). His son Abimelech then tries to establish himself as king by killing all his brothers (Judges 9:1-6). We now have Israelites killing other Israelites. Eventually this develops into civil war (Judges 12:1-6), culminating in a horrifying crime: a group of Israelites from the tribe of Benjamin rape and murder the wife of an Israelite from the tribe of Levi (Judges 19:22-26). Retaliation for this crime almost destroys the tribe of Benjamin. Far from being a blessing, the descendants of Abraham are threatening to annihilate each other.

The question posed by the book of Judges is this: Who can break the cycle? Who can lead the people of Israel out of this pattern of sin and suffering to help them become secure in the land promised to Abraham's descendants? Toward the end of the book, a key statement is repeated four times: "In those days there was no king in Israel" (Judges 17:6, 18:1, 19:1, and 21:25). In two of these cases the following conclusion is drawn: "All the people did what was right in their own eyes" (Judges 17:6, 21:25). Clearly the revolving door of leadership portrayed in the book of Judges is not working. Even though the descendants of Abraham are living in the Promised Land, they are hardly a blessing to themselves or others, and their hold on the land is tenuous. How will God lead these people to become the blessing they were meant to be?

Ruth

Before answering that question, the Bible digresses into a short story that seems to have little relevance to the Bible's plot. "In the days when the judges ruled, there was a famine in the land, and a certain man of Bethlehem in Judah went to live in the country of Moab, he and his wife and two sons (Ruth 1:1)." On top of the political chaos in the time of the judges, there is now a famine. (How many times have we seen God's chosen people threatened by a famine?) In Hebrew the word Bethlehem means "House of Bread," but there is no bread in Bethlehem. So Elimelech, his wife Naomi, and their two sons are forced to leave the Promised Land to find food among foreigners in Moab. Then their situation gets worse. Elimelech, the main "breadwinner," dies, and his sons marry Moabite women. This had disastrous consequences for the people of Israel earlier in their history (Numbers 25:1-3). To top it off, the sons die, leaving Naomi widowed with two foreign daughters-in-law.

When Naomi returns to her home town of Bethlehem she says to her old friends, "Call me no longer Naomi [which in Hebrew means 'pleasant'], call me Mara [which in Hebrew means 'bitter'], for the Almighty has dealt bitterly with me" (Ruth 1:20). That may be how the whole people of Israel were feeling at that moment.

But God has provided Naomi with an asset more valuable than she realizes: her daughter-in-law Ruth. At first Naomi is reluctant to let her daughters-in-law accompany her back to Bethlehem. She says to them, "Do I still have sons in my womb that they may become your husbands?" (Ruth 1:11). This refers to the practice mentioned earlier in connection with the story of Tamar. When a young woman is widowed without children, the husband's brother is responsible to produce and raise children for the widow. These children will inherit the dead husband's property and provide for the widow. But Naomi has no sons left to perform this duty. So she urges her daughters-in-law to go back to their families and seek husbands in Moab.

But Ruth begs to go with Naomi. She says, "Do not press me to leave you or to turn back from following you! Where you go, I will go; where you lodge, I will lodge; your people shall be my people, and your God my God" (Ruth 1:16). I find it ironic that this verse is quoted at weddings, since it refers not to a wife's pledge to her husband but to a widow's pledge to her mother-in-law!

Yet when seen in the light of the Bible's plot, this verse has special significance. God promised to bless Abraham's descendants and make them a blessing to all the nations. Wouldn't it be ironic if God blessed Naomi, a descendant of Abraham, through a foreigner named Ruth?

This is exactly what happens. In chapter 2 Ruth goes out to glean in the fields of a man named Boaz. Gleaning is a practice mentioned in the law of Moses: "When you reap the harvest of your land, you shall not reap to the edges of your field, or gather the gleanings of your harvest; you shall leave them for the poor and for the alien. I am the Lord your God" (Leviticus 23:22). Notice the reference to providing for "aliens" in the land as well as the poor. This again illustrates one of the important plot patterns of the Bible: that God is concerned for the economic as well as the spiritual well-being of all people.

It turns out that Boaz is a rich relative of Naomi's deceased husband. Now the plot takes a new turn. Naomi has no more sons to marry Ruth and give her children. But what about a relative of her husband? Could he be the one to fulfill that role? Naomi does not leave the issue to chance. She senses that Boaz is attracted to Ruth, because he has given her special treatment. So she instructs Ruth on how to put herself into a position with Boaz that will entice him (or perhaps coerce him) into taking Ruth as a wife.[1]

But Boaz does not need persuasion. He is glad to play the role of "next of kin" for Ruth and marry her. The result is that Ruth has a son and Naomi a grandson. After feeling cursed by God, Naomi is now considered blessed. Once again the promise of God's blessing to Abraham's descendants is saved. And once again a foreigner is included in the blessing.

But there is more. At the end of the book, the story of Ruth is placed within the family line of Israel (Jacob). We learn that Ruth's husband Boaz is descended from Judah's son Perez, the one who was born out of the illicit affair with Tamar! At the same time we are given a list of Ruth's descendants, including a grandson named Jesse, and a great-grandson named David. At this point these names mean nothing to us, but we will soon discover their significance.

The Call for a King

Meanwhile, the problems of Israel continue. The first seven chapters of Samuel contain many of the same plot dynamics as the book of Judges. A childless couple gives birth to a son who will become an important leader for the people of Israel. (Compare the story of Samuel's birth in I Samuel 1 to Samson's birth in Judges 13.) But the cycle of sin and defeat continues. Because of their sin, the people of Israel are defeated by the Philistines (I Samuel 4). Once again they cry out to God for help (I Samuel 7:2), and God gives them a judge, Samuel, to deliver them (I Samuel 7:3-14). But Samuel's sons turn out to be corrupt (I Samuel 8:3), and there is good reason to fear that after Samuel dies, the cycle of sin and defeat will continue, just as it did in the book of Judges.

At this point the people of Israel attempt to solve a spiritual problem with a political solution. They ask for a king. They hope that a king will unite their tribes against their enemies and provide more stable leadership than the haphazard appearance of judges.

God is decidedly ambivalent about this proposal. The Lord says to Samuel, "Listen to the voice of the people in all that they say to you; for they have not rejected you, but they have rejected me from being king over them" (I Samuel 8:7). In this one sentence God condemns the idea of a king, and then goes along with it. The same ambivalence continues for the next several chapters. The rest of chapter 8 is an eloquent warning against a king's abuse of power. But in chapter 9 the Lord picks out a man for Samuel to anoint as king: an Israelite named Saul from the tribe of Benjamin. Saul's choice is confirmed in chapter 10 by the drawing of lots—a sign that this is God's choice.

Let me note here that in ancient Israel kings were not "crowned;" they were "anointed" by having a small amount of oil poured on their heads. This is important because the Hebrew word for an "anointed person" is *Messiah*. The Greek word for an anointed person is *Christ*. The Messiah or Christ is first and foremost a king.

At first Saul proves to be a capable leader defeating Israel's enemies, just as the judges had done (I Samuel 11). But Samuel warns the people that a king will not save them unless they are obedient to God's commands (I Samuel 12). In other words, the problems of Israel will not be solved by political means if their relationship to God is in disarray.

This proves true in the chapters that follow. Saul, afraid that he might lose his hold on the people, usurps the authority of the priest and offers his own sacrifice to God. Presumably he did this to assure the people that he had God's authority and backing for his war effort.[2] But Samuel confronts him and says,

> You have done foolishly; you have not kept the commandments of the Lord your God, which he commanded you. The Lord would have established your kingdom over Israel forever, but now your kingdom will not continue; the Lord has sought out a man after his own heart; and the Lord has appointed him to be ruler over his people, because you have not kept what the Lord commanded you (I Samuel 13:13-14).

This short statement is loaded with important implications. First, it suggests that God was prepared to make Israel's kingship *permanent*. This is surprising given the ambivalence God expressed about it. Second, it implies that God has already chosen someone to take Saul's place. Saul will continue as king for the rest of I Samuel, but his fate has already been sealed, as has the identity of his successor.

From this point on Saul has limited success in defeating Israel's enemies. The success comes more from his son Jonathan and from a young man called to play soothing music for Saul's frazzled nerves.

David

I Samuel 16 provides another turning point in the Bible's plot. Samuel is sent by God to a man in Bethlehem named Jesse. Here we suddenly discover the significance of Ruth's descendants (see Ruth 4:18-22). Samuel is told to anoint a new king from among Jesse's sons. Samuel assumes that the chosen one is Eliab: 1) because he is the oldest, and 2) because he is tall. (Height was one of the impressive qualities of King Saul; I Samuel 9:2.) But Eliab was not the chosen one, nor were any of the other brothers whom Jesse brought forward. Puzzled, Samuel asks Jesse, "Are all your sons here?" Jesse says, "There remains yet the youngest, but he is keeping the sheep." Apparently, Jesse considered him such an unlikely candidate he was not invited to the auditions.

That, of course, is the person God chose. We have seen already that God often chooses the least likely people to be the instruments of God's work in the world. Only after Samuel anoints him as king do we hear his name: David (I Samuel 16:13).

While David is secretly anointed as king in chapter 16, he does not actually become king for another 17 chapters. Instead he becomes a servant (I Samuel 16:14-23). Keep this pattern in mind when we come to the New Testament where a descendant of David is anointed king in a hidden way and spends his life being a servant before being recognized as a king.

David was still a shepherd boy and a palace musician when he met Goliath (I Samuel 17). Most people know the details of this story: how the huge, powerful, and well-armored Goliath is defeated by a shepherd boy with a slingshot. This is certainly an example of God's ability to deliver Israel through an unlikely person. But it is also our first hint of the amazing things God intends to do for Israel through David. In the next chapter David has so much success against Israel's enemies he becomes the subject of a song. The women sing, "Saul has killed his thousands, and David his ten thousands."

This sparks jealousy in Saul, setting in motion a conflict between Saul and David that will run through the rest of the book. On several occasions Saul tries to kill David even while David faithfully serves him in the palace and on the battlefield. Here again we see a recurring plot-pattern: God's deliverance comes through a person rejected by God's people. Joseph saves his brothers from starvation after they sell him as a slave. Moses brings the Israelites to the Promised Land after they reject his leadership and suggest going back to Egypt. David delivers Israel from the Philistines even though Saul tries to kill him. All of this foreshadows a pattern we will see again in the New Testament.

Despite Saul's hostility, David remains loyal to Saul. He is best friends with Saul's son Jonathan. He is married to Saul's daughter Michal. While Saul pursues David, David twice has an opportunity to kill Saul, but refuses to take it (I Samuel 24 and 26). When Saul is killed in battle, David is the first to mourn (II Samuel 1), and later David shows special kindness to Saul's crippled grandson (II Samuel 9).

By these examples the Bible emphasizes that David did not take the throne away from Saul, God did. To be sure, David's general, Joab, used pitched battles and treachery to prevent the descendants of Saul from claiming the throne (see II Samuel 2-4). David also helped his own cause through success in battle (II Samuel 5:1-2). There are many political reasons why David became king. But the ultimate reason was God.

The work of God and the work of politics are not identical. God was not responsible for the treacherous way Joab killed Abner, Saul's commander (II Samuel 3:22-30), nor for the way Saul's son was murdered by his own officers (II Samuel 4:1-7). Nevertheless, God's plan that David would succeed Saul was fulfilled. God cannot be identified with a political party or a political movement. But God is not afraid to work in the realm of politics, sometimes in ironic ways, to fulfill God's purpose.

The Second Pivotal Promise

We now come to what I consider the second most important passage in the Old Testament (the most important being God's promise to Abraham in Genesis 12:1-3). In II Samuel, chapter 7, David announces his desire to build a house for God—a permanent temple in Jerusalem for the ark of God's covenant. Up to this point the ark had been carried by the Israelites from place to place while they were traveling through the wilderness or settling in the Promised Land. But David wants to give it a permanent home. He may have had political motives for doing this: wanting to consolidate political power and religious power by housing both in his capital city of Jerusalem. [3]

God declines the gesture. Through the prophet Nathan, God reminds David in verse 6, "I have not lived in a house since the day I brought up the people of Israel from Egypt to this day, but I have been moving about in a tent and a tabernacle." Apparently God prefers it that way. In verse 7 God says, "Whenever I have moved about among all the people of Israel, did I ever speak a word with any of the tribal leaders of Israel, whom I commanded to shepherd my people Israel, saying, 'Why have you not built me a house of cedar?'" God seems uninterested in a permanent "house," perhaps because God does not want to be bound to a place—to be in anyone's pocket, so to speak. God's power to work in our lives is always free. It cannot be captured or guaranteed through a building.

Then comes the surprise. Having rejected David's attempt to capture God's presence and blessing in a building, God offers that presence and blessing to David in a freely given promise—II Samuel 7:12-16:

> When your days are fulfilled and you lie down with your ancestors, I will raise up your offspring after you, who shall come forth from your body, and I will establish his kingdom. He shall build a house for my name, and I will establish the throne of his kingdom forever. I will be a father to him, and he shall be a son to me. When he commits iniquity, I

will punish him with a rod such as mortals use, with blows inflicted by human beings. But I will not take my steadfast love from him, as I took it from Saul, whom I put away from before you. Your house and your kingdom shall be made sure forever before me; your throne shall be established forever.

It is hard to overstate the importance of this promise for the rest of the Old Testament. You may recall that God's promise to Abraham included the promise of a land in which to dwell. That promise is repeated to David: "I will appoint a place for my people Israel and will plant them, so that they may live in their own place, and be disturbed no more" (II Samuel 7:10). God also promised to make Abraham's name great. That promise is refocused on David: "I will make for you a great name, like the name of the great ones of the earth" (II Samuel 7:9). The promise of God to Abraham is repeated and refocused on David and his descendants.

At the same time the promise is given a new twist. God promises to give David's descendants an *eternal* kingdom. In doing this, God acknowledges that David's descendants may sin, as Saul did. (Given what we have seen of human beings, this is a sure bet.) God also acknowledges that the sin of David's descendants may have devastating consequences, including defeat at the hands of their enemies (note the reference to blows inflicted by human beings). Nevertheless, God promises to maintain steadfast love toward David's descendants. The throne of David shall be established forever.

The eternal and unconditional nature of this promise is breathtaking. Through this promise God is bound to David's family more tightly than David could have ever hoped to achieve through building a temple.

This is another critical juncture at which the Bible's plot becomes narrowly focused in order that it may later expand. Out of all the people in the world God chose Abraham and his descendants to bring blessing to the world. Out of the descendants of Abraham, God chose Isaac and then Jacob to be the bearers of the promise. Eventually the promise became focused in a nation: the people of Israel, Jacob's descendants. Now God again focuses the promise—this time upon one family within the nation of Israel: the descendants of David. And yet, as David makes plain in the prayer that follows, David's family is chosen to be a vehicle of blessing to all Israel just as Abraham's descendants were chosen to bring blessing to all nations.

The connection between God's promise to Abraham and God's promise to David is made explicit in Psalm 72. The psalm begins, "Give the king your justice, O God, and your righteousness to a king's son." It then prays for numerous blessings to come through the king, including justice, security, prosperity, and peace. Near the end of the psalm is this statement, a direct echo of God's promise to Abraham: "May all the nations be blessed in him; may they pronounce him happy" (Psalm 72:17).

This promise is later described as a covenant, just like the promise to Abraham. In Psalm 89:3-4 the people of Israel say to God, "You said, 'I have made a covenant with my chosen one, I have sworn to my servant David: I will establish your descendants forever, and build your throne for all generations.'"

As in the case of Abraham, there are no conditions placed on the covenant. The covenant is not dependent on the people's obedience but on God's promise.

Sin and Its Aftermath

It did not take long for this promise to be tested. Four chapters later in II Samuel 11, David commits one of the most heinous betrayals of God and his people recorded in the Bible. While his troops are out fighting for him, David sleeps with Bathsheba, the wife of Uriah, one of his soldiers. David then arranges to have Uriah killed in combat so he can take Bathsheba as his wife. This is adultery, murder, lying, and coveting all rolled into one. And it is committed by the very person called "a man after God's own heart" (I Samuel 13:14).

To his credit, when confronted by the enormity of his sin, David accepts responsibility and admits his wrong. He says simply, "I have sinned against the Lord." In Psalm 51 we have a fuller account of David's prayer to God—one of the most eloquent pleas for forgiveness in all literature.

God forgives David, but there are still consequences of his sin that must be faced. As we have seen, sin has a ripple effect. The first effect is the death of the child David conceived with Bathsheba (II Samuel 12:14). Why does the child die? Isn't David the one who should be punished? The Bible offers no explanation for this. Why do children suffer for the sins of their parents? We don't know, but it often happens that way. Wars between adults consume the lives of children. The scars of alcoholism, abuse, or addiction damage the lives of generations to come. That is the ripple effect of sin. The true horror of sin is the damage it can do to human lives over many generations.

So it is with David. The consequences of his affair with Bathsheba ripple through the rest of II Samuel. In chapter 13 David's daughter is raped by her half-brother, Amnon. In retaliation Amnon is killed by David's son Absalom. For this act Absalom must flee into exile. Now David has not only lost his child by Bathsheba, he has seen his daughter raped, his oldest son murdered, and another son become a fugitive. But there is more. Absalom leads a rebellion against his father, and David must flee into exile (II Samuel 15). With David out of the way, Absalom proceeds to have sex with all of his father's wives, one after the other, on the roof of the palace. It was on the roof of the palace that David first spied Bathsheba and hatched his plan to have sex with her. Once again, the ripple effect of sin has come full circle.

Eventually Absalom is killed, his rebellion quashed, and David is restored to his throne. But the loss of his son leaves a gaping wound in his heart. David cries, "O my son Absalom, my son, my son! Would I had died instead of you, O Absalom, my son, my son!" (II Samuel 18:33).

Despite all this, the promise of God to David is not forgotten. In II Samuel 22 David sings a song of thanksgiving that concludes with these words: "For this I will extol you, O Lord, among the nations, and sing praises to your name. He is a tower of salvation for his king, and shows steadfast love to his anointed, to David and his descendants forever" (II Samuel 22:50-51).

Even in the horrible aftermath of David's sin, there is a sign of God's enduring covenant with David and his offspring. After the child David conceived with Bathsheba dies, David and Bathsheba have another child: Solomon. We are told that this child is especially loved by God (II Samuel 12:24-25). You get the feeling that this child is chosen for something special.

Succession

As David's life nears its end, the question becomes: Who will inherit God's unconditional promise to David? In Genesis we read about the intrigues of Jacob and Esau over who would inherit the promises of God to Abraham. Isaac wanted his older son Esau to inherit this blessing, but his wife Rebekah conspired with Jacob, the younger son, to claim it. A similar pattern unfolds at the beginning of I Kings. Adonijah, David's oldest remaining son, assumes that he will inherit the kingdom.[4] But Bathsheba conspires to make her son Solomon the heir to the throne and to God's promise. She does this by deceiving her husband David, just as Rebekah deceived her husband Isaac. She says to the elderly and feeble King David, "My lord, you swore to your servant by the Lord your God, saying: 'Your son Solomon shall succeed me as king, and he shall sit on my throne'" (I Kings 1:17). Actually, we have no record that David ever said such a thing. But the prophet Nathan conspires with Bathsheba to confirm her words, and David believes them. (At this point King David may have trouble remembering things, just as Isaac had trouble seeing.) So David proclaims Solomon to be the heir to his throne. After David's death, Solomon leaves nothing to chance. He eliminates his rival Adonijah, along with the general and the priest who had supported Adonijah (I Kings 2). And that is how Solomon becomes king.

Did God choose Solomon to be king? At one point Adonijah says to Bathsheba, "You know that the kingdom was mine, and that all Israel expected me to reign; however, the kingdom has turned about and become my brother's *for it was his from the Lord*" (I Kings 2:15; my emphasis). Whether Adonijah believes this or is saying it simply to gain favor with Bathsheba, we do not know. But in II Kings 3, God promises to bless Solomon's reign, and later, after the dedication of the temple, God repeats to Solomon the promises God had made to David (I Kings 9:3-5). The deceptions and executions that made Solomon king were not God's doing; they were the actions of people, just like Jacob's deception of his father Isaac. Nevertheless, God uses these human actions to make Solomon the recipient of the promise, just as God did for Jacob. Why? That is left to the mystery of God's grace.

The Temple

The temple is, first of all, the preeminent sign that God is working through Solomon to fulfill the promises made to David. In II Samuel 7 God told David,

> When your days are fulfilled and you lie down with your ancestors, I will raise up your offspring after you, who shall come forth from your body, and I will establish his kingdom. He shall build a house for my name, and I will establish the throne of his kingdom forever.

By building the temple, Solomon establishes himself as the heir to this promise (see Solomon's speech to the people of Israel in I Kings 8:20-21). In this sense the temple had a political purpose: to consolidate Solomon's authority.

But God also uses the temple for a religious purpose: to consolidate God's authority over the people. Years earlier in Deuteronomy 12, Moses told the people of Israel, "You must destroy completely all the places where the nations whom you are about to dispossess served their gods, on the mountain heights, on the hills, and under every leafy tree" (Deuteronomy 12:2). These are what the Bible calls the "high places"—the places people set up for themselves to worship God. In contrast to this, Moses says to the people of Israel, "Take care that you do not offer your burnt offerings at any place you happen to see. But *only at the place that the Lord will choose in one of your tribes*—there you shall offer your burnt offerings and there you shall do everything I command you" (Deuteronomy 12:13-14, my emphasis).

In my 30 years of ministry I cannot count how many times people have told me, "I don't need to go to church to worship God. I feel closest to God when I am out in the woods by myself."

To be sure, God is not confined to a building. Solomon admits this in his prayer of dedication for the temple. He says, "But will God indeed dwell on the earth? Even heaven and the highest heaven cannot contain you, much less this house that I have built!" (I Kings 8:27). Can God be worshiped in nature? Of course!

But here is the danger. When we worship God on our own, we end up with a God of our own making. That is the danger of the "high places." In I and II Kings we will see numerous examples of how worshiping God on the high places leads people to create their own new gods (look ahead to I Kings 12:25-33).

Worshiping God at a central sanctuary is one of the ways God tries to limit this temptation. The temple cannot contain or capture God. But it reminds people of whom they are serving. Turning toward the temple to pray, as Solomon recommends in his dedication prayer, reminds people of the kind of God to whom they are praying—a God of steadfast love and faithfulness, who demands love and faithfulness from us.

Apostasy

Unfortunately, Solomon and many of the kings that follow him turn away from the Lord to worship other gods, gods that will support their political ambitions. After building the temple, Solomon builds an even larger palace for himself. (Compare the dimensions of the temple in I Kings 6:2 with the dimensions of the palace in I Kings 7:1-2.) He did this by conscripting labor from his own people (I Kings 5:13). He also required huge amounts of food and provisions to be supplied by the people of Israel on a rotating basis (I Kings 4:7-28). This created a simmering resentment that would haunt Solomon's son (see I Kings 12:1-19).

More dangerous, however, is the relationship Solomon has with foreign wives. Moses warned the people of Israel about this in Exodus 34:15-16:

> You shall not make a covenant with the inhabitants of the land, for when they prostitute themselves to their gods and sacrifice to their gods, someone among them will invite you, and you will eat of the sacrifice. And you will take wives from among their daughters for your sons, and their daughters who prostitute themselves to their gods will make your sons prostitute themselves to their gods.

We have seen cases where Israelites took foreign wives, and the wives turned to worshiping the Lord. Ruth is the preeminent example of this. But more often it turns out badly. In I Kings 11, when Solomon takes for himself foreign wives, he ends up worshiping their foreign gods, and the result is disastrous. The same Lord who had blessed Solomon now says to him,

> Since this has been your mind and you have not kept my covenant and my statutes that I have commanded you, I will surely tear the kingdom from you and give it to your servant. Yet for the sake of your father David I will not do it in your lifetime; I will tear it out of the hand of your son. I will not, however, tear away the entire kingdom; I will give one tribe to your son, for the sake of my servant David and for the sake of Jerusalem, which I have chosen (I Kings 11:11-13).

Two important aspects of the Bible's plot come together in this statement. 1) We again see the ripple effect of sin. Solomon's apostasy will haunt his descendants. Why does the son suffer for the father's sin? It is the nature of sin to have ripple effects extending to future generations. 2) Nevertheless, God's promise to David is preserved. God gave David an unconditional promise. Even if his descendants sinned,

God would punish them, but not revoke the promise. Politically, this is the high water mark of Israel in the Bible. In terms of power, security, and prosperity, the reigns of David and Solomon were as good as it gets. From here on Israel's national existence and the promises God has given them will be under constant threat.

The Divided Kingdom

The seeds of civil war were sown by Solomon's own ambitious building program. To accomplish his projects he used forced labor of his own people. After his death, the people petition his son King Rehoboam to lighten the load. But Rehoboam thinks that lightening the load shows weakness. So he threatens to make it greater. In response, Jeroboam, a man from the tribe of Ephraim, leads a rebellion of the northern ten tribes of Israel against the tribe of Judah, which remained loyal to David's heir (I Kings 12). You might say this is opposite of the American Civil War. In America the south seceded from the north in order to preserve slavery. In Israel the north seceded from the south in order to abolish it.

Though the civil war in Israel had a political cause, it was also the fulfillment of God's judgment against Solomon. In fact, Jeroboam was commissioned by a prophet of God named Ahijah to carry out this rebellion (I Kings 11:29-39). This will not be the last time God sends a prophet to intervene in the politics of a kingdom.

Even though he was commissioned by God to lead the rebellion, Jeroboam would not trust God for the security of his reign. He feared that if people continued to worship God at the temple in Jerusalem—the capital of the southern kingdom—people would become loyal to Rehoboam, the southern king. So he created his own places of worship in the northern cities of Bethel and Dan. At each of these new sanctuaries he set up a golden calf, reminiscent of the golden calf the people of Israel worshiped at Mt. Sinai (Exodus 32:1-6). Frequently the people of Judah did the same thing. They created alternative sanctuaries, called "high places," at which they worshiped new gods—gods like Molech, whose worship included child sacrifice, and Asherah, who was worshiped through sacred prostitution. When people worship God on their own, they end up creating their own god to worship!

For the next 200 years the Bible follows both kingdoms simultaneously. Each new king is introduced in relationship to the ruler of the other kingdom. For example, I Kings 15:9 says, "Now in the twentieth year of King Jeroboam of Israel, Asa began to reign over Judah." Later, I Kings 15:33 says, "In the third year of King Asa of Judah, Baasha the son of Ahijah began to reign over all Israel." The introduction of each king is followed by a summary judgment on his reign: "He did what was right in the sight of the Lord," or "He did what was evil in the sight of the Lord."

Most of the time it was the latter. Not one king of Israel is called righteous, and very few kings of Judah. Even the kings of Judah called "righteous" are given only qualified approval. For example, the Bible says King Jehoshaphat of Judah did "right in the sight of the Lord; yet the high places were not taken away, and the people still sacrificed and offered incense on the high places" (I Kings 22:43).

A modern historian would evaluate these kings quite differently than the Bible. In terms of fame and accomplishments one of the greatest kings of Israel was Omri. In the Louvre Museum in Paris there is a Moabite stone inscribed by a king of Moab in the ninth century B.C.E. It says, "As for Omri, king of Israel, he humbled Moab for many years."[5] For a Moabite king to admit that he was "humbled" by an Israelite king is quite a statement. For a time Omri and his son Ahab totally dominated Moab, ordering the people of that country to pay taxes to them. Omri also built the city of Samaria, which became the capital of the northern kingdom. Omri established a dynasty so powerful that, many years after his death, other nations referred to Israel as "the land of the house of Omri."[6]

But the Bible says very little about Omri. It mentions that he built the city of Samaria, but otherwise it dismisses him with this terse evaluation: "Omri did what was evil in the sight of the Lord; he did more evil than all who were before him. For he walked in all the way of Jeroboam son of Nebat, and in the sins he caused Israel to commit, provoking the Lord, the God of Israel, to anger by their idols" (I Kings 16:25-26). In the plot of the Bible, political power is less important than faithfulness to God.

Prophets

Unfortunately neither the kings of Israel nor the kings of Judah show much faithfulness to God. Still, God does not give up on them, and the sign of this is the sending of prophets.

Often God sends prophets to the kings of Israel with a message of judgment because of their wrongdoing.

- Nathan confronts David over his affair with Bathsheba (II Samuel 12:1-15)
- Ahijah gives part of the kingdom to Jeroboam because of Solomon's idolatry (I Kings 11:29-39)
- Ahijah confronts Jeroboam's idolatry (I Kings 14:1-16)
- Jehu announces doom to King Baasha (I Kings 16:1-4)
- Elijah challenges King Ahab and the prophets of Baal (I Kings, chapters 18-21)
- Micaiah gives bad news to Ahab and Jehoshaphat (I Kings 22:13-28)

But the prophets are also messengers of hope:

- Elijah offers hope for relief from a famine in order to show that the Lord, not Baal, is the ruler of the storms (I Kings 18).
- An unknown prophet promises victory for Ahab against Aram (Syria) because the Arameans think the Lord only protects Israel in the hills, not in the valleys (I Kings 20:27-28).
- Elisha promises not only an end to famine but a victory for Israel against Moab (II Kings 3:13-19).
- Elisha announces that the siege of the Syrians against Israel will be broken and the people will have food again (II Kings 7:1).
- Isaiah declares that the Lord will defeat the Assyrians

and save Jerusalem (II Kings 19:20-34).

The challenge is how to discern when a prophet's message is from the Lord and when it is wishful thinking or political expediency. This issue is illustrated in the story of the prophet Micaiah (I Kings 22:1-28). Before going into battle against Aram, King Jehoshaphat, one of the few righteous kings of Judah, wants to consult the Lord. So he asks King Ahab to gather some prophets of the Lord. This must have embarrassed King Ahab, since his wife Jezebel had killed many of the Lord's prophets. But like most kings, Ahab knows how to find advisors who tell him what he wants to hear. So he gathers 400 government-appointed prophets, all of whom tell him that the Lord will give Aram into his hand. Only one prophet, Micaiah, dares to speak otherwise. He even suggests that the Lord put a lying spirit in the mouth of these other prophets in order to deceive Ahab, so that Ahab would go ahead with the war and be killed in the process.

In this situation how do we know that Micaiah is the true prophet? After all, there have been times when a true prophet of God predicted victory for the people of Israel (see the examples above). How do we know that in this case Micaiah is right to predict doom?

Micaiah himself proposes an answer. He says to Ahab, "If you return in peace, the Lord has not spoken by me" (I Kings 22:28). The true prophet will be known by the fulfillment of his word. When Ahab and Jehoshaphat are defeated by the Arameans, then we will know that Micaiah is the true prophet.

Unfortunately, this works only in hindsight. How do we know at the time whether a prophet is speaking for the Lord or for some other motive? The answer is to view the prophet's message in light of God's commandments and in light of the character of God shown to us in God's previous actions (see Deuteronomy 13:1-5). Previously God had announced through Elijah that dogs would lick up Ahab's blood because of the innocent blood Ahab had shed (I Kings 21:17-19). This, by itself, should give pause to any prophet who speaks of victory for Ahab. Secondly, Ahab himself initiates this war after a period of peace with Aram in order to take back some of Aram's territory. This war was not the Lord's idea; it was the king's. Finally, one should inquire into the motives of the prophets who predict Ahab's victory. Jezebel has been known to kill prophets who opposed her husband. Could this not be sufficient motive for these prophets to lie? On the other hand, what political advantage would Micaiah gain from his message of doom? What possible motive would Micaiah have for opposing the war, except that it is wrong? These are important considerations in discerning a true prophet from a false one.

The Fate of the Promise

Despite the ups and downs of the descendants of Abraham in the time of the kings, the promises of God are not forgotten. Surprisingly, through all of this turmoil the people of Judah hang on, and a descendant of David continues to rule in Jerusalem. This is not the case in the northern kingdom of Israel. The northern kingdom goes through periodic changes of dynasty, where a new king takes power after wiping out the entire family of the previous king (I Kings 15:27-30 and II Kings 10:1-11). But this did not happen in the southern kingdom of Judah. For the entire 240 year history of Judah, there was always a descendant of King David on the throne. Even when that descendant of David sinned against God, God still preserved the dynasty (I Kings 15:4-5). In one episode the descendants of David came close to being destroyed by a murderous queen mother (II Kings 11:1). But the dynasty was saved by a daughter who managed to rescue one of the infant sons of the previous king and hide him until it was safe for him to take the throne (II Kings 11:2-12). Recall the story we read earlier of how God saved Moses.

During most of this time, Israel's relationship to other nations is antagonistic. But there are glimmers of God's grace reaching out through Israel to other nations:

- The visit of the Queen of Sheba (I Kings 10:1-13)
- Elijah caring for a foreign widow (I Kings 17:8-24)

- Elisha healing Naaman, an Aramean army commander (II Kings 5:1-19)

The promises of God to Abraham and David are not forgotten in these stories, but at the end they are placed in serious jeopardy. In II Kings 17 the ripple effect of generations of apostasy against God and injustice toward God's people finally comes to a head. In 722 B.C.E. Israel is conquered by the Assyrians. In the process many Israelites are killed or sent into exile, and the land is settled by foreigners who worship other gods (II Kings 17:24-41). In 587 B.C.E. a similar catastrophe happens to Judah: the Babylonian army captures Jerusalem, destroys the temple, kills many of the people, and takes the rest, including the king, into captivity in Babylon (II Kings 25).

It is hard to imagine a more devastating end to the promises God made to Abraham. Instead of being a great nation, the descendants of Abraham are displaced refugees. Instead of living in the Promised Land, they are in exile. Instead of being a blessing to other nations, they are cursed by other nations. And the throne that God promised to David's descendants has been destroyed.

In this dark situation there is one ray of hope. At the end of II Kings we are told that Jehoiachin, the last descendant of David to reign as king in Jerusalem, survives in captivity. The Babylonian king invites him to live in the palace and eat at the king's table. That is all we are told. The promises of God to Abraham and David seem totally lost. But somewhere in captivity a descendant of David still survives.

Chronicles: The Story Revisited

At first glance the books of I and II Chronicles seem to repeat the same story we just read in II Samuel and I and II Kings. Indeed many of the same stories are told, sometimes in the same words. But there are major differences, and by retelling the story with a different slant, Chronicles prepares us for a new era in the lives of Abraham's descendants.

The first obvious thing about Chronicles is the long genealogical tables contained in chapters 1-9. This obsession with lists of leaders and descendants continues through Ezra and Nehemiah. For what purpose are we given these exhaustive lists? One possibility is to assure the true lineage of the people of Israel who return from exile to repopulate the Promised Land. At the end of Nehemiah, the people of Israel are told to separate from all those of foreign descent (Nehemiah 13:3). The genealogical records helped people prove their descent from one of the tribes of Israel and, hence, their right to be included among the people of God living in Judah.

But in terms of the Bible's plot, the genealogies have a deeper significance. They indicate that even in exile the descendants of Abraham are preserved. This is particularly important in relation to the descendants of David, because of the promise in II Samuel 7. I Chronicles 3 lists the descendants of David and Solomon past the time of the exile. For example, verse 17 mentions "the sons of Jeconiah, the captive." This is an alternate spelling of the same Jehoiachin mentioned as being alive at the end of II Kings. I Chronicles 3 tells us that this surviving son of King David himself had descendants who survived. That will prove crucial later in the story.

The special theme of Chronicles is worship. While I and II Kings focuses almost exclusively on kings and prophets, Chronicles highlights the clergy—the special role played by priests, Levites, and other leaders in worship. For example, I Chronicles 23-26 give extensive lists of the Levites, priests, temple musicians, and gatekeepers who led worship in the time of King David, even before the temple was built. II Chronicles 11:13-17 notes that after the division of the kingdom between David's son Rehoboam and the rebel leader Jeroboam, the priests and Levites from both northern and southern tribes joined with Rehoboam to support the worship of God in Jerusalem. Chronicles even notes that these priests and Levites helped Rehoboam stay faithful to God longer than he would have if they had not been there. These details are not found in I Kings.

A particularly interesting story is found in II Chronicles, chapter 20. The people of Judah are attacked by the Moabites and Ammonites. The people cry out to God for help, and a prophet named Jahaziel gives this response:

> Thus says the Lord to you: "Do not fear or be dismayed at this great multitude; for the battle is not yours but God's.…This battle is not for you to fight; take your position, stand still, and see the victory of the Lord on your behalf, O Judah and Jerusalem" (II Chronicles 20:15-17).

King Jehoshaphat of Judah then executes a highly unusual battle plan. He puts the choir—those who sing praises to the Lord—at the front of his army, and when they begin to sing, the Ammonites and Moabites start attacking each other. They destroy each other without the army of Judah lifting a finger (II Chronicles 20:21-23). The battle is won by worship, reminiscent of the victory by Joshua at the battle of Jericho (Joshua 6). This episode is not found in II Kings.

The emphasis on worship is important, because the worship of God in the temple is crucial to the identity of Abraham's descendants. The book of II Chronicles ends with these words:

> In the first year of King Cyrus of Persia, in fulfillment of the word of the Lord spoken by Jeremiah, the Lord stirred up the spirit of King Cyrus of Persia so that he sent a herald through all his kingdom and also declared in a written edict: "Thus says King Cyrus of Persia: the Lord, the God of heaven has given me all the kingdoms of the earth, and he has charged me to build him a house at Jerusalem, which is in Judah. Whoever is among you of all his people, may the Lord his God be with him! Let him go up" (II Chronicles 36:22-23).

There are two striking things about this statement. First, the Lord God of Israel is giving instructions to Cyrus, a Persian king, and Cyrus is listening! Here is another hint that the Lord is working in other nations than Israel. Second, the purpose of going back to the Promised Land is not freedom, independence, prosperity, or the pursuit of happiness. It is worship. The people are sent to rebuild the temple and to reestablish the worship of God in Jerusalem.

Remember the message God gave Pharaoh centuries earlier: "Let my people go, so that they may worship me'" (Exodus 8:1). The goal of creation was the Sabbath, the day of rest and worship. God's goal for the people of Israel is the same: that they may glorify God and enjoy God forever.

Return to the Land

Ezra and Nehemiah tell the story of the descendants of Abraham who returned to the Promised Land to rebuild the temple. The people who make this journey to Jerusalem in the land of Judah are called Jews. (Except for a brief reference in II Kings 25, Ezra is the first place in the Bible where the people of Israel are called Jews—people of Judah.) They immediately meet opposition from the people living in the land. These are the people from other nations whom the Assyrians resettled in the land after destroying the kingdom of Israel and taking its people into exile. (Refer back to the story in II Kings 17:24-34.) These people mixed the worship of the Lord with the worship of other gods. Because they occupied a part of Israel whose capital city was Samaria, they are later referred to as Samaritans.

The battle between the Jews and Samaritans is waged through correspondence with the Persian emperor. The Samaritans wait until King Cyrus is replaced by a new emperor of Persia named Ahasuerus. In a letter they tell Ahasuerus that the Jews are rebuilding the foundations and walls of the city of Jerusalem in order to declare their independence from Persia, thus taking away tax money (Ezra 4:11-16). Ahasuerus immediately orders a moratorium on building.

However, when King Darius replaces King Ahasuerus, the Jews resume building the temple, and Darius grants them permission based on the previous decree of Cyrus (Ezra 6:1-13). The temple is completed, and Ezra leads the people in a rededication of their commitment to God. Part of this is a commitment by the people of Judah to separate from their foreign wives, on the grounds that foreign wives are what got Israel into trouble in the first place.

The danger of foreign wives was certainly true for Solomon (I Kings 11:1-13), Ahab (I Kings 16:31-33), and other kings of Israel. But the Bible also contains counter-examples. Tamar, Rahab, and Ruth were foreign wives who came to believe in the Lord and who brought great blessing to the Israelites who married them. Their children became ancestors of the kings of Israel. The relationship to foreigners will be an on-going struggle for the people of Israel. How do they preserve their identity by separating themselves from other nations, while trying to become the blessing to other nations that God wants them to be?

Esther

The issue of marrying foreign wives is addressed in reverse form by the story of Esther. Esther is a Jewish girl who marries the Persian King Ahasuerus. Esther has been raised by her Jewish uncle Mordecai, who was carried away into exile by the Babylonians with King Jeconiah (Jehoiachin). Placing the story of Esther at this point in the Bible tells us three things relevant to the Bible's plot: 1) many of the descendants of Abraham are still living in exile, even after Nehemiah leads some of them back to the Promised Land, 2) in exile the Jewish people face constant threats to their existence, and 3) in exile the Jewish people sometimes became a blessing to their captors, fulfilling God's promise to Abraham in unexpected ways.

Both Esther and Mordecai become a blessing to King Ahasuerus: Esther by becoming his wife, and Mordecai by alerting the king to a plot against his life. Despite this, a conspiracy is hatched by a man named Haman to hang Mordecai and destroy all the Jews in the empire. It is up to Esther to use her influence with the king to save them. This is a risky proposition. Unless a wife is summoned by the king, she cannot ask for an audience with him without risking death. Mordecai asks Esther to risk going uninvited to King Ahasuerus to ask for help. In one of the great speeches of the Bible Mordecai reminds her:

Do not think that in the king's palace you will escape any more than all the other Jews. For if you keep silence at such a time as this, relief and deliverance will rise for the Jews from another quarter, but you and your father's family will perish. Who knows? Perhaps you have come to royal dignity for just such a time as this (Esther 4:13-14).

In this short speech Mordecai eloquently describes two great plot patterns of the Bible: 1) how God repeatedly saves Abraham's descendants when they are on the verge of annihilation, and 2) how God uses human actions to accomplish God's purposes in ironic ways. When Esther wins the beauty pageant to be queen, neither she, nor Ahasuerus, nor Mordecai dream that this will be used by God to save the Jews. But it is. To complete the irony, the very gallows on which Haman hopes to hang Mordecai become the site of his own execution.

Interestingly, God is not mentioned anywhere in the book of Esther. Imagine a book of the Bible that does not mention God! Yet without being mentioned, God works in this story from multiple angles to save the descendants of Abraham and make them a blessing.

At this point the Bible's plot hits the pause button. The temple and walls of Jerusalem have been rebuilt by a small group of Jews led by Ezra and Nehemiah. They have recommitted themselves to the Lord, and their numbers are growing. But they are living under an army of occupation: the Persians. A few descendants of King David are still alive, but none of them sits on a throne. Meanwhile, the majority of Abraham's descendants still live in exile. The fate of God's promises is very much up in the air. The remaining books in the Old Testament are reflections on this situation, ranging from despair to hope.

Suggested Readings for Chapter 4

All of Judges, Ruth, I and II Samuel, and I and II Kings. This long section of the Bible tells a continuous, coherent, and gripping story. These books, along with Deuteronomy and Joshua, are sometimes called the Deuteronomic history.

While they contain stories from many different sources, they are put together in a continuous narrative that is meant to be read as a whole. Again, don't worry about understanding all the details of every story. Follow the major lines of the plot as highlighted in this chapter.

Questions for Reflection

1. In what ways does God use government to do good? In what ways does government use God to do harm?
2. How did God's promises to David and his descendants interact with their on-going proclivity toward sin? How does this work in your own life?
3. What role does a church building have in your life of faith?
4. How do you discern true preaching from false preaching?

5

Sages and Singers

In the movie *Forrest Gump* is a scene where Forrest Gump, played by Tom Hanks, goes with his friend Jenny back to the abandoned, ramshackle house where as a young child she was sexually abused by her father. As she stares at the house, all the memories of that abuse well up inside her, and she starts picking up rocks and throwing them at the empty house. One after another, tears streaming down her face, she throws rocks as hard as she can against the side of that empty house until she collapses in the yard sobbing. Forrest comes over, sits next to her, and says, "Sometimes there just aren't enough rocks."

I suspect the people of Israel felt the same way in exile, which may explain why some of the most anguish-filled writings of the Bible are found precisely at this point in the story. In the Hebrew version of the Bible, the books of Job, Psalms, Proverbs, Ecclesiastes, and Song of Solomon are found near the end of the Old Testament. But most Christian Bibles follow more closely the Greek version of the Old Testament. Job, Psalms, Proverbs, Ecclesiastes, and Song of Solomon come after the people of Israel have gone into exile (II Kings-Esther) but before the message of the prophets (Isaiah-Malachi).

The order of these books in the Christian Bible suggests something about their place in the plot. These books are meant to be read in the middle of the plot, not at the end. Job, Psalms, Proverbs, Ecclesiastes, and Song of Solomon have a timeless quality making them valuable to read in any situation. But coming as they do at this particular point in the story, when many of the people of Israel are in exile, gives them new meaning.

Job

In January of 2006, Pat Robertson, a conservative Christian minister, suggested on his television program that God "smote" Ariel Sharon, the former prime minister of Israel, with a stroke to punish him for withdrawing from the Gaza strip and handing over some of the Promised Land to Palestinians. I disagree with Pat Robertson on two points. First, I have previously noted several occasions when Abraham's descendants made peace with their neighbors.[1] In light of this, I do not find it a violation of God's promises for an Israeli prime minister to attempt peaceful co-existence with the Palestinians. Second, I disagree that a stroke is a sign of God's judgment against a person. Suffering is not always the result of sin, as the story of Job makes clear.

Job is a righteous man. Even God says so (Job 1:8). Yet Job experiences devastating loss in his life coupled with incredible personal suffering. His servants are killed and his livestock are carried away by invaders. Then a house collapses on his sons and daughters, killing them. Finally, Job is afflicted with terrible sores from head to toe making him wish he were dead. Why does God allow a good man to suffer in this way?

It is not obvious how the story of Job is connected to the story of Israel. We do not even know if Job was a descendant of Abraham. We are told only that he was a man living in the land of Uz. He could have been from any ethnic group. In this sense, the story of Job is a reminder that God has regard for all the families of the earth.

Yet, for an Israelite living in exile, the story of Job would have struck a special chord. First, the suffering of Job's family is reminiscent of the suffering Israel experienced when conquered by the Assyrians and Babylonians. Homes were destroyed, family members were killed, and livestock were seized. Note that in Job 1:17 the raiders are called Chaldeans, which is a name associated with the Babylonians (see the reference to Chaldeans in II Kings 25). Second, the Israelites in exile would have identified with the problem of suffering by innocent people. Even if the kings of Israel sinned against God and deserved to be killed or sent into exile, what about the Israelites and their families who quietly went about their daily lives trying to obey God? Why did God's judgment fall on them? Finally, Job's feeling of being abandoned by God must have been the feeling of many Israelites in exile. Job cries out for God to hear his case. It feels as if he is throwing rocks at God's house, trying to get God's attention. But there is no response until the very end. Job's situation parallels the anguish of the people of Israel in exile.[2]

In Job the plot takes place on two levels. The first level is the dialogue between God and Satan in heaven. The Hebrew word *satan* means "adversary." Sometimes it refers to a political or military adversary (I Kings 11:14, 23). But sometimes it refers to an adversary in a legal proceeding (Psalm 109:6-7). Building on this usage, the Greek Old Testament translates the word *satan* by the Greek word *diabolos* which means "accuser." Satan is like the accuser or prosecutor in a trial. He argues the case that people are guilty and should be condemned.

At their meeting in heaven God sticks up for humanity against the old Prosecutor. God says to Satan, "Have you considered my servant Job? There is no one like him on the earth, a blameless and upright man who fears God and turns away from evil" (Job 1:8). Yes, Satan may have a case against many people, but Job is exhibit A that not all people are bad. Job proves that humanity can be worth saving.

But Satan scoffs, "Does Job fear God for nothing? Have you not put a fence around him and his house and all that he has, on every side? You have blessed the work of his hands, and his possessions have increased in the land. But stretch out your hand now, and touch all that he has, and he will curse you to your face" (Job 1:9-11).

On the heavenly level Job is a test case. Will people serve God, even if there is no reward for it, even if they find themselves in a situation of terrible suffering?

Meanwhile, there is another dialogue taking place on earth between Job, his wife, and his friends. In the heavenly dialogue we learn that there is a great purpose being played out. Job is a test case for vindicating humanity against Satan's accusations. But Job does not know that. Neither does his wife or his friends. They must wrestle with Job's situation without benefit of the heavenly perspective.

Their answers for Job's suffering are not helpful. His wife suggests giving up on God. Job's friends are more pious. They tell Job, "Admit your sin and the justice of God's punishment. Then maybe God will be merciful to you." When Job protests his innocence, his friends reply: "How then can a mortal be righteous before God? How can one born of woman be pure? If even the moon is not pure in his sight, how much less a mortal, who is a maggot, and a human being, who is a worm?" (Job 25:4-6).

This is not the recommended approach to pastoral care. Apparently Job's friends feel a need to defend God when God does not need defending. The friends might have been better off listening to Job without comment.

At times the friends try to be encouraging to Job. They suggest that his suffering is a form of discipline or training by which God will make him stronger (Job 5:17-18). But Job rejects these solutions. He will not give up on God, as his wife suggests. He curses the day of his birth, but not God. To the end he begs God for a hearing. Despite his inability to make sense of what has happened to him, Job seeks vindication from God and no one else. He says, "For I know that my Redeemer lives, and that at the last he will stand upon the earth; and after my skin has been thus destroyed, then in my flesh I shall see God" (Job 19:25-26).

Finally in chapters 38-41 God responds. But God does not tell Job about the contest between God and Satan in heaven. Nor does God answer any of Job's questions or complaints.

Instead God asks Job a series of counter-questions:

- "Where were you when I laid the foundation of the earth?" (Job 38:4).
- "Or who shut in the sea with doors when it burst out from the womb?" (Job 38:8).
- "Do you give the horse its might? Do you clothe its neck with mane?" (Job 39:19).
- "Is it by your wisdom that the hawk soars, and spreads its wings toward the south?" (Job 39:26).

Basically God asks Job: "Who is the Creator here? Was God created for you, or were you created for God?"

This brings us back to the original issue raised by Satan in chapter 1: Do we worship the Lord for our benefit, or do we worship the Lord because the Lord is God?

This was one of the deepest issues faced by the people of Israel in exile. Do we continue to worship God even when we have lost everything: family, home, farms, temple, and national sovereignty?

Many of the Jewish exiles answered yes. A classic example is the story of Shadrach, Meshach, and Abednego in the fiery furnace (Daniel 3). Shadrach, Meshach, and Abednego were three Jewish exiles living in Babylon after the fall of Jerusalem. When ordered to worship a statute of King Nebuchadnezzar of Babylon, they refused. Warned that refusal could get them thrown into a fiery furnace, they give this memorable reply: "If our God whom we serve is able to deliver us from the furnace of blazing fire and out of your hand, O king, let him deliver us. But if not, be it known to you, O king, that we will not serve your gods and we will not worship the golden statue that you have set up" (Daniel 3:17-18).

Near the end of the novel *Uncle Tom's Cabin*, a beaten and dejected slave named Tom faces his cruel master Simon Legree. Legree says, "Well, old boy, you find your religion don't work, it seems! I thought I should get that through your wool at last!...Come, Tom, don't you think you'd better be reasonable?—heave that ar old pack of trash in the fire, and join my church."

"The Lord forbid!" Tom replies.

Legree says, "You see the Lord an't going to help you; if he had been, he wouldn't have let me get you! This yer religion is all a mess of lying trumpery, Tom. I know all about it. Ye'd better hold to me. I'm somebody, and can do something!"

"No, Mas'r," says Tom. "I'll hold on. The Lord may help me, or not help; but I'll hold to him, and believe him to the last!"[3]

Simon Legree embodies the voice of Satan; Tom the response of Job. Job has no assurance that faithfulness to God will pay off in any earthly benefit, but he continues to put his life in God's hands, not in the hands of anyone else.

In the end Job's home, family, and livestock are restored, just as the people of Israel in exile hope that one day their families, homes, and farms will be restored in the Promised Land. But in the meantime, Job gave them encouragement to keep praying, to keep seeking God, to keep crying out for God's vindication and deliverance, even in their anguish. For in the very act of seeking God, Job experienced God (Job 42:1-6).[4] And that, in the deepest part of our heart, is what we yearn for most.

Psalms

It may not be immediately obvious how the psalms are connected to the Bible's plot. How is a hymnbook connected to the history of America? Yet, in the case of the psalms there are numerous connections.

First, many of the psalms have a superscription or heading that connects them to the stories we have read so far. Seventy three of the psalms are entitled "Psalms of David." This does not necessarily mean they were written by David. The Hebrew phrase *leDavid* does not always mean "by David." It can also mean "concerning David" or "for David" (in the sense of being dedicated to David).[5] The title connects these psalms to the plot we have read by connecting them to the story of David. In some cases a specific story of David is noted. For example, Psalm 3 is entitled "A Psalm of David, when he fled from his son Absalom." We read this story in

II Samuel, chapters 15-18. You can hear the anguish of that situation in the opening verse of the psalm: "O Lord, how many are my foes! Many are rising against me." Remembering the story of David's exile gives hope to the people of Israel in exile. So does his expression of trust in verse 6: "I am not afraid of ten thousands of people who have set themselves against me all around." Most of us do not have ten thousand enemies. But David did, and if he can trust God in such a situation, maybe we can trust God with our problems.

Many other psalms are also connected to stories in David's life, especially to the time he lived as a refugee fleeing from King Saul (see Psalms 18, 52, 54, 56, 57, 59, and 63.) These psalms would also have special meaning to the people of Israel living as refugees in exile.

Sometimes the psalms retell the Bible's plot from different angles. Psalm 105 tells the stories of Abraham, Joseph, Moses and the journey of Israel through the wilderness as a hymn of praise. (See Psalm 136 for another example of how the Bible's plot becomes a hymn of praise.) Psalm 106 recounts these same stories, but emphasizes Israel's disobedience. In this psalm the story of Israel becomes an extended prayer of confession.

Sometimes the psalms are quoted within the plot of the Bible itself. In II Samuel 22 David is finally safe from his enemies. He then sings a psalm of praise, which turns out to be Psalm 18. In I Chronicles 16 when the ark of God is brought to Jerusalem, a song of praise is led by Asaph and his singers. This is a medley from Psalm 96, Psalm 105, and Psalm 106.

Psalm 89 is particularly relevant to the Bible's plot. It begins with a reminder of God's covenant with David (II Samuel 7:4-17): "You [God] said, "I have made a covenant with my chosen one, I have sworn to my servant David: 'I will establish your descendants forever, and build your throne for all generations'" (Psalm 89:3-4). But later the psalm cries out to God, "But now you have spurned and rejected him; you are full of wrath against your anointed. You have renounced the covenant with your servant; you have defiled his crown in the dust" (Psalm 89:38-39). This could apply to many occasions during Israel's monarchy, but it applies particularly to the exile when foreign armies plundered Judah and the throne of David's descendants was literally thrown down. This psalm gives eloquent expression to the feelings of the people of Israel at this moment in the Bible's plot. They are wondering, "Lord, where is your steadfast love of old, which by your faithfulness you swore to David?" (Psalm 89:49).

Another psalm which gives unmistakable expression to the anguish of the people of Israel in exile is Psalm 137. It begins, "By the rivers of Babylon—there we sat down and there we wept when we remembered Zion." (Zion is the word for the hill in Jerusalem on which the temple was located.) They are asked by their captors to sing one of the songs of Zion for entertainment, but they cannot do it. "How could we sing the Lord's song in a foreign land?" (Psalm 137:4). Their grief then spills over to bitterness and anger: "O daughter of Babylon, you devastator! Happy shall they be who pay you back what you have done to us! Happy shall they be who take your little ones and dash them against the rock!" (Psalm 137:8-9) Sometimes, there just aren't enough rocks!

That is how the people of Israel felt in exile, and perhaps at other times in their story. (Psalm 109 is another example of a very angry psalm.) At this point it is important to remember that the psalms are not always God's word to us. They are our words to God. But by including them in the Bible we are given permission to be angry, depressed, afraid, hopeful, joyful, and thankful in the presence of God, just like the people of God in the Bible.

I have noted how individual psalms connect with parts of the Bible's plot. But in a sense the book of Psalms itself unfolds with a certain flow to it, almost like a plot. The first two chapters involve remembrance. Psalm 1 is a reminder of the law given to Moses and the blessings promised in the book of Deuteronomy to those who keep the law. Psalm 2 is sometimes called an "enthronement" psalm—a song for the anointing of a new king. It recalls the promises God gave to David, especially when God said of David's offspring: "I will establish the throne of his kingdom forever. I will be a father to him, and he shall be a son to me" (II Samuel 7:13-14). In Psalm 2 the new king recalls that promise when he says, "I will tell of the decree of the Lord: He said to me, 'You are my son; today I have begotten you.'" The psalm goes on to promise that the new king will rule the nations with a rod of iron (Psalm 2:9). Psalm 1 reminds the people of God's covenant with Moses, and Psalm 2 recalls God's covenant with David.[6]

But then the book of Psalms plunges into series of laments or complaints to God. Psalm 3 begins, "O Lord, how many are my foes! Many are rising against me." This could be the cry of any individual, but it would make particular sense if it were the cry of one of Judah's kings. Psalm 6 says, "Be gracious to me, O Lord, for I am languishing; O Lord, heal me, for my bones are shaking with terror" (Psalm 6:2). This too is a psalm asking for deliverance from enemies (see verses 9-10). One of the most powerful psalms of complaint, Psalm 22, begins with these words, later quoted by Jesus on the cross: "My God, my God, why have you forsaken me?" In these psalms the people of Israel complain because the blessings promised in Psalm 1 and 2 have not materialized.

Interspersed within the psalms of complaint are statements of trust in God. Psalm 3 says, "But you, O Lord, are a shield around me, my glory, and the one who lifts my head" (Psalm 3:3). Not only are statements of trust mixed into the individual psalms, but entire psalms of trust are mixed into the collection of psalms as a whole. One of the most famous is Psalm 23: "The Lord is my shepherd, I shall not want."

Often the elements of remembrance, complaint, trust, thanksgiving, and praise are mixed together within an individual psalm. But these elements also characterize the book of Psalms as a whole, and in general the book of Psalms moves from complaint to praise. The psalms of complaint or lament are more concentrated in the early part of the book, while the psalms of thanksgiving and praise are more concentrated toward the end.[7] In the book of Psalms as a whole there is a kind of flow, not unlike the plot of the Bible, moving from promise to adversity to deliverance to praise. The book of Psalms itself is a reminder that the world does not end with a bang or a whimper but with a song of praise to God (Revelation 19:1-8), and we are invited to join the chorus.

Proverbs

I once heard a story about a college professor who was approached after class about a failing grade. The seductively dressed female student came into the professor's office, leaned over his desk and said, "I will do anything to pass this class. Anything!" The professor raised his eyebrows. "Anything?" he asked. "Anything," she nodded. The professor stood up, leaned over his desk, and whispered, "Then study!"

That is the perspective of the book of Proverbs. Proverbs is a call for God's people to use their heads. It is a call to study, to make use of our experience, our powers of observation, and the intelligence God has given us to discern how we should live.

Like the book of Job, it is not readily apparent how Proverbs is connected to the Bible's plot. Proverbs contains no references to any events of the Bible. The key link between Proverbs and the rest of the Bible is the figure of Solomon, who is mentioned at the beginning as the source for many of the proverbs. In I Kings 3 God appears to Solomon in a dream and invites Solomon to ask for whatever he wants. Solomon responds, "Give your servant therefore an understanding mind to govern your people, able to discern between good and evil; for who can govern this your great people" (I Kings 3:9). In answer to this prayer God gives Solomon a wise and discerning mind, and the book of Proverbs is part of that gift of wisdom.

The title of this book in Hebrew is *Mashalim*, usually translated "Proverbs." The Hebrew word *mashal* has two derivations. It comes from a Hebrew word which means "to be like," and it also comes from a Hebrew word which means "to rule."[8] The first meaning, "to be like," reflects the fondness in the book of Proverbs for similes or figures of speech. The second meaning, "to rule," indicates Proverbs particular focus on kings and rulers. If Solomon is understood to be the speaker, then the child to whom he speaks in each of the first seven chapters will be the future king. This is confirmed by the number of references in Proverbs to the king. (For examples see Proverbs 14:28, 16:10, 20:28, 25:5, 29:4, 29:14, and all of chapter 31 which is couched as the advice of a queen mother to her son.)

Given where we are in the Bible's plot, it would be fair to ask why so much attention is given in Proverbs to instructions for a king. At this point in the story, Israel had no king. Even the group that returned to the Promised Land with Ezra and Nehemiah did not have a king. For the remainder of the Bible, the people of Israel are governed by foreign powers. (Even King Herod in the New Testament is a puppet king.) So why would they preserve and treasure these instructions for kings to rule wisely?

There are signs that even in exile the people of Israel were given significant governing responsibilities. The book of Esther is about a Jewish girl who becomes a queen of Persia and her uncle Mordecai who becomes a trusted advisor to the Persian king. The book of Daniel is about a Jew who becomes an official and trusted advisor for two kings of Babylon, and later for the king of Persia. These people follow in the footsteps of Joseph, who was sold as a slave to the Egyptians but became the second in command to Pharaoh himself.

Even at this point in the plot, there is great relevance for the people of Israel to have wise instruction in governing. In fact, some of the proverbs are aimed not at the king himself but at officials who serve the king. (See Proverbs 22:11 and 23:1-3 for examples.)

But there is an even deeper connection in Proverbs to the plot of the Bible. Proverbs is instruction on the life of blessing. Proverbs 3:1-2 says, "My child, do not forget my teaching, but let your heart keep my commandments; for length of days and years of life and abundant welfare they will give you."

Blessing is a key theme of the Bible's plot. God promised to bless Abraham and his descendants and to make them a blessing to all the nations (Genesis 12:2). Moses told the people of Israel that they would be blessed by keeping God's commandments (Deuteronomy 28:1-14). This point is repeated at the beginning of the book of Psalms: "Happy [or blessed] are those who do not follow the advice of the wicked, or take the path that sinners tread, or sit in the seat of scoffers; but their delight is in the law of the Lord, and on his law they meditate day and night" (Psalm 1:1-2).

The book of Proverbs continues this focus on blessing but looks at it from a different angle. Like the Old Testament law, Proverbs stresses that the life of blessing begins with the fear of the Lord (Proverbs 1:7, 9:10, 10:27, 14:26-27, 15:33, 19:23, and others). But the proverbs are different than the Old Testament law. The proverbs are based not on revelation but on experience. They are not commandments chiseled by God in stone. They are the accumulated experience of people on how to live in a way that will honor God and bring God's blessing. They are a call to study!

One indication that the proverbs are not the same as God's commandments is their international flavor. The superscriptions at the beginning of the first two sections of the book (Proverbs 1:1 and 10:1) ascribe the proverbs to Solomon, an Israelite. But the beginning of the third section (22:17) ascribes them to "the words of the wise." Interestingly, this section borrows heavily from an Egyptian book of wisdom known as the "Instruction of Amenemopet."[9] The last two sections of Proverbs (chapters 30 and 31) are ascribed to people who do not appear to be Israelites at all. Because the proverbs are based on experience rather than the laws given to Moses, the source of these proverbs can come from people of any nation.

The second indication that proverbs are not the same as commandments is their highly situational and sometimes contradictory nature. A good example is the observations in Proverbs about wealth. Proverbs clearly recognizes the value and power of money:

- "The wealth of the rich is their fortress; the poverty of the poor is their ruin" (10:15)
- "Wealth brings many friends, but the poor are left friendless" (19:4)
- "The rich rules over the poor, and the borrower is the slave of the lender" (22:7)

These are not commandments. They are observations about life. Maybe life should not be this way, but it is.

However, wealth is not the only thing to consider when it comes to having a blessed life:

- "Better is a little with the fear of the Lord than great treasure and trouble with it" (15:16)
- "Better is a dinner of vegetables where love is than a fatted ox and hatred with it" (15:17)
- "Better is a dry morsel with quiet than a house full of feasting with strife" (17:1)
- "Better to be poor and walk in integrity than to be crooked in one's ways even though rich" (28:6).

The tenth commandments say, "You shall not covet." Proverbs would certainly agree. But Proverb's attitude toward money and possessions is more nuanced. Poverty is destructive. It isolates and enslaves people. So taking care of your finances is part of wise living and one of the means by which God brings blessing into your life. But there is a limit to how compulsively you should pursue wealth. Proverbs 23:4-5 says, "Do not wear yourself out to get rich; be wise enough to desist. When your eyes light upon it, it is gone; for suddenly it takes wings to itself, flying like an eagle toward heaven." Proverbs stresses the importance of sharing. Proverbs 11:24-25: "Some give freely, yet grow all the richer; others withhold what is due, and only suffer want. A generous person will be enriched, and one who gives water will get water."

Proverbs supports the idea "you shall not covet," not only because it is God's command but because it is proven wise by experience. At the same time Proverbs goes beyond the simple command: do not covet. It encourages us to look more deeply at the role of money and possessions, and at how God might use them to bless us and make us a blessing to others.

This brings us back to the Bible's plot. God wants to bring blessing to the descendants of Abraham and through them to all nations. Proverbs is a collection of observations which can help accomplish that. Many important topics are covered in the book of Proverbs: money, sex, hard work, conflict resolution, watching your mouth, even etiquette. By living wisely in these areas, we can participate in fulfilling God's promise to Abraham and God's purpose for creating us.

Ecclesiastes

The book of Ecclesiastes not only seems unconnected to the Bible's plot, it is anti-plot. The "teacher" who speaks in the book of Ecclesiastes sees no evidence of a grand plan that gives meaning to human life.[10] "Vanity of vanities, says the Teacher, vanity of vanities! All is vanity" (Ecclesiastes 1:2).

His first argument is that the creation is not going anywhere except in circles. "The sun rises and the sun goes down, and hurries to the place where it rises. The wind blows to the south, and goes around to the north; round and round goes the wind, and on its circuits the wind returns" (Ecclesiastes 1:5-6).

As we saw in Genesis, chapter 1, the Bible sees creation as unfolding in a progression toward a certain end: the Sabbath—the day of rest and worship. But the Teacher in Ecclesiastes does not see it that way. The creation goes nowhere; it simply repeats itself in an endless cycle.

The same is true for human life. "What has been is what will be, and what has been done is what will be done; there is nothing new under the sun" (Ecclesiastes 1:9). People may think they are doing something new, but they are only reinventing the past that they no longer remember (Ecclesiastes 1:10-11).

If God has a plan, we do not know what it is. Chapter 3 presents a poignant poem often read at memorial services:

"For everything there is a season, and a time for every matter under heaven" (Ecclesiastes 3:1). But here is the teacher's comment about this poem: "God has made everything suitable for its time; moreover he has put a sense of past and future into their minds, yet they cannot find out what God has done from the beginning to the end" (Ecclesiastes 3:11). There may be a time for every matter under heaven, but we do not know what it is, and we cannot see where it is all going. You don't often hear that part read at a memorial service!

The one thing we know, according to the Teacher, is that life is headed toward death. In chapter 2 we discover why the Teacher identifies himself as Solomon, the son of David, king in Jerusalem (1:1). In I Kings 10 we are told that Solomon had extravagant wealth, wisdom, and fame. In Ecclesiastes, chapter 2, the Teacher talks about this wealth, wisdom, and fame and concludes, "All was vanity and chasing after wind." It is vain because all alike end up dead and forgotten (Ecclesiastes 2:14-16).

It is striking to compare Ecclesiastes to Job. Job is not struggling with the meaning of life in the face of death. Job is struggling with the injustice of life in the face of innocent suffering. Perhaps existential angst is a luxury of the privileged. In any event, the Teacher of Ecclesiastes is not looking for an intervention by God. He cannot imagine God providing anything for him that he does not already have. It is all pointless.

So what is the Teacher's conclusion from all this? Enjoy what you can of life here and now, including relationships, because that is all there is (see Ecclesiastes 5:18-20). Note that the Teacher does not reject God. He says that any enjoyment in life comes from God, so enjoy it. He even recommends a certain piety: be respectful of God because your life will be better if you do (Ecclesiastes 5:1-6). But he does not expect from God anything more than that.

One of the pleasures of this life that the Teacher encourages is relationships with other people: "Two are better than one, because they have a good reward for their toil. For if they fall, one will lift up the other; but woe to one who is alone and falls and does not have another to help" (Ecclesiastes 4:9-10).

It is all very practical. Relationships with other people make life better. The Song of Solomon, which follows Ecclesiastes in the Christian Bible, is a testimony to the joy that sex and marriage can bring. (Solomon was certainly an expert on that subject!) The Teacher of Ecclesiastes would applaud that, as long as you don't expect it to have any deeper meaning.

Robert Gordis, a Jewish commentator, summarizes the perspective of Ecclesiastes in these words: "Koheleth has two fundamental themes—the essential unknowability of the world and the divine imperative of joy."[11]

But the editor of Ecclesiastes has one final word. At the end of the book the unknown editor acknowledges the wisdom and thoughtfulness of the Teacher's words. But he makes this concluding comment:

> The end of the matter; all has been heard. Fear God, and keep his commandments; for that is the whole duty of everyone. *For God will bring every deed into judgment, including every secret thing, whether good or evil* (Ecclesiastes 12: 13-14; my emphasis).

In other words, there is still a plot yet to unfold. There is a future of judgment and hope that the Teacher of Ecclesiates has not yet reckoned with, and the contours of that future are about to be revealed by the prophets, as well as by the New Testament.

Suggested Readings for Chapter 5

Job, chapters 1-21, 38-42. There is value in reading all of Job, but these chapters will take you through the first two cycles of Job's dialogue with his friends and give you God's reply, as well as the conclusion to the story.

Psalms 1 and 2 and a sampling of as many psalms as you would like to read from throughout the rest of the book.

Proverbs, chapters 1-8, and a sampling of other chapters as you have time.

Ecclesiastes, chapters 1-12.

Questions for Reflection

1. In what ways does serving God benefit your life? In what ways does it not benefit your life?

2. What would you say to God in a psalm of complaint? A psalm of trust? A psalm of thanksgiving or praise?

3. What are the best pieces of advice you have ever received? How is that advice consistent or inconsistent with what you have learned about God in the Bible?

4. What gives your life meaning given the fact that one day you will die and that a few generations from now you will probably be forgotten?

6

A Stern and Fearful Hope

The late Fred Speakman, who for many years was the pastor of the Third Presbyterian Church in Pittsburgh, tells of a man who went to an old friend named John to ask for a loan. Since the man wanted the loan with no interest and no collateral, John was unenthusiastic. He told the man, "I don't think our friendship is that close."

The friend was shocked. "John," he said, "how can you sit there and say that to me? We spent our childhood together! In school we were inseparable. If you have forgotten all the past years of devotion, still, how could you forget the time I saved you from drowning, the hours spent coaching you in calculus, the months I spent persuading my cousin to marry your sister, the fact that it was through my friendship that you got your start in business?"

"Oh, I remember all that," John replied. "But what have you done for me lately?"[1]

In the time of the exile the people of Israel asked the same question of God.

> Then they remembered the days of old, of Moses his servant. Where is the one who brought them out of the sea with the shepherds of his flock? Where is the one who put within them his holy spirit, who caused his glorious arm to march at the right hand of Moses, who divided the waters before them to

make for himself an everlasting name, who led them through the depths? (Isaiah 63:11-13)

Living in ruined cities or as refugees in a foreign land, the people of Israel remember the stories of what God did in the time of the Exodus and cry to God, "What have you done for us lately?" But in asking such a question, the people show that they do not understand what the exile means in terms of their past or future. So God sends the prophets to explain it to them.

The Prophets and the Plot

The prophetic writings of the Old Testament (Isaiah-Malachi) are connected to the Bible's plot in three ways.

1. Some of the prophets are mentioned by name in parts of the story we have already covered:
   - Isaiah delivers a message of hope when Jerusalem is attacked by the Assyrians (II Kings 19 and 20).
   - Jeremiah speaks God's word in the time of King Zedekiah (II Chronicles 36:12, 21-22).
   - Jonah prophesies a partial restoration of Israel in the time of King Jeroboam II (II Kings 14:25).
   - Haggai and Zechariah prophesy to the Jews who return to Jerusalem to rebuild the temple (Ezra 5:1, 6:14).

2. In other cases the writings of the prophets expand on events that have been described earlier in the story:
   - Isaiah's conversation with King Ahaz during the attack by Syria (Isaiah 7; expanding on II Kings 16:5).
   - Jeremiah's imprisonment by King Zedekiah during the Babylonian invasion (Jeremiah 37-39; expanding on II Kings 24:18-25:7).
   - Ezekiel's experience of exile in Babylon and Daniel's experience of exile in Babylon and Persia (expanding on II Kings 24:12-17).
   - Haggai's encouragement to the returning exiles to rebuild the Lord's temple (expanding on Ezra 5:1-2).

3. Frequently the writings of the prophets are connected to the plot of the story by identifying the kings who reigned

during the time of their prophecy. (See the opening verses of Isaiah, Jeremiah, Ezekiel, Daniel, Hosea, Amos, Micah, Zephaniah, Haggai, and Zechariah.)

In light of these connections, it would seem logical to insert the prophets at their chronological point in the story. Many editions of the Bible include charts showing where different prophets would fit into a timeline of the Old Testament (see Appendix B). But this is not how the Christian Bible was finally arranged. Why are the writings of the prophets collected at the end of the Old Testament instead of interspersed into the story according to the time period of their ministry?

The issue gets even more complicated. In some cases Bible scholars have identified different parts of a single prophetic book that come from different time periods. For example, Isaiah, chapters 40-55 are thought to come from the time of the exile, about two centuries later than the events portrayed in chapters 1-39. Isaiah, chapters 56-66 are thought to come from an even later time. These three sections of the book of Isaiah are known as First Isaiah, Second Isaiah, and Third Isaiah. Yet, in its final form the Bible groups all three sections of Isaiah together and then groups the whole book of Isaiah with all of the other prophetic writings. Why?

The Bible itself does not answer this question. But in terms of the Bible's plot I think there may be a reason that the writings of the prophets are collected at the end of the Old Testament. *The writings of the prophets, individually and as a whole, represent a new twist in the plot.* When the promise of land to the descendants of Abraham is lost, and when the promise of eternal kingship to the descendants of David comes to an end, then the future hope of Israel and the other families of the earth requires a new work of God. But this new work can be understood only when the failure of the old promises and covenants is honestly faced.[2]

Note on terminology: As I mentioned in chapter 4, after the reign of King Solomon the nation of Israel was divided by a civil war. The northern ten tribes were known as the kingdom of Israel, and the southern two tribes, who continued to be ruled by the descendants of David in Jerusalem, were known as the kingdom of Judah. However, in the writings of the prophets it is not always certain whether the term Israel is used only to refer to the northern kingdom or whether it refers to the whole people of Israel descended from Abraham's grandson. In this chapter I will use the term Judah to refer specifically to the southern kingdom. When speaking of the northern kingdom I will call it "the northern kingdom of Israel." I will use the expression "people of Israel" to refer to the whole of God's chosen people descended from Abraham.

The Broken Covenant

The book of Isaiah begins much like the story told by Fred Speakman. God, sounding like an unappreciated friend, says to the people of Israel: "Hear, O heavens, and listen, O earth; for the Lord has spoken: I reared children and brought them up, but they have rebelled against me. The ox knows its owner and the donkey its master's crib; but Israel does not know, my people do not understand" (Isaiah 1:2-3).

God did many things for the people of Israel: creating them miraculously from a barren Sarah, saving them from slavery and genocide in Egypt, bringing them to the Promised Land, and delivering them from their enemies. Yet they turned their back on God.

The book of Jeremiah begins with the same theme: "Thus says the Lord: What wrong did your ancestors find in me that they went far from me, and went after worthless things and became worthless themselves?" (Jeremiah 2:5). God makes a similar point through the prophet Hosea: "When Israel was a child, I loved him, and out of Egypt I called my son. The more I called them, the more they went away from me; they kept sacrificing to the Baals, and offering incense to idols" (Hosea 11:1-2).

Having followed the Bible's plot up to this point, you will appreciate the pathos of the situation. God went to extraordinary lengths to save the people of Israel and bring them to the Promised Land. God did this not only to bring blessing to the people of Israel but to bring blessing to all the families of the earth. But the people of Israel broke their covenant relationship to God. First, they broke the covenant by worshiping other gods. Hosea compares the people of Israel to a prostitute who abandons her husband and goes off to make love with other gods (Hosea 2:13). Jeremiah uses the same image: "The Lord said to me in the days of King Josiah: Have you seen what she did, that faithless one, Israel, how she went up on every high hill and under every green tree, and played the whore there?" (Jeremiah 3:6).

If you remember from chapter 4, the high places were the sites where the kings of Israel set up shrines to other gods. When Jeremiah says that Israel "prostituted herself" on every high hill, he compares Israel's idolatry to adultery. This may have been true literally, since some of the gods of the ancient Middle East were worshiped through ritual prostitution.

In this particular verse Jeremiah uses the word "Israel" to mean the northern kingdom. But the southern kingdom of Judah was just as bad:

> She saw that for all the adulteries of that faithless one, Israel, I had sent her away with a decree of divorce; yet her false sister Judah did not fear, but she too went and played the whore. Because she took her whoredom so lightly, she polluted the land, committing adultery with stone and tree (Jeremiah 3:8-9).

Jeremiah is not talking literally about having sex with a stone or tree. He is talking about Judah worshiping gods of stone or wood.

In some cases the people of Israel and Judah worshiped other gods while claiming to worship the Lord. Jeremiah points out that they turn their backs on God, but in the time of trouble they say to God, "Come and save us!" To change the gender of the metaphor: they are like a philandering husband. They want their marriage and their mistresses. They serve other gods when they think it serves their purposes, but they still want their relationship to the Lord.

As the Bible says on numerous occasions, the Lord is a jealous God, meaning that the Lord will not accept rivals for our ultimate allegiance. Later in the Bible Jesus puts it this way: "You cannot serve God and wealth" (Matthew 6:24). Israel and Judah broke their covenant with God by committing religious adultery. They forsook their exclusive commitment to the Lord in order to pursue relationships with other gods. This metaphor of adultery foreshadows a later reversal. At the end of the story, the new Jerusalem will be pictured as the faithful bride of Christ (Revelation 21:9-10).

Israel and Judah also broke their covenant with God through injustice toward other people. Referring to Jerusalem, Isaiah says,

> How the faithful city has become a whore! She that was full of justice, righteousness lodged in her—but now murderers!...Your princes are rebels and companions of thieves. Everyone loves a bribe and runs after gifts. They do not defend the orphan, and the widow's cause does not come before them (Isaiah 1:21, 23).

Having turned their back on God, they forgot their mission to be a blessing to the families of the earth. They exploited the poor for their own gain.

Amos makes a similar point:

> Thus says the Lord: For three transgressions of Israel, and for four, I will not revoke the punishment; because they sell the righteous for silver, and the needy for a pair of sandals—they who trample the head of the poor into the dust of the earth, and push the afflicted out of the way; father and son go into the same girl, so that my holy name is profaned; they lay themselves down beside every altar on garments taken in pledge; and in the house of their God they drink wine bought with fines they imposed (Amos 2:6-8).

Notice how in this paragraph economic sins (exploiting the poor), sexual sins (father and son having sex with the same woman), and religious sins (laying themselves down beside every altar and doing so in clothes seized from the poor who could not pay their debts) are all mentioned in the same breath. Here again we see one of the recurring plot patterns of the Bible: concern for the real world of economics, power, and family relationships. Faithful worship, marital fidelity, and economic justice are all important to God.[3]

Is This the End?

This is certainly not the first time Israel has broken God's covenant. When Moses came down from Mt. Sinai with the Ten Commandments, he caught the people of Israel in the act of breaking those commandments through their orgy of worship around a golden calf (Exodus 32). In response Moses smashed the tablets containing the Ten Commandments as a sign that God's covenant had been broken. But God made new tablets for Moses, indicating God's determination to continue the covenant relationship.

But in the time of the exile, breaking the covenant has more devastating consequences. The prophet Joel compares it to a plague of locusts: "What the cutting locust left, the swarming locust has eaten. What the swarming locust left, the hopping locust has eaten, and what the hopping locust left, the destroying locust has eaten" (Joel 1:4). How ironic that the nation of Israel would be destroyed by the same means that God used to save them from slavery in Egypt (Exodus 10:3-7). It may be that the locust plague described by Joel is symbolic for the invasion of a foreign army. But if so, the effect is equally devastating: "To you, O Lord, I cry. For fire has devoured the pastures of the wilderness, and flames have burned all the trees of the field. Even the wild animals cry to you because the watercourses are dried up, and fire has devoured the pastures of the wilderness" (Joel 1:19-20). As in the case of Noah and the flood, as in the case of Pharaoh and the plagues of Egypt, human sin ripples beyond human beings to affect the whole creation.

This is eloquently described by the prophet Hosea:

Hear the word of the Lord, O people of Israel; for the

Lord has an indictment against the inhabitants of the land. There is no faithfulness or loyalty, and no knowledge of God in the land. Swearing, lying, and murder break out; bloodshed follows bloodshed. Therefore the land mourns, and all who live in it languish; together with the wild animals and the birds of the air, even the fish of the sea are perishing (Hosea 4:1-3).

Notice how the breaking of the Ten Commandments causes harm not only to human relationships but to the land, animals, birds, and fish. It is the ripple effect of sin on the creation.

Isaiah describes the desolation of land using the image of Israel as an unfruitful vineyard: "And now I will tell you what I will do with my vineyard. I will remove its hedge, and it shall be devoured; I will break down its wall, and it shall be trampled down" (Isaiah 5:5).

This image has a double meaning. At one level it could be taken almost literally. When the northern kingdom of Israel and the southern kingdom of Judah were conquered by foreign armies, their vineyards were literally destroyed, along with their cities. But at a deeper level this passage signals not only the destruction of their land but the end of their vocation as God's people. They were created to be a fruitful vineyard. God called them into existence through Abraham so they could be a blessing to themselves and others. But that possibility appears to be over.

For Jeremiah, the damage seems irreversible. In chapter 19 God tells Jeremiah to buy an earthenware jug and says to Jeremiah, "Then you shall break the jug in the sight of those who go with you, and shall say to them: Thus says the Lord of hosts: So will I break this people and this city, as one breaks a potter's vessel, *so that it can never be mended*" (Jeremiah 19:10-11, my emphasis).

This is followed by a particularly poignant prophecy in Jeremiah 22. You may recall from chapter 4 that the book of II Kings ended on a slight ray of hope. Among the exiles living in captivity was a descendent of King David named

Jehoiachin, also known as Jeconiah or Coniah. This was important because Jeconiah was a surviving link to God's promise to David. Jeconiah was a slim thread of hope that one day a descendant of David would again reign as king. But Jeremiah dashes even this hope. Jeremiah says of Jeconiah: "Thus says the Lord: Record this man as childless, a man who shall not succeed in his days; for none of his offspring shall succeed in sitting on the throne of David, and ruling again in Judah" (Jeremiah 22:30).

Here is another scripture passage that would make no sense unless you follow the Bible's plot. God promises to give Abraham many descendants who would become a great nation and bring blessing to all the families of the earth. Later God promises to make David and his descendants an eternal dynasty to rule Israel and help them fulfill their purpose as God's people. Now Jeconiah, the last king descended from David, has been deposed from his throne and is living in exile, and Jeremiah tells us that he will die childless! It appears that all hope for God's promise to David is over.

The prophet Amos shares this disturbing pessimism: "'The end has come upon my people Israel; I will never again pass them by. The songs of the temple shall become wailings in that day,' says the Lord God; 'the dead bodies shall be many, cast out in every place. Be silent!'" (Amos 8:2-3). For God to tell a prophet to be silent suggests that God has given up. God is finished with trying to warn the people of Israel or call them back.

You cannot appreciate the message of the prophets without understanding how dire they perceived the situation to be. At this point in the story, the Bible's plot appears headed for a tragic end.

False Hopes of Fake Prophets

Meanwhile the prophets of the Bible battle rival prophets who offer false hope. Isaiah gives us a sarcastic version of their message: "Because you have said, 'We have made a covenant with death, and with Sheol we have an agreement; when the overwhelming scourge passes through it will not come to us; for we have made lies our refuge, and in false-hood we have taken shelter'" (Isaiah 28:15).

The false prophets claimed that Israel and Judah had a "covenant with death," meaning an agreement that death would not consume them. They based this idea on the promises of God given earlier in the Bible, particularly the promise to King David: "Your house and your kingdom shall be made sure before me; your throne shall be established forever" (II Samuel 7:16). The false prophets regarded the temple in Jerusalem as a sign of God's enduring presence, something God would never allow to be destroyed.

But the prophets of the Bible warn that Israel cannot rely on God's covenant and flout God's commandments at the same time. Standing in the very temple on which the false prophets based their hope, Jeremiah thunders:

> Will you steal, murder, commit adultery, swear falsely, make offerings to Baal, and go after other gods that you have not known, and then come and stand before me in this house, which is called by my name, and say, "We are safe!"—only to go on doing all these abominations? Has this house, which is called by my name, become a den of robbers in your sight? (Jeremiah 7:9-11).

Later in the Bible, this statement will be quoted by Jesus when he too stands in the temple warning of God's judgment (Mark 11:17).

Repeatedly the prophets confront their rivals who offer a false hope. Isaiah says to the false prophets:

> Then your covenant with death will be annulled, and your agreement with Sheol will not stand; when the overwhelming scourge passes through, it will take you; for morning by morning it will pass through, by day and by night; and it will be sheer terror to understand the message (Isaiah 28:18-19).

For a particularly dramatic confrontation between Jeremiah and a false prophet, read Jeremiah, chapter 28.

At this point we come to a dilemma. If the false prophets are wrong, what hope is there for God's people? If the covenant between God and the descendants of Abraham is broken, what will happen to God's promises? More specifically, what will happen to God's whole plan to reverse the curse of sin by bringing blessing through Abraham's descendants to all the families of the earth?

A Glimmer of Hope

One of the most heart-wrenching passages of the Old Testament, and one of the most important, is Hosea 11:1-9. The first four verses describe how God cared for the people of Israel like a parent caring for a child: rescuing them from Egypt, feeding them in the wilderness, teaching them how to live, and protecting them in the Promised Land. But now, because of Israel's disobedience, those blessings have been lost:

> They shall return to the land of Egypt, and Assyria shall be their king, because they have refused to return to me. The sword rages in their cities, it consumes their oracle priests, and devours because of their schemes. My people are bent on turning away from me. To the Most High they call, but he does not raise them up at all (Hosea 11:5-7).

Up to this point Hosea echoes the pessimism of the other prophets. But suddenly we come to a turning point. God says,

> How can I give you up, Ephraim? How can I hand you over, O Israel? How can I make you like Admah? How can I treat you like Zeboiim? [Note: Admah and Zeboiim were two cities destroyed along with Sodom and Gomorroh; see Deuteronomy 29:23.] My heart recoils within me; my compassion grows warm and tender. I will not execute my fierce anger; I will not again destroy Ephraim; for I am God and no mortal, the Holy One in your midst, and I will not come in wrath (Hosea 11:8-9).

Normally God's holiness would imply that God must

separate from an unholy people. But here God's holiness means that God has the power to be faithful to Israel, even when Israel is not. Though Israel does not repent, God repents.[4] Though Israel does not turn away from sin; God turns away from destroying them.

Isaiah describes this change of heart in images very similar to Hosea. The Lord says to the people, "Can a woman forget her nursing child, or show no compassion for the child of her womb? Even these may forget, yet I will not forget you" (Isaiah 49:15).

We also see God's dramatic change of heart in Jeremiah, chapter 30.[5] Verses 12-15 echo the grim assessment of Israel's condition that I have discussed above.

> For thus says the Lord: your hurt is incurable, your wound is grievous. There is no one to uphold your cause, no medicine for your wound, no healing for you. All your lovers have forgotten you; they care nothing for you; for I have dealt you the blow of an enemy, the punishment of a merciless foe, because your guilt is great, because your sins are so numerous. Why do you cry out over your hurt? Your pain is incurable. Because your guilt is great, because your sins are so numerous, I have done these things to you.

Because God's chosen people have rejected God, God has rejected them. The other gods whom they worship (their "lovers") will not save them. They have crossed a point from which they cannot return.

The next verse (verse 16) begins with the ominous word "therefore." The word "therefore" usually introduces God's judgment on Israel for breaking God's commandments (see Micah 3:11-12 and Hosea 4:1-3). At this point we expect God to say, "Therefore you shall be devoured by your enemies, and your people shall go into captivity."

But suddenly God reverses direction. Verses 16-17:

> Therefore all who devour you shall be devoured, and all your foes, everyone of them, shall go into

captivity; those who plunder you shall be plundered, and all who prey on you I will make a prey. For I will restore health to you, and your wounds I will heal, says the Lord, because they have called you an outcast: "It is Zion; no one cares for her!"

What a dramatic turn of events. The enemies whom God has used to punish Israel will themselves be punished, and the incurable wound in God's people will be cured by God.

This determination by God to do a new work among the people is the source of hope sprinkled throughout the writings of the prophets. Isaiah is particularly eloquent at describing this new work of God. In Isaiah 43:18-19 God says to the people, "Do not remember the former things, or consider the things of old. I am about to do a new thing; now it springs forth, do you not perceive it? I will make a way in the wilderness and rivers in the desert."

The new work of God will be like a new Exodus. Just as God parted the waters of the Red Sea and led the Israelites through the wilderness to the Promised Land, so God will lead Israel out of captivity from Babylon and bring them through the wilderness back to the Promised Land. This explains the imagery in Isaiah 40:3: "A voice cries out: 'In the wilderness prepare the way of the Lord, make straight in the desert a highway for our God.'" Here the words "In the wilderness prepare the way of the Lord" mean to prepare a path by which God can bring the descendants of Abraham through the wilderness back to their homes in the land of Israel. This is the first step in the new work of God. (Later the gospel writers will associate this verse with John the Baptist, who prepares the way for the new work of God in Jesus.)

The radical nature of this new work of God is captured in Ezekiel, chapter 37. In a vision Ezekiel is led to a valley full of dry bones. God tells Ezekiel to preach to these dead, dry bones. Talk about an unresponsive congregation! But Ezekiel speaks God's word to them, and suddenly there is a rattling among the bones, and the bones come together, joined by muscles and tendons. They are covered with flesh, and the breath of God enters them, causing them to stand on their feet, a vast living multitude. That is the magnitude of God's new work in the life of Abraham's descendants.

The New Covenant

But what will keep the pattern from repeating, as it did in the time of the judges? If God brings the people of Israel back from captivity and reestablishes them in the Promised Land, what will prevent the cycle of sin and judgment from happening over again?

The difference is a *new covenant*. Jeremiah 31:31-34:

> The days are surely coming, says the Lord, when I will make a new covenant with the house of Israel and the house of Judah. It will not be like the covenant that I made with their ancestors when I took them by the hand to bring them out of the land of Egypt—a covenant that they broke, though I was their husband, says the Lord. But this is the covenant that I will make with the house of Israel after those days, says the Lord: I will put my law within them, and I will write it on their hearts; and I will be their God, and they shall be my people. No longer shall they teach one another, or say to each other, "Know the Lord," for they shall all know me, from the least of them to the greatest, says the Lord; for I will forgive their iniquity, and remember their sin no more.

In the new covenant obedience is not a condition; it is a gift of the covenant. The new covenant will be secured by God's power and faithfulness, not ours. This does not mean that our obedience is unimportant. A life of righteousness and peace, a life of glorifying God and enjoying God forever, is the purpose for which we were created. But in the future God's power will bring that goal to fruition in our lives, not our own faithfulness.

The Other Families of the Earth

In the prophets the other nations appear first as the tools

that God uses to bring judgment on the people of Israel. Isaiah describes how God uses Assyria as an instrument of punishment (Isaiah 10:5-6). In Jeremiah, God uses the nation of Babylon for the same purpose:

> Therefore thus says the Lord of hosts: Because you have not obeyed my words, I am going to send for all the tribes of the north, says the Lord, even for King Nebuchadrezzar of Babylon, my servant, and I will bring them against this land and its inhabitants, and against all these nations around; I will utterly destroy them and make them an object of horror and hissing, and an everlasting disgrace (Jeremiah 25:8-9).

God refers to Nebuchadrezzar, the king of Babylon, as his servant. Of course, Nebuchadrezzar does not see himself as God's servant. He sees himself as a military conqueror. But unbeknownst to King Nebuchadrezzar, God is using him to carry out God's purposes. Here again is the sovereign irony of God.

God uses foreign powers not only to bring judgment on Israel but also to save them. Isaiah says to the people of Israel,

> Thus says the Lord, your Redeemer, who formed you in the womb: I am the Lord, who made all things, who alone stretched out the heavens, and who by myself spread out the earth;...who says to Cyrus, "He is my shepherd, and he shall carry out all my purpose"' and who says of Jerusalem, "It shall be rebuilt," and of the temple, "Your foundation shall be laid" (Isaiah 44:24, 28).

At the end of II Chronicles we read how Cyrus, the king of Persia, issued a decree allowing the Jews to return from exile to the land of Israel to rebuild the temple. Cyrus, of course, is doing this for his own political reasons (perhaps to reduce the size of a potentially explosive refugee population). But Isaiah sees it as another example of God's sovereignty displayed through the ironic use of human actions and decisions.

Meanwhile the other nations come under the scathing judgment of God, just like Israel. The prophet Amos handles this in a particularly intriguing way. In chapters 1-2 Amos delivers repeated announcements of doom to all of Israel's neighbors: the Syrians (1:3-5), the Philistines (1:6-8), the people of Tyre (1:9-12), the Ammonites (1:13-15), and the Moabites (2:1-3). All the while the people of Israel are cheering: "Yeah, preach it, brother Amos!" But suddenly Amos turns the same message of judgment against the kingdoms of Judah and Israel (Amos 2:4ff), and that message of judgment continues for the rest of the book. If the kingdoms of Israel and Judah want God's judgments to fall on other nations, they had better prepare for God's judgment against themselves. In the New Testament letter to the Romans the apostle Paul uses the same strategy to remind first the Gentiles then the Jews of their need for God's grace in Jesus Christ (Romans 1:18-3:20).

Other prophets also devote large sections to God's judgment against other nations. Examples are Isaiah 13-24, Ezekiel 25-32, the visions of Daniel, and the entire books of Obadiah and Nahum.

Yet the promise of God to bring blessing to the other nations of the earth is not forgotten. In fact it is given a new prominence. Following the pronouncement of judgment against all the nations in Isaiah 13-24, Isaiah announces this vision of hope in chapter 25:

> On this mountain the Lord of hosts will make for all peoples a feast of rich food, and a feast of well-aged wines, of rich food filled with marrow, of well-aged wines strained clear. And he will destroy on this mountain the shroud that is cast over all peoples, the sheet that is spread over all the nations; he will swallow up death forever. Then the Lord will wipe away the tears from all faces, and the disgrace of his people he will take away from all the earth, for the Lord has spoken (Isaiah 25:6-8).

This vision foreshadows a theme we will see prominently displayed in the New Testament: the Kingdom of God as a great banquet.

At one point Jeremiah sends a letter to the people of Israel who are in exile in Babylon with these instructions:

> Thus says the Lord of hosts, the God of Israel, to all the exiles whom I have sent into exile from Jerusalem to Babylon: Build houses and live in them; plant gardens and eat what they produce. Take wives and have sons and daughters; take wives for your sons, and give your daughters in marriage, that they may bear sons and daughters; multiply there, and do not decrease. But seek the welfare of the city where I have sent you into exile, and pray to the Lord on its behalf, for in its welfare you will find your welfare (Jeremiah 29:4-7).

Even in exile the people of Israel are meant to be a blessing to themselves and the people around them. A good example of this is the story of Daniel, mentioned in the previous chapter. There are two striking episodes in the book of Daniel where Nebuchadnezzar, the Babylonian king, is converted to faith in the Lord God of Israel (Daniel 3:1-30 and 4:28-37). The exiles become evangelists, something that also happens to the followers of Jesus in the book of Acts.

One of the most poignant examples of Israel's mission to be a blessing to other nations is the story of Jonah. God tells Jonah to preach God's message of judgment against Nineveh. Nineveh was the capital city of Assyria. If you recall from chapter 4, in 722 B.C.E. the Assyrian army destroyed the northern kingdom of Israel, killing many of its people, taking others into exile, and resettling the land with foreigners. Now God wants Jonah to go to its capital city and preach God's word to them.

Jonah will have nothing to do with this assignment: 1) because he hates the Assyrians for what they did to his people, and 2) because it isn't safe. An unarmed Jewish prophet would not last 24 hours standing in the middle of Nineveh telling the Assyrian king to repent.

Since Nineveh is east of Israel, Jonah books passage on a boat going west across the Mediterranean Sea as far away from Nineveh (and the Lord) as he can get. But, of course, you can't get away from the Lord on a boat. Ironically, the foreign sailors seem to understand this better than Jonah. When a fierce storm comes up, the captain wakes Jonah and says, "Get up, call on your god! Perhaps the god will spare us a thought so that we do not perish" (Jonah 1:6). How ironic that a pagan ship captain would tell a prophet of God to pray!

When the storm continues unabated, the crew draws lots to see whose sin is responsible for the storm. The short lot is drawn by Jonah. After telling them that he was fleeing from the presence of the Lord, Jonah urges them to throw him overboard. Apparently he would rather die than go to Nineveh. But the ship's crew rows hard to bring the ship back to land in order to save Jonah. As in the case of Rahab and Ruth, the foreigners try to save the Israelite.

When they cannot make it to land, they reluctantly agree to throw Jonah overboard, praying to Jonah's God for deliverance. For his part Jonah does not utter a single prayer. He wants only to find escape from the Lord at the bottom of the sea.

But God will not let him off the hook, so to speak. God sends a great fish to swallow him and spit him back on the shore, and then God's voice comes to him again saying, "Go to Nineveh." So Jonah goes and preaches to the people of Nineveh saying, "Forty days more and Nineveh shall be overthrown." He is expecting, of course, to be arrested and executed. But instead the king hears Jonah's message, gets down from the throne, puts on sackcloth and ashes, and decrees that everyone should turn from their evil ways and ask God's forgiveness. When God sees their repentance, God "repents," just as God had done in the case of Israel. God spares the people of Nineveh, much to Jonah's dismay.

This story is about so much more than a wayward prophet swallowed by a fish. The story of Jonah is a microcosm of the Bible's plot. God formed the people of Israel to bring blessing to all nations. But Israel turned its back on God. As a result they were cast out of the boat—driven out of the Promised Land into exile. But God did not forget them, anymore than God forgot Jonah. God preserved

Israel during its exile and eventually brought them back to the Promised Land, so that they could still be a blessing to other nations. The hope that Israel can fulfill that mission is proven by the success that God gives to Jonah.

One of the most extraordinary visions in all of the prophetic writings is found in Isaiah, chapter 19. Verse 19 says, "On that day there will be an altar to the Lord in the center of Egypt, and a pillar to the Lord at its border." The people of Egypt will turn to the Lord, just as the people of Nineveh did in the time of Jonah. But that is not all. Verses 23-25 tell us,

> On that day there will be a highway from Egypt to Assyria, and the Assyrian will come into Egypt, and the Egyptian into Assyria, and the Egyptians will worship with the Assyrians. On that day Israel will be the third with Egypt and Assyria, a blessing in the midst of the earth, whom the Lord of hosts has blessed, saying, "Blessed be Egypt my people, and Assyria the work of my hands, and Israel my heritage."

Not only will Egypt turn to the Lord but so will Assyria. Then there will be peace between Egypt, Assyria, and Israel, and across their open borders will flow the blessing that God intends for all the families of the earth. Insert into this sentence Israel and Palestine, India and Pakistan, or any other chronic world conflict, and yet get a feel for the breathtaking scope of this vision.

The Messiah

At various points in the writings of the prophets, Israel's future relationship to God is connected to the hope for a new king descended from David—a king who would bring God's righteousness and peace to the world. Isaiah says, "A shoot shall come out from the stump of Jesse, and a branch shall grow out of his roots. The spirit of the Lord shall rest on him, the spirit of wisdom and understanding, the spirit of counsel and might, the spirit of knowledge and the fear of the Lord" (Isaiah 11:1-2).

Notice in this scripture that the "shoot" does not come from the stump of David, but from the stump of Jesse, David's father. In other words, the new king is not simply a descendant of David like all the previous kings of Israel, most of which were miserable failures. The new king will be a new David, a fundamentally new beginning for the kingdom of Israel.[6]

The prophet Micah echoes this point. Micah 5:2: "But you, O Bethlehem of Ephrathah, who are one of the little clans of Judah, from you shall come forth for me one who is to rule in Israel, whose origin is from of old, from ancient days." One would expect a king of Israel to be born in Jerusalem, the capital city where the palace was located, where all the previous kings of Israel had been born. But David was not born in Jerusalem. He was born in Bethlehem. Micah therefore looks forward, not to a typical king born in a palace, but to a new king like David, born in the humble surroundings of Bethlehem. This new king will finally bring the peace and security for which the people of Israel have always yearned.

Though this new king will not be like the other kings of Israel, he will still be descended from David and fulfill God's promises to David. Ironically, the prophet most adamant about this is Jeremiah. If you remember, Jeremiah declared that Jeconiah, David's descendant, would die childless and that none of his offspring would again sit on the throne of David and rule in Judah (Jeremiah 22:30). But later Jeremiah says, "The days are surely coming, says the Lord, when I will fulfill the promise I made to the house of Israel and the house of Judah. In those days and at that time I will cause a righteous Branch to spring up for David; and he shall execute justice and righteousness in the land" (Jeremiah 33:14-15). The shoot from the stump of Jesse will not be a rejection of God's promises to David and his descendants; it will be a fulfillment of those promises in a new way.

Zechariah pictures this new king using a different image: "Rejoice greatly, O daughter Zion! Shout aloud, O daughter Jerusalem! Lo, your king comes to you; triumphant and victorious is he, humble and riding on a donkey, on a colt, the foal of a donkey" (Zechariah 9:9). The image of a king riding triumphantly into Jerusalem on a donkey again suggests a different kind of king—a king whose power comes from the Lord, not from military might. This is confirmed in the verse that follows: "He will cut off the chariot from Ephraim and the war horse from Jerusalem; and the battle bow shall be cut off, and he shall command peace to the nations; his dominion shall be from sea to sea, and from the River to the ends of the earth" (Zechariah 9:10).

Later in the Bible, Jesus rides a donkey into Jerusalem to claim these words of Zechariah for himself.

A crucial part of Zechariah's vision is that the promised king will bring peace not only to Israel but to the whole world. In other words, this new king will be the one through whom the descendants of Abraham fulfill their mission to bring blessing to all the families of the earth.

Isaiah takes this a step further. In chapter 11, after describing the shoot that shall come from the root of Jesse, Isaiah envisions how this new king shall bring justice and peace to the whole earth (Isaiah 11:3-4). The result is not just a transformation of the relationship between people but a transformation of the whole creation:

> The wolf shall live with the lamb, the leopard shall lie down with the kid, the calf and the lion and the fatling together, and a little child shall lead them. The cow and the bear shall graze, their young shall lie down together; and the lion shall eat straw like the ox. The nursing child shall play over the hole of the asp, and the weaned child shall put its hand on the adder's den. They will not hurt or destroy on all my holy mountain; for the earth will be full of the knowledge of the Lord as the waters cover the sea (Isaiah 11:6-9).

Notice the reference to children playing with snakes. In Genesis 3, as a result of the first sin, the offspring of humans and snakes become mortal enemies (Genesis 3:14-15). Here the relationship is repaired. It is a sign that the ripple effect of sin—the destruction sin wrecks on the whole creation—is about to be reversed!

Among the people of Israel this new king came to be known as "the Messiah"—from the Hebrew word meaning "anointed one." Kings in ancient Israel were not crowned but anointed with oil. Hence the term "anointed one" could refer to any anointed king of Israel (see Psalm 2:2). But in the time between the Old and New Testaments, the term "Messiah" came to refer to the ultimate king—the king who would one day fulfill the promises made by the prophets.

The Servant

The prophet Isaiah refers not only to a promised king but to a promised servant, a unique figure with a unique calling (see parts of Isaiah 41-45, 48-50, 52 and 53). In many cases the servant is identified collectively as the people of Israel (Isaiah 41:8; 43:10; 44:1, 21; 48:20; 49:3), and many of the things said about the servant in these chapters could be applied to the people of Israel as a whole. But in at least one case the servant cannot be identified simply as the people of Israel, because the servant is given a specific mission to the people of Israel.

> And now the Lord says, who formed me in the womb to be his servant, to bring Jacob back to him, and that Israel might be gathered to him, for I am honored in the sight of the Lord, and my God has become my strength—he says, "It is too light a thing that you should be my servant to raise up the tribes of Jacob and to restore the survivors of Israel; I will give you as a light to the nations, that my salvation may reach to the end of the earth (Isaiah 49:5-6).

Notice how in this passage the "servant" is given a mission beyond Israel to bring light and salvation to all the nations. Here we see a glimpse of another recurring plot pattern of the Bible: the narrowing of God's focus in order later to expand it. Out of all the people in the world God chose Abraham to be the bearer of a special promise. Out of all the nations God chose Israel to be God's special servant to bring blessing to all the nations. But now Isaiah hints that

God will choose a special servant within Israel to be a channel of God's blessing both to Israel and the other nations.

This sets the stage for one of the pivotal sections of the Bible. In Isaiah 52:13-53:12, Isaiah again describes the Lord's servant. But this time Isaiah uses terms unprecedented in the Old Testament. Far from being blessed, the servant is despised. Far from being a light to others, the servant is an embarrassment. But the startling truth is that the servant's suffering is the means of God's blessing to others:

> But he was wounded for our transgressions, crushed for our iniquities; upon him was the punishment that made us whole, and by his bruises we are healed. All we like sheep have gone astray; we have all turned to our own way, and the Lord has laid on him the iniquity of us all (Isaiah 53:5-6).

Here we see captured two more recurring plot patterns of the Bible: 1) God's tendency to choose unexpected people, and 2) the fulfillment of God's promises through a person rejected by God's people.

In certain ways the prophets themselves were like this suffering servant. Most of them did not choose to be prophets. They were called. Jeremiah complained, "Ah, Lord God! Truly I do not know how to speak, for I am only a boy" (Jeremiah 1:6), sounding reminiscent of Moses. Amos demurs, "I am no prophet, nor a prophet's son; but I am a herdsman, and a dresser of sycamore trees, and the Lord took me from following the flock, and the Lord said to me, 'Go, prophesy to my people Israel'" (Amos 7:14-15). We have already seen how Jonah reacted to God's command to prophesy. The call of the prophets reflects God's tendency to choose unexpected people to do God's work.

But the ministry of the prophets also involved rejection and suffering. Isaiah was told from the beginning that people would not listen to his message (Isaiah 6:9-10). Jeremiah was imprisoned and threatened with death (Jeremiah, chapters 37-38). In anguish he cried out to God in laments rivaling those of Job (see especially Jeremiah 20:7-18). Hosea suffered the betrayal of his wife. Daniel was put in a lion's den. Ezekiel was taken into exile with others from Jerusalem and suffered numerous indignities including being bound and forced to lie on his side for 390 days (Ezekiel 4:4-8). God's comment to Ezekiel is particularly revealing:

> Then lie on your left side, and place the punishment of the house of Israel upon it; you shall bear their punishment for the number of days that you lie there. For I assign to you a number of days, three hundred and ninety days, equal to the number of years of their punishment; and so you shall bear the punishment of the house of Israel (Ezekiel 4:4-5).

Here we have a distant echo of the suffering servant in Isaiah 53.

And yet, the work of the suffering servant in Isaiah 53 goes far beyond anything experienced or accomplished by the people of Israel or the prophets of the Old Testament. None of their suffering had the effect of redeeming people or bringing blessing to the other nations. At the end of the book of Malachi the people of Israel are still awaiting cleansing from their sin and restoration of their relationship with God and others. The entire thrust of the prophetic books at the end of the Old Testament points forward to a new work of God, foreshadowed by the proclamation and suffering of the prophets, but still awaiting its arrival.

Suggested Readings for Chapter 6

Isaiah, chapters 1-12, 25, 40-55, and 61
Jeremiah, chapters 1-7, 21-45
Ezekiel, chapters 1-6, 34 and 37
Daniel, chapters 1-6
Hosea, chapters 1-3 and 11
Amos, chapters 1-2, 7-9
Jonah, chapters 1-4
Micah, chapters 1-6
Malachi, chapters 3-4

Questions for Reflection

1. In what ways has your relationship to God been damaged or broken by your actions?
2. When has God done something new in your life or taken your life in an unexpected direction?
3. How has God used people of other races or nationalities in your life? How has God used you in their lives?
4. Describe your ideal ruler, such as a king, president, or prime minister. How does your ideal ruler compare to the future ruler envisioned by the prophets?

7

Good News in Quadraphonic

The four gospels at the beginning of the New Testament are like four speakers on a compact disk player. All four speakers carry music from the same performance, but each amplifies a different channel, emphasizing different parts of the music. The result is a depth of sound not possible from a single speaker. In the same way each of the four gospels emphasizes different aspects of Jesus' life and ministry, giving us the story of Jesus in quadraphonic.

We have already encountered this phenomenon in reading the Old Testament. The story of the kings in I Samuel through II Kings is told again from a different perspective in I and II Chronicles. Sometimes the Old Testament gives us two or more angles on a given event without separating the perspectives into different books. I mentioned in chapter 1 that many Bible scholars regard Genesis 2 as a second version of the creation story, giving us a different perspective on the relationship of God, humans, and creation than we get in Genesis 1. These two different perspectives are sometimes assigned to different sources that have been woven together along with other sources to form the Old Testament.[1]

It is not my purpose here to analyze the Old Testament into different sources, only to show that the Bible is not averse to telling us the same story more than once from different angles. It does this so that we will see the Bible's plot with a depth perspective. The Bible is not a linear retelling of events in chronological order. It is an exploration of different meanings and implications of these events as they bear on the Bible's plot.

By including four gospels instead of one, the Bible exposes itself to discrepancies, even contradictions, between the different accounts. For example, Matthew says that there was an angel at Jesus' tomb on Easter, Mark says it was a young man, Luke says it was two men, and John says it was two angels. But from very early in the church's history, Christians believed it was better to have these four accounts of Jesus' life rather than one, even if at times it made the picture confusing.[2]

In this chapter I will look at the story of Jesus' life as a whole to show 1) how Jesus connects to the plot that preceded him in the Old Testament, and 2) how Jesus provides a dramatic new point of departure for the rest of the plot in the New Testament. Along the way I will note some of the different perspectives that each gospel gives on the meaning and implications of Jesus' life.

Beginnings

Each of the four gospels begins its story in a different way, but each in its own way connects the story of Jesus to the plot we have followed so far. Matthew's gospel begins in the most boring fashion imaginable: "An account of the genealogy of Jesus the Messiah, the son of David, the son of Abraham." The next 17 verses trace in excruciating detail the line of descent from Abraham to David and then from David to Jesus.

Why does Matthew care so much about Jesus' ancestry? If you have been following the Bible's plot so far, you know the answer. Because of the promises! In chapter 2 I noted that God's promise to Abraham was the key to the entire Old Testament. God promises to bless Abraham's descendants and make them a blessing to all the families of the earth, thus reversing the world-wide curse that had spread through creation because of sin. Then in chapter 4 we saw that God refocused this promise on David and his descendants, promising to give them an eternal kingdom. By tracing Jesus' ancestry to Abraham and David, Matthew makes Jesus the heir to these promises.

But in the process Matthew throws in a few unexpected details. If you look carefully at Matthew, chapter 1, you will discover that in four cases Matthew mentions the mother who gave birth to the next ancestor: Tamar (v.3), Rahab (v. 5), Ruth (v. 5), and the wife of Uriah (v. 6). Why out of 52 generations does Matthew mention these four moms?

There are several theories, but the best, I think, is the connection to Gentiles—those who are not Israelites descended from Abraham. Tamar, as you may recall from chapter 2, was a Canaanite woman who tricked Judah into getting her pregnant when he refused to give one of his sons to be her husband. Rahab, whom we read about in chapter 3, was a Canaanite prostitute in Jericho who helped the Israelites spy out the Promised Land. Ruth was a Moabite woman, mentioned in chapter 4, who helped her mother-in-law Naomi survive during a famine. We are not specifically told Bathsheba's nationality, but if you notice Matthew does not identify her as Bathsheba. He identifies her as the wife of Uriah, a Hittite. The connection uniting these four women is that they are all Gentiles, or married to Gentiles, and yet they are included in Jesus' ancestry. For Matthew this foreshadows the future inclusion of Gentiles in Jesus' family.

But there is an even bigger surprise in Matthew's genealogy. Jesus' ancestry is traced through Joseph, but Joseph is not Jesus' biological father. Jesus is born of a virgin named Mary, who is engaged to Joseph but has not yet had sexual relations with him. Why does Matthew go to such lengths to trace Jesus' ancestry through Joseph, only to tell us in the next paragraph that Jesus was not really Joseph's son?

In this first chapter of the New Testament Matthew wants us to understand two things about Jesus: 1) In Jesus, God continues the plot of the Old Testament in order to fulfill the promises given to Abraham and David (the genealogy), and 2) In Jesus, God begins a radically new work (the virgin birth).

Up to this point, the descendants of Abraham have been

caught in a vicious cycle. Each new generation repeated the sins of the previous one. That is why Jeremiah envisioned a new covenant, or using the Latin word a new testament (see Jeremiah 31:31-34 quoted in the previous chapter). The virgin birth of Jesus is one of the ways that Matthew and Luke indicate that God has begun a new covenant in Jesus. The virgin birth means that Jesus is no longer simply a product of his heredity. He is a new work of God.

We have seen numerous examples of the ripple effect of sin passed on generation after generation to Abraham's descendants. The virgin birth is about breaking this cycle. The virgin birth foreshadows the possibility that God will bring about a new birth through the Holy Spirit for all the descendants of Abraham.

The virgin birth also indicates something about Jesus' unique relationship to God as God's Son. Luke makes this explicit in the angel's announcement to Mary: "The Holy Spirit will come upon you, and the power of the Most High will overshadow you; therefore the child to be born will be holy; he will be called the Son of God" (Luke 1:35). This introduces the theme of Jesus' identity, which is central to all four gospels.

In Matthew's gospel the first people to visit Jesus after his birth are foreign astrologers (Matthew 2). The visit of the wise men foreshadows several later developments in the story. At first the wise men from the east do not know where to find Jesus. The star tells them that a new king of the Jews has been born, but at this point the star does not tell them where to find him. They go to Jerusalem because Jerusalem is the capital of the Jews, the home of the reigning Jewish king. To them it only makes sense that the new king would be born in the palace of the old one. But this new king is not like the other kings descended from David. He is not found in Jerusalem but in Bethlehem.

How did the wise men learn to look for the new king in Bethlehem? Not from the star but from the scriptures—scriptures read to them by the Jewish priests and scribes! This reinforces Matthew's view that the Old Testament points us to Jesus.

Ironically, the Jewish priests and scribes did not go with them. They knew where to look for the new king, but they did not bother to go. Instead they sent some Gentiles to look for him. For Matthew this foreshadows the future fate of the gospel. The Messiah will be rejected by the Jewish leaders but find an unexpected welcome among Gentiles.

Luke describes the beginning of Jesus' life from a different perspective. In Matthew the recipient of God's communication is Joseph. But in Luke the angel appears and speaks to Mary (Luke 1:26-38). Luke hardly mentions Joseph. The focus is on how Mary accepts God's word while pondering all these events in her heart. In Luke's gospel Mary is not simply a passive conduit for a new work of God, but an example of discipleship: someone who trusts in God's promises and acts accordingly (Luke 1:38, 45, 46-55). This foreshadows a particular interest Luke has in the women who follow Jesus (see Luke 8:1-3, 23:49).

In Matthew, the Jewish leaders show disinterest, if not hostility, to the news of Jesus' birth. But Luke tells of faithful Jewish men and women, descended from Abraham, who welcomed Jesus' birth: Zechariah, Elizabeth, Mary, Simeon, Anna, and even the shepherds. Luke mentions no foreign wise men. However, in the early chapters of his gospel, Luke foreshadows Jesus' mission to the Gentiles in three significant ways:

1. The statement of Simeon in Luke 2:32 calling Jesus "a light for revelation to the Gentiles and for glory to your people Israel."
2. Luke's genealogy of Jesus which traces him back not just to Abraham and David but to Adam, signifying Jesus' importance for all humanity (Luke 3:23-37).
3. Jesus' first sermon at his hometown in Nazareth where he notes that of all the widows in Israel at the time of Elijah, Elijah was sent to a Gentile woman from Sidon; and out of all the people with leprosy Elisha healed a foreign army commander (Luke 4:25-27).

Mark's gospel contains none of these stories of Jesus' birth. Instead he goes straight to the story of Jesus' baptism by John the Baptist. The clothing of John the Baptist—camel's hair with a leather belt around his waist—reminds us of the prophet Elijah (II Kings 1:8). Malachi, in the last two verses of the Old Testament, had said, "Lo, I will send the prophet Elijah before the great and terrible day of the Lord comes. He will turn the hearts of the parents to their children and the hearts of the children to their parents, so that I will not come and strike the land with a curse" (Malachi 4:5-6). Mark presents John the Baptist in that role. Like Elijah he calls people to repentance in preparation for the coming of God's promised salvation.

Mark highlights a special significance to Jesus' baptism. When he is baptized the heavens are "torn apart" (Mark 1:10). The Greek word used is *schizein*. There is only one other place in Mark's gospel where that unusual Greek word is used: the moment of Jesus' death when the curtain of the temple is torn apart (Mark 15:38). Jesus' baptism at the beginning of his ministry foreshadows the culmination of his ministry on the cross.

At the same time the baptism of Jesus is like the secret anointing of a king. A voice from heaven says, "You are my Son" (Mark 1:11). This is a reference to Psalm 2:7, where God says to the newly anointed king: "You are my son; today I have begotten you." Recall the secret anointing of David by Samuel years before David actually became king (I Samuel 16:1-13). After that secret anointing, David was rejected by King Saul and nearly killed. In Jesus' baptism Mark foreshadows a similar plot pattern in the life of Jesus. Jesus is proclaimed king at his baptism, but his kingship is hidden from everyone except those who are given the eyes to see it.

John's gospel begins with the story of creation: "In the beginning was the Word, and the Word was with God, and the Word was God" (John 1:1). Where Matthew highlights the relationship of Jesus to the promises God made to Abraham and David, John starts by connecting Jesus to the creation. John then emphasizes Jesus' unique relationship to God: "And the Word became flesh and lived among us, and we have seen his glory, the glory as of a father's only son, full of grace and truth" (John 1:14). Jesus is not *a* son of God but the *only* Son of God.

In different ways all four gospels emphasize two key themes at the beginning of their accounts: 1) Jesus is the hope of Israel, the key to fulfilling God's promises to Abraham and David, and 2) Jesus is the hope of the world, the one in whom God will reverse the curse that has fallen on creation and bring blessing to all the families of the earth.

Acceptance

In all four gospels Jesus' ministry begins by calling disciples, though the process is described in strikingly different ways. In Mark's gospel Jesus calls and the disciples follow (Mark 1:16-20). That's it. There is no explanation of why God chose these particular people or why they immediately decided to follow Jesus. Mark gives no indication that they even knew Jesus before he called them. Mark's account emphasizes that we are disciples of Jesus only because of God's gracious call to us, not because of any special knowledge or worthiness on our part. Matthew is similar to Mark in this respect. Both remind us of a recurring plot pattern of the Bible: God chooses unlikely people for no apparent reason to be the key to God's blessing.

But Luke and John remind us that calling people to faith involves a process. In Luke's gospel Jesus calls Peter, James, and John to follow him only after having spent some time with them, healing Peter's mother-in-law and helping them secure an enormous catch of fish (Luke 4:38-5:11). This reflects Luke's perspective, frequently illustrated in the book of Acts, that people come to faith in Jesus through acts of mercy done in his name. Note here another example of God's concern for the real world of environment, economics, and family.

John's gospel gives us yet another perspective on how people come to faith. In John's gospel the first disciples of Jesus are referred to him by John the Baptist (John 1:35-37). One of those sent by John the Baptist was Andrew. Andrew finds his brother Simon Peter and invites him to follow Jesus (John 1:40-42). We are then told that Jesus found a man named Philip and said to him, "Follow me" (John 1:43). This sounds like Mark's version of how Jesus' called disciples. But notice the little detail added by John: "Now Philip was from Bethsaida, the city of Andrew and Peter" (John 1:44). We are led to suspect that Philip heard about Jesus from Andrew and Peter. Philip then finds his brother Nathanael and invites him to meet Jesus (John 1:45-46). And that is how Jesus gets his first disciples: John the Baptist sends Andrew, Andrew invites Peter, Peter and Andrew talk to Philip, and Philip invites Nathanael.

We are disciples of Jesus because of God's gracious call to us. We did not choose him; he chose us (John 15:16). But more often than not God's call comes to us through other people. Hence, in one way or another all four gospels portray Jesus commissioning his disciples to be witnesses— inviting others to know him and believe in him.

Beyond the disciples there are others who rejoice at Jesus' coming. All four gospels report how excited people were by Jesus' miracles. Often Jesus' miracles provoke a reaction of amazement among those who witness them.

In the Bible's plot Jesus' miracles are connected to his identity. John's gospel makes this clear by calling Jesus' miracles "signs" and pairing each miracle with a speech by Jesus revealing its significance.

- In John 6 when Jesus feeds 5000 people with a few loaves of bread, he tells the crowd, "I am the bread of life" (John 6:35).
- In John 9 when Jesus gives sight to a man born blind, he tells his disciples, "I am the light of the world" (John 9:5).
- In John 11 when Jesus raises Martha's brother Lazarus from the dead he tells Martha, "I am the resurrection and the life" (John 11:25).

Perhaps the most dramatic example of the relationship between Jesus' miracles and Jesus' identity is the story of Jesus healing a paralyzed man brought to him on a stretcher (Mark 2:1-12). When the paralyzed man is laid in front of him, Jesus says, "Son, your sins are forgiven." This provokes a surprised response from the Jewish scribes, "Why does this fellow speak in this way? It is blasphemy! Who can forgive sins but God alone?"

If you think about it, the scribes are right. If you do something to hurt me, I have the right to forgive you. But what right do I have to forgive you for something you do to someone else? How presumptuous of Jesus or anyone else to claim the authority to forgive people for all the wrongs they have done to others, let alone the wrongs we have done to God! Who has the right to forgive except God, the one who made us and to whom we are ultimately accountable?

Jesus responds with a counter-question: "Which is easier to say to the paralytic, 'Your sins are forgiven,' or to say, 'Stand up and take your mat and walk'?" This is an interesting question. Which is easier? In one sense it is easier to say, "Your sins are forgiven." Who can prove you wrong? But if you say, "Rise up and walk," then people will see whether you can actually do what you claim.

When Jesus heals the paralyzed man, he does it as a sign. He does the visible act (helping a lame man walk) as a sign that he has authority to do the invisible act (forgiving sins).

There are other incidents where Jesus claims an authority that belongs only to God. One Sabbath Jesus and his disciples are walking through a grain field plucking off heads of grain to eat. The Jewish religious leaders considered this a form of work (harvesting) that was prohibited on the Sabbath. Remember that the command to do no work on the Sabbath was part of the Ten Commandments given by God to Moses. When confronted about this, Jesus could have said, "Quit being so picky. We're not really harvesting, just plucking a few grains to eat." Instead Jesus said, "The Sabbath was made for humankind, and not humankind for the Sabbath; so the Son of Man is lord of the Sabbath" (Mark 2:27-28). "Son of man" is a phrase Jesus often uses to refer to himself. Thus Jesus claims to be lord of the Sabbath! Who can make a claim like that except God?

An even more dramatic claim is found in the gospel of John. Jesus tells the Jewish people, "Your ancestor Abraham rejoiced that he would see my day; he saw it and was glad."

The Jews then say to him, "You are not yet fifty years old, and have you seen Abraham?" Jesus replies, "Very truly, I tell you, before Abraham was, I am" (John 8:56-58). The phrase "I am" is the explanation God gives to Moses of God's own holy name (Exodus 3:14). If Jesus had said, "Before Abraham was, I was," the people would have thought he was crazy. When he says, "Before Abraham was, I am," the people think he is blasphemous.[3]

Opposition

All four gospels describe a steadily growing opposition to Jesus, even as his popularity increases. As the gospels progress this opposition becomes more serious. When Jesus heals a man with a withered hand on the Sabbath, immediately the Pharisees conspired with the Herodians to destroy him (Mark 3:6). Later, two days before the Passover celebration in Jerusalem, the chief priests and the scribes look for a way to arrest Jesus secretly and execute him (Mark 14:1).

John's gospel also portrays the growing opposition to Jesus but with more nuances. In John's gospel some reject Jesus because they can not understand him. After feeding 5000 people with a few loaves of bread, Jesus says, "I am the living bread that came down from heaven. Whoever eats of this bread will live forever; and the bread that I will give for the life of the world is my flesh" (John 6:51). Mystified, the Jewish people say among themselves, "How can this man give us his flesh to eat?" (John 6:52).

This is one of several cases in John's gospel where Jesus and his audience seem to talk past each other. During a visit by a Pharisee named Nicodemus, Jesus says, "Very truly, I tell you, no one can see the kingdom of God without being born from above" (John 3:3). Nicodemus replies, "How can anyone be born after having grown old? Can one enter a second time into the mother's womb and be born?" (John 3:4). Nicodemus thinks Jesus is talking about physical birth when in fact Jesus is talking about a new life made possible only by God's spirit given to us from above.

A similar misunderstanding happens when Jesus meets

a Samaritan woman at a well. He offers to give her living water, but she says, "Sir, you have no bucket, and the well is deep. Where do you get that living water?" (John 4:11). She thinks Jesus is talking about ordinary well water, while Jesus offers to quench a deeper thirst in her life, a thirst that well water cannot satisfy.

Eventually the Samaritan woman catches on and becomes a witness for Jesus in her village. Whether Nicodemus becomes a believer in Jesus, we do not know. But John tells us that Nicodemus defended Jesus before the chief priests and Pharisees (John 7:50-51), and after Jesus' death he helps to bury him (John 19:39).

Nicodemus proves that not all Jewish religious leaders were opposed to Jesus. Some were simply struggling to understand him. But others cared only about finding reasons to discredit him. Mark's gospel says that the scribes dismissed some of Jesus' healings by calling him "Beelzebul"—a kind of head demon (Mark 3:22). In John's gospel they take a similar tack. In chapter 9, when Jesus heals a man born blind, the Jewish leaders try to discredit the miracle by questioning whether the man was really born blind. They also call Jesus a sinner for working (healing) on the Sabbath.

In Luke's gospel the opposition to Jesus comes not only from the Jewish religious leaders but from the people of his own hometown. Speaking at his home town synagogue in Nazareth Jesus says, "Truly I tell you, no prophet is accepted in the prophet's hometown" (Luke 4:24). He then reminds his Israelite listeners how Elijah was sent not to any of the widows in Israel but to a foreign widow from Sidon. He also reminds them that Elisha was sent not to any of the Israelites with leprosy but to a Syrian army commander. Hearing this, the people in the synagogue were so enraged that they tried to throw Jesus off a cliff (Luke 4:28-29). In Luke's gospel Jesus' ministry almost ends before it begins.

All of this illustrates a recurring plot pattern that we have seen throughout the Bible: the fulfillment of God's promises through a person rejected by God's people.

• Joseph is sold into slavery by his brothers and becomes

the one who saves them from famine
- Moses is rejected by the people of Israel and becomes the one God uses to bring them out of Egypt
- David is rejected by King Saul who tries to kill him, yet David is the one who delivers Saul and the people of Israel from the Philistines

Jesus is also rejected by the very people who should have welcomed the Messiah and yet, as we will see, he is the key to the fulfillment of God's promises.

The plot lines of acceptance and opposition come to a head on Palm Sunday. When Jesus enters Jerusalem on a donkey, fulfilling the expectations of Zechariah 9:9, the crowd goes wild. They spread tree branches and coats on the road, signs of welcoming a king, and they shout, "Hosanna to the Son of David! Blessed is the one who comes in the name of the Lord" (Matthew 21:9). All four gospels tells this story with slightly different details and wording, but all mention a king or kingdom and one "who comes in the name of the Lord." This seems like a culmination of Jesus' career—his acclamation as the promised king. But at this very moment the opposition intensifies. Jesus enters the temple where he drives out the merchants and moneychangers, after which the chief priests and scribes look for a way to kill him. But they must move cautiously because of his popularity with the crowd (Mark 11:18).

The Unexpected Twist

We come now to the defining event of the Bible's plot: Jesus' death and resurrection. If God's promises to Abraham and David set the stage for the plot in the Old Testament, Jesus' death and resurrection set the stage for the plot of the New Testament.

If you did not already know what was going to happen, the gospels give plenty of warning. The fate of Jesus is foreshadowed in the attempt of King Herod to kill him shortly after he was born (Matthew 2:16). It is also foreshadowed in the fate of John the Baptist. At the beginning of Jesus' ministry we are told that John the Baptist has been arrested (Mark 1:14). Later we are told that he has been beheaded by another King Herod (Mark 6:14-29). Even more ominously, King Herod thinks that Jesus is John the Baptist raised from the dead (Mark 6:16).

In this case, however, you don't need subtle foreshadowing. Jesus himself tells the disciples plainly on numerous occasions that he is going to Jerusalem to suffer and die (see Matthew 16:21, Mark 9:31, Luke 18:31-33). Jesus also alludes to his coming death when a woman (John says it was Mary, the sister of Lazarus) anoints his feet with expensive ointment. Some of those with Jesus criticize the woman for wastefulness. They say, "This ointment could have been sold for more than three hundred denarii [about a year's pay for a laborer] and given to the poor" (Mark 14:5). But Jesus says, "Let her alone; why do you trouble her? She has performed a good service for me. For you always have the poor with you, and you can show kindness to them whenever you wish; but you will not always have me. She has done what she could; she has anointed my body beforehand for its burial" (Mark 14:6-8).

If someone spent $3,000 to fly to Paris for the weekend on a sudden whim, one might call that extravagant, if not wasteful. But what if the person bought an expensive ticket to Paris in order to see a dying father or mother? In that case I doubt anyone would say, "The money was wasted; it should have been given to the poor." Criticizing the woman shows that the disciples do not understand what is about to happen to Jesus. They do not comprehend that they are about to lose him.

The disciples cannot imagine Jesus' death, because in their minds it does not fit with the Bible's plot. Here are some Old Testament verses associated with the coming of the Messiah:

- Psalm 2:7-9: "I will tell of the decree of the Lord: He said to me, 'You are my son; today I have begotten you. Ask of me, and I will make the nations your heritage, and the ends of the earth your possession. You shall break them with a rod of iron, and dash them in pieces like a potter's vessel.'"
- Isaiah 11:1, 4: "A shoot shall come out from the stump

of Jesse, and a branch shall grow out of his roots,…with righteousness he shall judge the poor, and decide with equity for the meek of the earth; he shall strike the earth with the rod of his mouth, and with the breath of his lips he shall kill the wicked."

- Jeremiah 33:15: "In those days and at that time I will cause a righteous Branch to spring up for David; and he shall execute justice and righteousness in the land."

None of these expectations for the Messiah include watching him die. The Messiah was supposed to defeat his enemies, not be executed by them. No wonder the disciples did not understand Jesus' statements about his death. After Jesus' first prediction of his death, Peter tells him, "God forbid it, Lord! This must never happen to you" (Matthew 16:22). After the second prediction of his death, Mark says, "But they did not understand what he was saying and were afraid to ask him" (Mark 9:32). After the third prediction of his death, James and John come asking to sit at his right and left hand in his kingdom (Mark 10:35-37). They are clearly not expecting to be at his right and left hand on a cross.

One day in 1984 while Presbyterian missionary Ben Weir was a hostage of Shiite extremists in Lebanon, a guard noticed him reading a small Arabic New Testament. The guard asked what it was, and Ben said it was about the life of Jesus. The guard replied, "We know that Jesus was not really executed; Judas died in his place, deservedly, because he was not faithful. God rescued Jesus and took him up to heaven. He was a good man, and God would not allow him to be harmed."[4] Like the Arab guard, the disciples could not believe that God would let Jesus die.

The motives for Jesus' execution were complex. The Jewish religious leaders regarded him as blasphemous for claiming rights that belong only to God. They may also have felt that their religious authority was undermined by Jesus, a fear aggravated by Jesus' act of driving merchants and money-changers out of the temple.

For Pilate the religious issues were meaningless. Pilate was not concerned about blasphemy, only sedition. The relevant question was whether Jesus constituted a threat to the Roman occupation. The Jewish leaders understood this. When they brought Jesus before Pilate they accused Jesus of claiming to be a king and opposing the payment of taxes to the Roman emperor. So Pilate asked Jesus if he was the king of the Jews (Luke 23:2-3).

Jesus' reply was evasive, which could have made Pilate suspicious. But in all four gospels Pilate is reluctant to condemn him. Instead he invokes a custom of releasing one Jewish prisoner in honor of the Passover and offers to release Jesus. But Luke says that the Jewish leaders ask Pilate to release Barabbas instead (Luke 23:18). Barabbas was in prison for leading a murderous insurrection against the Romans. The irony of this situation is overwhelming. The Jewish leaders ask Pilate to condemn Jesus, an unarmed teacher, for undermining Roman authority; then they ask Pilate to release Barabbas, an insurgent with a history of violent attacks against Roman soldiers.

All the gospels agree that Pilate considers Jesus innocent. But Pilate finally bows to pressure and hands Jesus over for crucifixion. In doing this Pilate demonstrates that those who refuse to stand up against injustice become collaborators with those who commit it.

It is one thing to understand the political motives for Jesus' crucifixion, but Jesus himself was aware of a greater motive. The most surprising comment Jesus makes about his approaching death is its necessity. In the following scriptures notice the use of the word "must":

- In Matthew 16:21 after Peter confesses Jesus to be the Messiah, Matthew says, "From that time on, Jesus began to show his disciples that he must go to Jerusalem and undergo great suffering at the hands of the elders and chief priests and scribes, and be killed, and on the third day be raised" (parallels in Mark 8:31 and Luke 9:22).
- In Matthew 26:53-54 when Jesus is arrested in the garden of Gethsemane he says, "Do you think that I cannot appeal to my Father, and he will at once send me more than twelve legions of angels? But how then would the

scriptures be fulfilled, which say it must happen in this way?"

- In Luke 22:37 at the last supper Jesus says, "For I tell you this scripture must be fulfilled in me, 'And he was counted among the lawless'; and indeed what is written about me is being fulfilled."

- In Luke 24:6-7 the two men at the empty tomb say to the women, "Remember how he told you, while he was still in Galilee, that the Son of Man must be handed over to sinners, and be crucified, and on the third day rise again."

- In John 3:14 Jesus tells Nicodemus, "And just as Moses lifted up the serpent in the wilderness, so must the Son of Man be lifted up."

Why is Jesus' death necessary? Jesus tries to explain this to his disciples at their last supper. In Mark 14:22, while Jesus shares the Passover meal with his disciples, he takes the unleavened bread, breaks it, and says, "Take, this is my body." (In some manuscripts of Luke's gospel Jesus says, "This is my body, which is given for you.") Then Jesus takes the cup of wine for the Passover and says, "This is my blood of the covenant [some manuscripts have "new covenant"], which is poured out for many" (Mark 14:24).

There have been great struggles in the history of the church over exactly what these words mean. But in the context, where Jesus has clearly told the disciples that this will be their last meal together, Jesus is trying to communicate the meaning of his death. His death is *for them*. It will not be just another miscarriage of justice in a world that is already quite familiar with the death of innocent people. It will be a gift given to his followers that saves them, just as the blood of the Passover lamb saved the people of Israel from the plague in Egypt.

The Meaning of Jesus' Death

How does this work? How does Jesus' death save any one? Does it not vindicate the power of the oppressors? Christians have struggled to explain this in many different ways, and each of the gospels use different images to describe the meaning of Jesus' death.

In Mark's gospel, Jesus' words at the last supper refer to a covenant. As we have seen, covenants mark decisive turning points in the story of God's relationship to people. Often a covenant between God and people is sealed with a sacrifice (see Genesis 15 on God's covenant with Abraham and Exodus 24 on God's covenant with Moses). Mark suggests that Jesus' death on the cross served as the sacrifice to inaugurate the new covenant promised by the prophets. If we accept the longer text of Luke 22:20, Luke echoes this view.

Matthew is more explicit in connecting Jesus' death to the forgiveness of sins. In Matthew's account of the last supper Jesus passes the cup and says, "Drink from it, all of you; for this is my blood of the covenant, which is poured out for many for the forgiveness of sins" (Matthew 26:27-28). This repeats a theme Matthew emphasizes even before Jesus was born. In announcing Mary's pregnancy to Joseph, the angel says, "She will bear a son, and you are to name him Jesus, for he will save his people from their sins" (Matthew 1:21). For Matthew, Jesus' death is an atoning sacrifice. I mentioned earlier the problem the Jewish scribes had with Jesus' claim to forgive sins. Only the person who has suffered for someone's sins has the right to forgive. But Matthew suggests that Jesus has suffered for all our sins, so that even in forgiving he has still satisfied the requirements of justice.

Interestingly, John has no account of Jesus celebrating the Passover with his disciples on the night before his death. In John's gospel Jesus is executed on the day of preparation for the Passover, at precisely the hour the Passover lambs were slaughtered.[5] In John's gospel Jesus is the Passover lamb who takes away the sin of the world (see John the Baptist's words about Jesus at the beginning of the gospel in John 1:29).

In light of this, Jesus' crucifixion becomes the greatest irony of all in the Bible's plot. Jesus' death is a necessary part of the plot, and the Jewish and Roman authorities play right into it. Pilate puts a sign on the cross that says, "The King of the Jews" (John 19:19). The sign is meant as mockery: this is the best king the Jews can muster! Pilate writes the sign in three languages: Hebrew, Latin, and Greek, so that everyone will get the joke. But without realizing it, Pilate has displayed the truth on his sign, and the message will soon reach people of all nations. The only person in the gospel of Mark who recognizes that Jesus is the Son of God is a Roman centurion standing at the foot of the cross. The very cross that was intended to get rid of Jesus ends up becoming the means by which he brings forgiveness and new life to all the families of the earth. Here again we see the sovereign irony of God.

The Great Reversal

By all rights the Christian faith should not have survived Jesus' death on the cross. This is not the case with many other religions. Most of the great world religions had no trouble surviving the death of their founder. Confucius and Buddha were considered great teachers, and their followers held on to their teaching even after they died. The laws of God delivered by Moses and Mohammed could still be followed even after Moses and Mohammed were dead. It is somewhat like the theory of Relativity. Albert Einstein may have originated the theory of Relativity, but the theory does not depend on what happened to Albert Einstein. It is just as valid whether Albert Einstein is alive or not.

But the Christian faith is different. To be sure Jesus impressed people with his teaching (Matthew 7:28-29), and his followers have always treasured his words (hence the publication of red-letter Bibles with the words of Jesus in red). But the disciples did not follow Jesus because of his teaching or because he gave a new law. They followed him because they believed him to be the Messiah—the Christ—God's chosen king to bring righteousness and peace to the world. At a critically important moment in the middle of Matthew, Mark, and Luke, Jesus asks his followers, "Who do people say that I am?" They reply, "John the Baptist; and others, Elijah; and still others, one of the prophets." But then

Jesus asks, "Who do you say that I am?" Peter replies, "You are the Messiah" (Mark 8:27-29).

Jesus was not the only person who ever claimed to be the Messiah. In 132 C. E. a man named Simon Bar Kokba led a Jewish revolt against the Roman emperor Hadrian. Initially he had so much success he proclaimed himself to be the Messiah and attracted thousands of followers. Three years later he was killed, and almost overnight his entire movement disappeared.

One would have expected the same result from Jesus' death. Jesus' execution on the cross should have shattered the disciples' faith in him. And at first, it did shatter their faith. Early in Luke 24 some women came back from Jesus' tomb and told the disciples that Jesus was raised from the dead. Verse 11 says, "But these words seemed to them an idle tale, and they did not believe them." Later in the same chapter we hear of two of Jesus' followers walking on the road from Jerusalem to Emmaus on the third day after Jesus' death. Luke tells us they look sad. They meet a stranger on the road and begin to tell the stranger about Jesus. In verse 21 they say, "We had hoped that he was the one to redeem Israel." You can sense their disappointment and disillusionment. None of the disciples say, "Well, if he's gone, at least we still have his teaching." The disciples were not counting on Jesus' teaching to save them; they were counting on Jesus himself. Which means their faith in him was buried in that borrowed tomb.

Yet somehow their faith was reborn. Somehow this discouraged, disillusioned group of disciples became the most fearless missionaries the world has ever seen. One minute they are dejectedly shuffling their feet toward Emmaus, the next minute they are racing back to Jerusalem with good news. One minute they are fearfully huddled in an upper room, the next minute they are courageously preaching all over the Mediterranean.

Something happened to the disciples between Good Friday and Pentecost. That something is Easter. The disciples did not proclaim Jesus as Lord because they liked his teaching or politics. They did it because they met him raised from the dead. It was not his principles but his presence—his living presence—which changed their lives forever.

All four gospels describe Jesus' resurrection. As I mentioned at the beginning of this chapter, there are some discrepancies in the details of their account. But all four gospels agree on one particularly striking detail: on the third day after Jesus' burial his tomb was empty.

This has crucial significance for the Bible's plot. The empty tomb means that Jesus' resurrection is not an event that happens only in the consciousness of his followers. It is an event that affects the real world of creation. In one of his books former President Richard Nixon wrote, "The resurrection symbolically teaches the great lesson that men who achieve the highest values in their lives may gain immortality."[6] That is not how the gospels understand Jesus' resurrection. Jesus' resurrection is not the enduring memory of a dead teacher. It is an earth shattering transformation of the creation. (Note the references to an earthquake.)

This fits with another consistent pattern in the gospels' portrayal of Jesus' resurrection. Jesus appears to the disciples bodily. According to Matthew's gospel, the women who came to the tomb met Jesus, and took hold of his feet (Matthew 28:9). In Luke's gospel, when Jesus appears to his disciples after his resurrection, he says to them, "Look at my hands and my feet; see that it is I myself. Touch me and see; for a ghost does not have flesh and bones as you see that I have" (Luke 24:39). He even eats a piece of boiled fish in their presence to underscore that he has a real body (Luke 24:42-43). In John's gospel after his resurrection Jesus appears to "doubting Thomas" and says, "Put your finger here and see my hands. Reach out your hand and put it in my side. Do not doubt but believe" (John 20:27).

To be sure, Jesus' bodily existence after the resurrection is different than it was before. In John's gospel he appears to the disciples in their house even though the doors are locked (John 20:19), not something an ordinary body can do. In Luke's gospel the risen Jesus breaks bread with two disciples in the village of Emmaus, and when they recognize him he vanishes from their sight. They race back to

Jerusalem as fast as they can to tell the other disciples, but before they can even finish their story Jesus himself appears in their midst.

Jesus' resurrection body is not the same as the body he had before his crucifixion. For one thing, it is a body that will never again die. For another, it is a body that crosses barriers to be with us even when we are locked in a room out of fear. But it is still a body. The continuity with Jesus' former body is emphasized by the marks of the nails in his hands (John 20:27 and Luke 24:40). In the resurrection Jesus has a body, but it is a transformed body, signaling that Jesus' resurrection is the beginning of a transformation of God's creation.

In his book *Miracles* C. S. Lewis writes:

> But Christian teaching by saying that God made the world and called it good teaches that Nature or environment cannot be simply irrelevant to spiritual beatitude in general, however far in one particular Nature, during the days of her bondage, they may have been drawn apart. By teaching the resurrection of the body it teaches that Heaven is not merely a state of the spirit but a state of the body as well: and therefore a state of Nature as a whole.[7]

If you recall from chapter 1, when human beings fell into sin, the whole creation was affected. The creation came under a curse (Genesis 3:17-18). The ripple effect of sin eventually resulted in the flood at the time of Noah. After Noah the creation still suffered, as witnessed by chronic famines in Israel, the plagues in Egypt, and the destruction of the land by the Babylonians. (For a commentary by the apostle Paul about the ripple effect of sin on the whole creation, see Romans 5:12 and Romans 8:22-23.)

Jesus' resurrection begins to reverse that damage. It is a clear, unmistakable sign that Jesus is the key to fulfilling God's promise to Abraham: to bring blessing back into a world that had fallen under the curse of sin.

One of the strangest accounts of the resurrection is in the gospel of Mark. Three women go to Jesus' tomb to anoint his body with spices, and they discover that the stone has been rolled away. When they enter the tomb a young man tells them, "Do not be alarmed; you are looking for Jesus of Nazareth, who was crucified. He has been raised; he is not here. Look, there is the place they laid him. But go, tell his disciples and Peter that he is going ahead of you to Galilee; there you will see him, just as he told you" (Mark 16:6-7). The next verse, the last verse of the gospel in most translations, says, "So they went out and fled from the tomb, for terror and amazement has seized them; and they said nothing to anyone, for they were afraid" (Mark 16:8). And with that the gospel ends! No joyful reunion with Jesus, no great commission, no stirring confession of faith like we find in the case of Thomas (John 20:24-29). The women flee in terror and say nothing to anyone. Mark does not even tell us if the disciples ever heard the news.

This ending is so abrupt and unsatisfying that some ancient Greek manuscripts have added new endings to Mark's gospel. You can read these endings in translations of Mark 16:9-20. But the oldest manuscripts of Mark's gospel end at verse 8.

There have been many attempts to explain this strange ending, but in terms of the Bible's plot the ending of Mark suggests two things. First it suggests that we today are in the same boat as the women at the tomb. We have been told of Jesus' resurrection, but we have not yet seen him for ourselves. We live in the frightening and uncertain time between Jesus' first coming and second coming, between the announcement of Jesus' resurrection and his appearance in glory.

Second, it suggests that the story of God's work in our lives through Jesus is not finished. If the story had ended at verse 8, the disciples would not have heard of Jesus' resurrection, they would not have gone to Galilee to meet him, and the Christian faith would have died before it started. But we know as a historical fact (and so did Mark's readers) that the Christian faith did survive and spread, which means that the message of Jesus' resurrection somehow got out, despite the fear of his followers. The three women may have failed to carry out the angel's command, but someone did, otherwise we would have no knowledge of what happened. Maybe the women themselves had a change of heart and later told the other disciples. The point is that the gospel is not thwarted even by our fear. The good news of new life in Jesus will be heard. The question for us, as for the women at the tomb, is whether people will hear it through us or in spite of us.

A Blessing to the Nations

Most of Jesus' earthly ministry was focused on the people of Israel. When he sent the disciples out on their first mission to preach and heal, he told them to go only to Israelites (Matthew 10:5-6). Later when a Canaanite woman asks him to heal her daughter, Jesus replies, "I was sent only to the lost sheep of the house of Israel." When she presses him, he says, "It is not fair to take the children's food and throw it to the dogs" (Matthew 15:26, parallel in Mark 7:27).

The primacy of Jesus' mission to Israel is highlighted by his selection of 12 disciples (Matthew 10:1-4, Mark 3:13-19, and Luke 6:12-16). The number 12 recalls the 12 tribes of Israel. This does not mean the disciples replace the people of Israel. The 12 disciples are themselves Israelites. It means they represent the people of Israel whom Jesus came to save.[8]

Yet, as mentioned above, not all Israel welcomed Jesus. John the Baptist anticipates this when talking about the coming Messiah. He warns the Jewish leaders, "Do not presume to say to yourselves, 'We have Abraham as our ancestor'; for I tell you, God is able from these stones to raise up children to Abraham" (Matthew 3:9). Biological descent from Abraham does not in itself make someone an inheritor of God's promise to Abraham. There is, in fact, a separation about to take place. John the Baptist says,

> I baptize you with water for repentance, but one who is more powerful than I is coming after me; I am not worthy to carry his sandals. He will baptize you with the Holy Spirit and fire. His winnowing fork

is in his hand, and he will clear his threshing floor and will gather his wheat into the granary; but the chaff he will burn with unquenchable fire (Matthew 3:11-12; parallel in Luke 3:16-17).

In both Matthew and Luke, Jesus affirms these words of John in his own self-description. In Matthew 10:34-36 Jesus warns that he will divide people, sometimes people within the same family (see similar words in Luke 12:49-53). Later this happened literally in some of the families of those who followed Jesus. But it also represents what happened within the family of Israel. John's gospel points out repeatedly that Jesus' words and actions produced division within the Jews who heard him (John 7:25-31, 7:40-44, 10:19-21).

Here we see again a pattern in the Bible's plot: the narrowing of God's focus in order later to expand it. Jesus focuses his ministry on Israel, and then on a sub-group within Israel. But the ultimate goal is ministry to all the families of the earth.

This begins even during Jesus' life on earth. Jesus heals the servant of a Roman centurion who shows more faith in Jesus than the people of Israel (Matthew 8:5-13; parallel in Luke 7:1-10). After telling the Canaanite woman, "It is not fair to take the children's food and throw it to the dogs," the woman replies, "Yes, Lord, yet even the dogs eat the crumbs that fall from their masters' table." For this response Jesus praises her faith and heals her daughter (Matthew 15:21-28, parallel in Mark 7:24-30). Thanks to a chance meeting at a well, Jesus has a significant mission among the Samaritans (John 4:1-42). Jesus may spend most of his time on earth with Jews, but the redemption of the world is always in view (John 3:16).

In John's gospel Jesus makes a tantalizing allusion to this when comparing himself to the Good Shepherd. He says, "I have other sheep that do not belong to this fold. I must bring them also, and they will listen to my voice. So there will be one flock, one shepherd" (John 10:16). This probably refers to the future inclusion of Gentiles in Jesus' flock.[9] At the very least it suggests that Jesus' ministry will bring salvation to people we have not yet imagined. This is reinforced by Jesus' final prayer for his disciples: "I ask not only on behalf of these [the first disciples], but also on behalf of those who will believe in me through their word, that they may all be one" (John 17:20-21). Jesus assumes that the ministry which began with 12 Jewish disciples will eventually encompass the world: "And I, when I am lifted up from the earth, will draw all people to myself" (John 12:32).

The ending of Matthew's gospel makes this clear. When Jesus meets the disciples after his resurrection, he says to them,

> All authority in heaven and earth has been given to me. Go therefore and make disciples of all nations, baptizing them in the name of the Father and of the Son and of the Holy Spirit, and teaching them to obey everything that I have commanded you. And remember, I am with you always, to the end of the age (Matthew 28:18-20).

Luke's gospel ends with similar words. Jesus says to the disciples, "Thus it is written that the Messiah is to suffer and to rise from the dead on the third day, and that repentance and forgiveness of sins is to be proclaimed in his name to all nations, beginning from Jerusalem" (Luke 24:46-47).

This poses an interesting challenge. If many among the people of Israel did not accept Jesus, why should the people of other nations? To answer that question we turn to the next stage of the plot.

Suggested Readings for Chapter 7

Read all four gospels. Notice their similarities and differences. In each gospel notice patterns of the plot highlighted in this chapter: how the disciples are called to follow Jesus, the differing reactions by people to Jesus, the inclusion of the Gentiles, the purpose of his death, and the great reversal brought about by his resurrection. Most of all notice how events in the story pose the question of Jesus' identity and ask you, the reader, to make a decision about Jesus.

Questions for Reflection

1. Why did the first disciples follow Jesus? Why do people follow him today?
2. Why did people in his own time oppose Jesus? Why do people oppose him today?
3. Why is Jesus' death necessary for the Bible's plot? What does it accomplish that God could not accomplish in some other way?
4. What does Jesus' resurrection mean for you and for the future of the world?

8

All the Families
of the Earth

One summer I served for a week as a chaplain at a Boy Scout camp in northern Idaho. During lunch a Jewish scout asked me questions about what Christians believe and why there are so many different Christian denominations. Then he said, "There's one thing I still don't understand. How can you Christians say that the Messiah has come when there is still so much suffering in the world?"

At the beginning of the book of Acts, the disciples wondered the same thing. Following his resurrection Jesus taught the disciples for 40 days about the kingdom of God. Finally they said to him, "Lord, is this the time when you will restore the kingdom to Israel?" (Acts 1:6). Notice that their focus was on Israel. The disciples expected a Messiah who would defeat Israel's enemies and establish righteousness and peace in their land, but their vision did not include the promise of blessing to all the families of the earth.

Preserved among the papers of John Ward, a citizen of England in the 18th century, is this prayer:

O Lord, Thou knowest I have nine estates in the City of London, and likewise that I have lately purchased an estate in fee-simple in the county of

Essex. I beseech Thee to preserve the two counties
of Middlesex and Essex from fire and earthquake;
and as I have a mortgage in Hertfordshire, I beg
Thee likewise to have an eye of compassion on that
country; and for the rest of the counties Thou mayest
deal with them as Thou art pleased.[1]

That, more or less, is the attitude of the disciples.

In response Jesus says, "It is not for you to know the
times or periods that the Father has set by his own authority. But you will receive power when the Holy Spirit has
come upon you; and you will be my witnesses in Jerusalem,
in all Judea and Samaria, and to the ends of the earth" (Acts
1:7-8).

Here we have the outline for the book of Acts and the
next stage of the Bible's plot. Jesus' earthly ministry was
restricted almost totally to the borders of Israel and the
descendants of Abraham. But now God brings the good
news about Jesus to a widening circle of people: starting in
Jerusalem, spreading through Judea and Samaria, rippling
across the Mediterranean Sea, and ultimately reaching the
ends of the earth.

The Unstoppable Gospel

At the end of Matthew's gospel Jesus says to his disciples, "And remember, I am with you always, to the end
of the age" (Matthew 28:20). However, at the end of Luke's
gospel, Jesus ascends to heaven, signifying that he is no
longer with the disciples in the same way that he had been
before (Luke 24:51 and Acts 1:9). But in the book of Acts he
promises to be with the disciples in a different way through
the Holy Spirit (Acts 1:8).

This promise is fulfilled at Pentecost. The disciples are
gathered together in one place when a sound like a strong
wind blows through the room, and tongues of fire appear
among the disciples and rest on them. Acts 2:4 says, "All of
them were filled with the Holy Spirit and began to speak in
other languages, as the Spirit gave them ability."

Pentecostal churches, which emphasize speaking in

tongues (a language previously unknown to the speaker), take their name from this story. But Pentecost is not just about speaking in tongues. It is about fulfilling Jesus' commission.

This becomes apparent in the next paragraph. We are told that devout Jews from many different countries were in Jerusalem at that time. Suddenly each of them hears the story of Jesus in his or her native language. At Pentecost the Holy Spirit enabled the disciples to communicate the story of Jesus across the barriers of language to people from other nations.

The response to this preaching is more miraculous than its multi-lingual delivery. In Acts 2:41 after hearing Peter's message three thousand people were baptized. The description of this new community of faith is also striking: "All who believed were together and had all things in common; they would sell their possessions and goods and distribute the proceeds to all, as any had need" (Acts 2:44-45). One of the recurring themes in the book of Acts is that faith in Jesus leads to concern for the economic well being of the community (see Acts 4:32-35).

Sometimes this produced tensions and conflicts among Jesus' followers. Acts 6:1 says, "Now during those days, when the disciples were increasing in number, the Hellenists complained against the Hebrews because their widows were being neglected in the daily distribution of food." Apparently Greek-speaking Christians (Hellenists) felt discrimination from Hebrew-speaking Christians when it came to distribution of food for widows. So the leaders of the church appointed seven people to oversee this ministry (Acts 6:5), and all of them have Greek names![2] The early church decided to appoint Greek-speaking Christians to oversee the distribution of food in order to protect the Greek-speaking widows from discrimination. Here again we see the Bible's concern for the real world of economics, politics, and family life.

As in the case of Jesus, the growing popularity of his followers provokes opposition. In Acts, chapter 4, some of the disciples are arrested. They are arrested again in chapter 5. In the second case they are released in the middle of the night by an angel who tells them to go back to the temple and resume preaching about Jesus. The angel did this without the guards realizing what happened. The next morning the Jewish authorities find the prison doors locked and the guards at their post, but they are guarding an empty cell. The disciples are preaching in the temple, which is the very thing the authorities were trying to prevent.

Besides its obvious humor, this story is a microcosm of what happens repeatedly throughout the book of Acts. Every time authorities try to stop people from preaching about Jesus, they spread the message farther:

- In Acts 8 the persecution of Christians in Jerusalem leads Philip to carry the gospel to Samaria.
- In Acts 9 a man named Saul goes to Damascus to arrest Christians and instead becomes one of them—the apostle Paul.
- Much later in the story when Paul visits Jerusalem, he is arrested (Acts 21). He is then put on a ship and taken to Rome to appear before the emperor. As a result he shares the message about Jesus in the capital of the Roman Empire, with his travel expenses paid for by the Romans (Acts 28).

A Presbyterian missionary in Pakistan once told of standing at a bus stop with two of his associates handing out scripture booklets. At that time Christians in Pakistan were allowed to worship but not to evangelize. The missionary and his friends were arrested by plainclothes policemen and taken to the magistrate's office. After questioning, they were released, but their scripture booklets were kept by the magistrate for inspection. Later the missionaries returned to retrieve their booklets but discovered they were gone. Lawyers passing through the magistrate's office had picked them up to read, and the whole stack had disappeared. Embarrassed, the magistrate offered to pay for the booklets, but the missionaries said, "By no means. We are grateful for your help in doing our work." That is the sovereign irony of God.

Connecting to the Plot

Many of the sermons in the book of Acts recall the Old Testament. Stephen's sermon in Acts 7 is particularly striking. Starting with Abraham, he retells the story of the Old Testament, highlighting some of the plot patterns we have noted so far:

1. promise, threat, and rescue
2. the ripple effect of sin as shown by the intractable disobedience of God's chosen people
3. the one rejected by people becomes the means of their salvation.

You can read Acts 7 to review many things we have covered in chapters 2-4 of this book.

In Acts 13 Paul preaches a similar sermon. He notes how God chooses key people at critical points and how Jesus fits that pattern. But his message is opposed by some of the Jews, and Paul concludes,

> It was necessary that the word of God should be spoken first to you. Since you reject it and judge yourselves unworthy of eternal life, we are now turning to the Gentiles. For so the Lord has commanded us, saying, "I have set you to be a light for the Gentiles, so that you may bring salvation to the ends of the earth" (Acts 13:46-47).

Paul reminds his listeners of the promises given by God to the prophets (Isaiah 49:6) and how the preaching of the apostles and even the rejection of the message by Jews works to fulfill that promise.

Later in Acts, Paul begins his defense before King Agrippa with these words: "And now I stand here on trial on account of my hope in the promise made by God to our ancestors..." (Acts 26:6). Paul goes on to connect the promise of blessing given to Abraham with the hope of new life made possible by Jesus' resurrection. Those who witness to Jesus in the book of Acts consciously connect the story of Jesus with the larger plot of the Bible.

Terms of Endearment

In Acts 10 an important milestone is crossed in the Bible's plot. Encouraged by a vision, Peter shares the story of Jesus with a Roman army officer and his household. Up to this point Peter had assumed that the message of Jesus was only for Jews, or at least for those who were willing to become Jews by being circumcised (the sign of God's covenant with Abraham in Genesis 17:9-14). All of those who heard the gospel at Pentecost were Jews, even though they came from different countries (Acts 2:5). But when Peter shared the good news of Jesus with Cornelius and his family, suddenly they were filled with the Holy Spirit, signaling their acceptance into the family of Christ. In light of this Peter approved baptizing them, even though they had not been circumcised.

This set off a controversy. Acts 15 begins with these words: "Then certain individuals came down from Judea and were teaching the brothers, 'Unless you are circumcised according to the custom of Moses, you cannot be saved.'" Here we encounter an issue that will come up several more times in the New Testament: Can a Gentile become a Christian without first becoming a Jew? Can you be baptized as a follower of Christ without first being circumcised as an heir to the covenant with Abraham? And if you go that far, are you not also responsible for keeping all the other ceremonial laws of the Old Testament: sacrifices, kosher foods, ritual observances, and so on?

The first Christians struggled with this issue and finally convened a council in Jerusalem to discuss the matter (Acts 15). First they heard reports from Peter, Paul, and others how God gave the Holy Spirit to Gentiles without waiting for them to be circumcised. Peter's speech is particularly telling:

> And God, who knows the human heart, testified to them by giving them the Holy Spirit, just as he did to us; and in cleansing their hearts by faith he has made no distinction between them and us. Now therefore why are you putting God to the test

by placing on the neck of the disciples a yoke that neither our ancestors nor we have been able to bear? On the contrary, we believe that we will be saved through the grace of the Lord Jesus, just as they will (Acts 15:8-11).

Peter notes that Jewish people had not achieved righteousness in their relationship to God through circumcision or keeping the law. So why expect that of Gentiles? We are all saved by grace, Peter says, and circumcision has nothing to do with it. (We will see a similar argument by the apostle Paul in his letters to the Romans and Galatians.)

Then James, a leader of the church in Jerusalem, recalls the words God spoke to the prophet Amos:

> After this I will return, and I will rebuild the dwelling of David, which has fallen; from its ruins I will rebuild it, and I will set it up, so that all other peoples may seek the Lord—even all the Gentiles over whom my name has been called. Thus says the Lord, who has been making these things known from long ago (Acts 15:16-18).

Given the Holy Spirit's work and the confirmation of scripture, the Jerusalem council decides to accept Gentiles into the family of Christ without requiring that they be circumcised.

The inclusion of Gentiles in the church sets the stage for Paul's extensive missionary journeys in Acts 16-28. By the end of the book of Acts, the gospel message has radiated out from Jerusalem to Samaria, Turkey, Greece, and finally to Rome. It has not yet reached the ends of the earth, but it is definitely on its way. But now comes the hard work of Jews and Gentiles learning to live together in a family of faith. To see how that works we turn to the letters of the New Testament.

The Blended Family

Paul's letter to the Romans is written to a mixed congregation of Jews and Gentiles.[3] In the thematic verse of the letter Paul says, "For I am not ashamed of the gospel; it is the power of God for salvation to everyone who has faith, to the Jew first and also to the Greek" (Romans 1:16).

He develops this point, first, by showing how Gentiles and Jews are both under the power of sin. Romans 1:18-32 is a scathing portrayal of the kind of sins for which Jews would have condemned Gentiles: idolatry, sexual immorality, murder, strife, deceit, arrogance, disrespect of parents, and ruthlessness, to name just a few. By the end of chapter 1, the Jews are nodding their heads in agreement with this grim assessment of Gentile religion. But Paul is setting them up, just as Amos did. Suddenly in Romans, chapter 2, Paul says,

> But if you call yourself a Jew and rely on the law and boast of your relationship to God and know his will and determine what is best because you are instructed in the law…you then, that teach others, will you not teach yourself? While you preach against stealing, do you steal? You that forbid adultery, do you commit adultery? You that abhor idols, do you rob temples? You that boast in the law, do you dishonor God by breaking the law? (Romans 2:17-18, 21-23)

In chapter 3 Paul answers his own question: "What then? Are we [Jews] any better off? No, not at all; for we have already charged that all, both Jews and Greeks, are under the power of sin" (Romans 3:9).

This brings Paul to one of his most important insights:

> But now, apart from law, the righteousness of God has been disclosed, and is attested by the law and the prophets, the righteousness of God through faith in Jesus Christ for all who believe. For there is no distinction, since all have sinned and fall short of the glory of God; they are now justified by his grace as a gift through the redemption that is in Christ Jesus… (Romans 3:21-24).

Since neither Jews nor Gentiles have been able to live righteous lives, their only hope for a right relationship to God is through Jesus.

Notice how Paul uses this statement to advance the Bible's plot. All along God wanted to bring blessing to Gentiles as well as Jews. But how will the two learn to live together in a blended family? They will do so by giving up their sense of superiority over one another. If we are saved by grace, boasting is excluded (Romans 3:27). Justification by grace levels the theological playing field between Jews and Gentiles. The letter to the Romans repeats this point numerous times:

- "Therefore just as one man's trespass [referring to Adam] led to condemnation for all, so one man's act of righteousness [referring to Jesus] leads to justification and life for all" (Romans 5:18).
- "For there is no distinction between Jew and Greek; the same Lord is Lord of all and is generous to all who call on him. For everyone who calls on the name of the Lord shall be saved" (Romans 10:12-13).
- "Welcome one another, therefore, just as Christ has welcomed you, for the glory of God. For I tell you that Christ has become a servant of the circumcised on behalf of the truth of God in order that he might confirm the promises given to the patriarchs, and in order that the Gentiles might glorify God for his mercy" (Romans 15:7-9).

This last sentence clearly brings Romans into the Bible's plot. "The promise given to the patriarchs" refers to the promise God gave to Abraham and his descendants—a promise through which God intended to bring blessing to the Gentiles. God fulfilled this promise through Jesus. The church in Rome—Jews and Gentiles together—is a testimony to this great work.

Unfortunately, many of the Jews, the very people who should have welcomed the Messiah, rejected him. This breaks Paul's heart (Romans 9:1-3). Paul never forgets how important are the people of Israel to God's plan for saving the creation. He says, "They are Israelites, and to them belong the adoption, the glory, the covenants, the giving of the law, the worship, and the promises; to them belong the patriarchs, and from them according to the flesh, comes the Messiah, who is over all. God blessed forever. Amen" (Romans 9:4-5). The word "adoption" refers to God's selection of Abraham and his descendants as God's chosen people. The reference to covenants recalls all the covenants God made with the people of Israel: the covenant with Abraham marked by circumcision, the covenant with Moses based on obedience to the law, and the covenant with David promising an eternal kingship. God's faithfulness to these covenants has been crucial to the plot of the Bible. God has remained faithful to Israel, even when Israel was not faithful to God.

But at this point Paul sees a new twist in the plot. Romans 11:25-27:

> So that you may not claim to be wiser than you are, brothers and sisters, I want you to understand this mystery: a hardening has come upon part of Israel, until the full number of the Gentiles has come in. And so all Israel will be saved; as it is written, "Out of Zion will come the Deliverer; he will banish ungodliness from Jacob" "And this is my covenant with them, when I take away their sins."

Notice the reference here to a "hardening" of the hearts of some of the people of Israel. You may recall that in the story of the Exodus Pharaoh's heart was hardened so that "the Egyptians will know that I am the Lord" (Exodus 7:5). The hardening of Pharaoh's heart happened so that people of other nations would come to know the Lord.

Paul understands the Jewish rejection of Jesus in the same light. He leaves ambiguous the question of whether God hardened their hearts or they hardened their own hearts. In the case of Pharaoh it was described both ways. But the purpose in both cases is the same: that people of other nations might come to know the Lord and share in God's blessing. Here again we see the sovereign irony of God working even through people's rejection of God's message.

But God's mission to bring blessing to the nations is not really complete if the descendants of Abraham are left out. So Paul anticipates yet another twist in the plot: "Now I am speaking to you Gentiles. Inasmuch then as I am an apostle to the Gentiles, I glorify my ministry in order to make my own people jealous, and thus save some of them" (Romans 11:13-14).

For Paul the church is not the replacement of Israel but the extension of God's promises through Israel to the Gentiles.[4] But if God does not continue to show faithfulness to Israel, despite its disobedience, what hope do Gentiles have that God will remain faithful to them?[5] For this reason Paul believes that God is not yet finished with the people of Israel. Just as the gospel came to the Gentiles because it was rejected by Jews, so God may use Paul's ministry among Gentiles to bring Jews into the salvation made possible by Jesus. Speaking to the Gentiles in the church Paul says, "Just as you were once disobedient to God but have now received mercy, so they have now been disobedient in order that, by the mercy shown to you, they too may now receive mercy" (Romans 11:30-31). In Paul's vision the day will come when Israel too will receive the gift of righteousness through Jesus that they cannot attain on their own. Then God's mission will finally be accomplished.

The Danger of Being Too Spiritual

In Romans Paul writes to a church of both Jews and Gentiles, helping them understand how to live together as one family in Christ. But in Corinth Paul faces a different situation. As in Rome, there were divisions in the Corinthian church. But the divisions were not between Jewish and Gentile Christians but between Gentile Christians trying to outdo one another spiritually. Paul spends much of the letter poking holes in the bubbles of their pride.

- They prided themselves on wisdom, so Paul emphasizes the foolishness of the gospel (I Corinthians 1:18-31).
- They prided themselves on their spiritual maturity, so Paul addresses them as infants in Christ (I Corinthians 3:1).
- They boast of their freedom in Christ; they say, "All things are lawful," but Paul tells them that not all things

are beneficial, not all things build up relationships within the family of Christ (I Corinthians 10:23).

Perhaps the worst example of Corinthian arrogance took place at their celebration of the Lord's Supper. Some brought sumptuous portions of bread and wine which they consumed for themselves, while others went hungry (I Corinthians 11:20-21). So Paul warns them: "For all who eat and drink without discerning the body, eat and drink judgment against themselves" (I Corinthians 11:29). Some commentators think he is talking about recognizing the real body of Christ in the bread of communion. But more likely he means respecting the church—the body of Christ—when taking communion.[6]

This is confirmed in the next three chapters (12-14) when Paul talks about spiritual gifts. Apparently some of the Corinthians felt they were more "spiritual" than others in the church because they displayed more visible and dramatic gifts of the Holy Spirit, like speaking in tongues. So Paul reminds them that "to each is given a manifestation of the Spirit for the common good" (I Corinthians 12:7). You cannot regard one person's spiritual gift above others, anymore than you regard an eye as more important than an ear. Both are needed, and both share the joys and sorrows of the whole body. The famous chapter about love—I Corinthians 13—comes precisely at this point. The discussion of love in I Corinthians 13 is not aimed at newlyweds. It is aimed at helping people get along with each other in the church.

Because the Corinthians are enamored with things spiritual, they have a general disrespect for earthly bodily life. They believe that as Spirit-filled Christians they are already raised up with Christ into a new spiritual existence. So they do not need or want a future resurrection of the body.[7] Paul spends an entire chapter setting them straight on this point (I Corinthians 15). He reminds them that Jesus was raised from the dead *bodily*. So if the dead are not raised bodily, Jesus was not raised. It is true that in the resurrection our bodies will be different. Just as you cannot imagine what a flower will be like from looking at its seed, so we cannot imagine what our resurrection bodies will be like from looking at our earthly bodies. But they will still be bodies, meaning they will still participate in God's bodily creation. And that is crucial for understanding the Christian faith.

Here we must go back to the Bible's plot. God's ultimate intention is to redeem the whole fallen creation. The blessing God promised to Abraham and his descendants was a very earthly tangible blessing. It was meant to counteract the curse that had fallen on creation because of sin. Paul describes this most eloquently in Romans 8:22-23: "We know that the whole creation has been groaning in labor pains until now; and not only the creation but we ourselves, who have the first fruits of the Spirit, groan inwardly while we wait for adoption, the redemption of our bodies." There is a connection between the resurrection of the body and the redemption of bodily creation which currently suffers from the ripple effect of sin.

But the Corinthians viewed salvation as Jesus drawing us out of this physical world instead of redeeming it. As a result, physical bodily life did not matter to them. So what if a man had sex with his father's wife (I Corinthians 5:1)? Or with a prostitute (I Corinthians 6:15)? These actions did not matter because bodily life was unimportant. Or conversely, a husband or wife might abstain from all sex with each other to prove their disregard for physical life (I Corinthians 7:1). In all of these cases the bodily life of creation is treated as irrelevant.

Against these attitudes Paul screams, "Or do you not know that your body is a temple of the Holy Spirit within you, which you have from God, and that you are not your own? For you were bought with a price; therefore glorify God in your body" (I Corinthians 6:19-20).

Bodily life is not something to disdain. It is the arena in which to serve God. When we serve God in bodily life we bear witness to the new bodily creation that God intends to give us through Jesus Christ. As J. Christiaan Beker puts it, Christian life is "life in the body for other bodies within the 'body of Christ.'"[8]

The Offering

This brings us to one of the recurring themes in Paul's letters, especially the Second Letter to the Corinthians. When Paul describes the Jerusalem meeting at which the mission to uncircumcised Gentiles was approved, he notes a provision that was not mentioned in Acts 15. He says,

> When James and Cephas [the Aramaic name for Peter] and John, who were acknowledged pillars, recognized the grace that had been given to me, they gave to Barnabas and me the right hand of fellowship, agreeing that we should go to the Gentiles and they to the circumcised. They asked only one thing, that we remember the poor, which was what I was eager to do (Galatians 2:9-10).

The poorest Christians, it turned out, were in Jerusalem. In Acts 11:27-30 we read about a severe famine over the whole world. Apparently it hit hardest in Jerusalem and Judea. (How many times in the Bible have we seen God's people hit with a famine?) Paul saw this as an occasion to fulfill his promise to James, Peter, and John. He took an offering among the Gentile converts around the Mediterranean to relieve the suffering of Christians in Jerusalem. He makes a pitch for this offering in both letters to the Corinthians (I Corinthians 16:1-3 and II Corinthians, chapters 8-9).

Paul explains the meaning of this offering near the end of the book of Romans:

> At present, however, I am going to Jerusalem in a ministry to the saints; for Macedonia and Achaia have been pleased to share their resources with the poor among the saints at Jerusalem. They were pleased to do this, and indeed they owe it to them; for if the Gentiles have come to share in their spiritual blessings, they ought also to be of service to them in material things (Romans 15:25-27).

This offering brings together three major plot patterns of the Bible. First, it shows the Bible's concern for the real world of economics and reinforces Paul's point that human bodily life really matters to God. Second, it shows in a material way how God's blessing has come to the Gentiles in partial fulfillment of God's promise to Abraham. The Gentiles have not only been blessed with the good news of the gospel but also with the resources to help others. Finally, the offering illustrates the ironic way that God works in this plot. Just as the descendants of Abraham were called to become a blessing to the Gentiles, so now in Christ the Gentiles are called to become a blessing to Israelites. In fact the offering is an economic version of the mystery Paul talked about in Romans 11. The Gentiles, who have been blessed by Israel's rejection of the gospel, now have the chance to share that blessing back with the people of Israel so that they too may be included in God's blessing.

Viruses in the Body of Christ

Paul, the apostle of grace, becomes downright harsh and judgmental when confronting attitudes or behaviors that could destroy the body of Christ and its mission. We see this dramatically portrayed in his letter to the Galatians. Paul tells the Galatians:

> But even if we or an angel from heaven should proclaim to you a gospel contrary to what we proclaimed to you, let that one be accursed! As we have said before, so now I repeat, if anyone proclaims to you a gospel contrary to what you received, let that one be accursed! (Galatians 1:8-9)

Paul is, shall we say, a little agitated. So-called Christian teachers have told the Galatians that to be a true Christian you must be circumcised and keep the Old Testament laws. (Note the similarity to Acts 15:5.) For Paul this a reversion to what did not work before. Our inability to keep the law of God in the Old Testament is precisely why we needed Christ. For Paul this is a step backward in the Bible's plot, a reminder of the recurring failures of God's people in the Old Testament. Paul tells the Galatians, "We ourselves are Jews by birth and not Gentile sinners; yet we know that a person is justified not by the works of the law but through faith in Jesus Christ" (Galatians 2:15-16). If a zealous Pharisee like the apostle Paul could not achieve a right relationship to God through obedience to the law, what chance did the Gentiles have? Paul is adamantly opposed to any subtle or not so subtle attempts to reintroduce ritual observances or works of obedience as the criteria for our inclusion in Christ's kingdom.

On the other hand, being saved by grace and set free from the condemnation of the law does not mean we are free to do whatever we want. Later in the letter Paul tells the Galatians,

> For you were called to freedom, brothers and sisters; only do not use your freedom as an opportunity for self-indulgence, but through love become slaves to one another. For the whole law is summed up in a single commandment, "You shall love your neighbor as yourself" (Galatians 5:13-14).

Salvation by grace through Jesus Christ gives us freedom from condemnation by the Old Testament law. But it does not give us license to be irresponsible. We are saved by grace, but we are saved for a life of service and love toward others in the name of Christ.

The letters of the New Testament are continually battling these two opposite viruses: 1) attempting to earn our salvation by works and 2) thinking that the works we do as Christians have no meaning.

Colossians addresses the first of these when it says, "Therefore do not let anyone condemn you in matters of food and drink or of observing festivals, new moons, or Sabbaths. These are only a shadow of what is to come, but the substance belongs to Christ" (Colossians 2:16-17). In Colossae, false teachers have urged Christians to combine their faith in Christ with the ritual observances of Judaism and even some pagan cults as a way of hedging their bets.[9] "Maybe Jesus will save you, but just in case try these other things, too." Such attitudes, if left unchallenged, would destroy our trust in God's grace through Jesus Christ, which is our only hope for inclusion in God's promised blessings.

But the second virus is also a danger to the church. We see this in the first letter to the Corinthians when Paul addresses the church's handling of a man having sexual relations with his father's wife. He tells the church, "When you are assembled, and my spirit is present with the power of our Lord Jesus, you are to hand this man over to Satan for the destruction of the flesh, so that his spirit may be saved in the day of the Lord" (I Corinthians 5:4-5). This sounds less like Jesus' response to the woman caught in adultery (John 8:3-11) and more like burning someone at the stake. We do not know for sure what Paul meant by "hand this man over to Satan," but it probably means removing the man from the fellowship of the church.[10]

Why does Paul react so harshly in this situation? Because there is more at stake here than one man's sinful action. There is danger that the Corinthians will regard the man's action as unimportant—a matter of bodily activity that has no real bearing on our spiritual life in Christ. As the Corinthians are fond of saying, "All things are lawful." Such a disregard for righteousness in bodily life undermines the new life Jesus came to bring.

The letter from James makes the same point. James says,

> What good is it, my brothers and sisters, if you say you have faith but do not have works? Can faith save you? If a brother or sister is naked and lacks daily food, and one of you says to them, "Go in peace; keep warm and eat your fill," and yet you do not supply their bodily needs, what is the good of that? So faith by itself, if it has no works, is dead (James 2:14-17).

In some ways James reads like a contradiction to the book of Galatians. But even in Galatians Paul urges Christians to act in love and exhibit the fruits of the Spirit: love, joy, peace, patience, kindness, generosity, faithfulness, gentleness, and self-control (Galatians 5:22-23). It was Paul himself who organized an offering so that brothers and sisters in Jerusalem who lacked food would have some. Paul insists that we are saved by grace through faith, but like James he insists that we are saved for a new life of righteousness and blessing—a life that bears witness to the new kingdom that will come when Jesus returns.

Already But Not Yet

This chapter began with a question by a Jewish Boy Scout: If we believe that the Messiah has come, why are we still waiting for his kingdom? This question is addressed in various ways by the book of Acts and the letters of the New Testament.

Sometimes the New Testament emphasizes the present reality of God's kingdom here and now. Jesus did that when he said, "The time is fulfilled and the kingdom of God has come near" (Mark 1:15). He did it again when he read a scripture from Isaiah about the year of the Lord's favor and said, "Today this scripture has been fulfilled in your hearing" (Luke 4:21). He did it again when asked about when the kingdom of God would come. He said, "For, in fact, the kingdom of God is among you" (Luke 17:21).

In one sense the kingdom of God—God's triumph over sin and death—is already present in Jesus. But in another sense we are still waiting for it. Jesus himself taught us to pray, "Thy kingdom come" (Matthew 6:10), recognizing that we are still waiting for that prayer to be fulfilled. He also spoke of the future coming of the Son of Man when "he will send out his angels, and gather his elect from the four winds, from the ends of the earth to the ends of heaven" (Mark 13:27).

Oscar Cullman compares it to the relationship between D-day and V-day in World War II.[11] By most accounts D-day was a decisive turning point in World War II. When the allied armies invaded Normandy, they established a beachhead for bringing massive numbers of troops, tanks, and equipment into Europe. At that point the fate of Nazi Germany was sealed. From a strategic point of view, the war was over. But the final victory was not yet achieved. There was still much struggle and fighting and dying to be done by allied troops. But they pressed forward in hope, knowing that the final victory would be theirs. It was just a matter of time.

The church in the New Testament and the church today are in much the same position. The death and resurrection of Christ has won the victory over sin, death, and any powers that might try to separate us from God or thwart God's kingdom. But the battle is not finished. We still face suffering and dying. But we do so in hope that the final victory will be ours through Jesus Christ. Our labor will not be in vain!

But why do we have this gap in time? Why does Jesus come twice? Why isn't his D-day also V-day—the day of his final victory over sin and death?

The book of Acts has already suggested an answer. The time between Jesus' first coming and second coming is the time for witness (Acts 1:6-8). Between D-day and V-day, the church is a beachhead for the kingdom of God. We allow Christ to exercise lordship over this community of faith in advance of the time when he will exercise lordship over the whole creation.

This explains the tension that exists in the New Testament about certain social issues such as slavery. Salvation by grace has not only abolished the distinction between Jew and Gentile, it has also abolished the distinction between slave and free (Galatians 3:28). Hence when a runaway slave named Onesimus comes to Paul in prison and becomes a Christian, Paul sends him back to his master Philemon with these words: "Perhaps this is the reason he was separated from you for a while, so that you might have him back forever, no longer as a slave but more than a slave, a beloved brother—especially to me but how much more to you, in both flesh and in the Lord" (Philemon, verse 15-16).

As a beachhead for the kingdom of God, the church has the opportunity to demonstrate within its own fellowship the freedom from slavery that God intends in the new creation. But until the kingdom comes, Christians must witness in a fallen world and deal with institutions that are not what God wants them to be. So Paul can tell Christians in Rome to be subject to the governing authorities, because all governing authorities are ultimately under the authority of

God (Romans 13:1). And to slaves he says, "You are called a slave? Don't dwell on it for yourself. But if you are able to be free, by all means make the most of it. For in the Lord the one called slave is a freeperson of the Lord; likewise the one called free is a slave of Christ" (I Corinthians 7:21; author's translation).[12]

In the kingdom of God there will be no slaves. Therefore in the church there can be no slaves, except in the sense that we are all slaves of Christ. But in the world these institutions still exist. So if Christians find themselves in that situation, they should serve faithfully, always doing what is right, not because they are slaves of earthly masters but because they are slaves of Christ. Meanwhile, if Christians find themselves in the role of masters, they must remember that they have a master over them in heaven (see Ephesians 6:5-9 and Colossians 3:22-4:1). The goal is to live as people already set free by Christ in a world where this freedom is not yet apparent.

The time between Jesus' first coming and second coming is not only a time for the church to embody the coming kingdom of God; it is a time to invite others into it. The anonymous letter to the Hebrews struggles with the delay of the kingdom as much as any letter in the New Testament. In chapter 11 it recalls many Bible stories and characters, in each case emphasizing the unfinished nature of God's work in their lives. Abraham is promised an inheritance that he never owns in his lifetime. Joseph dies in Egypt looking forward to a future Exodus. Moses leads the people out of Egypt but did not himself enter the Promised Land. But the chapter concludes, "Yet all these, though they were commended for their faith, did not receive what was promised, since God had provided something better so that they would not, *apart from us*, be made perfect" (Hebrew 11:39-40, my emphasis).

The very delay in the coming of God's kingdom has allowed us to be included in it, and while we continue waiting for the kingdom, we have the chance to invite others to share in its blessings.

Suggested Readings for Chapter 8

Read the whole book of Acts. It is an exciting story and displays many features of the Bible's plot. Read Romans, I Corinthians, Galatians, James, and Philemon to get a feel for the issues and struggles of those first Christian churches. Also read Hebrews 11 for an excellent review of the whole story.

Questions for Reflection

1. What events, people, or experiences has the Holy Spirit used to bring knowledge of Jesus to you? How is that similar or different to the way the Holy Spirit worked in Acts?

2. With what kind of people in the church do you have the hardest time getting along? For what reason might God have put you and them together in the same church?

3. What do you see as the greatest threats to the church from the inside?

4. Where do you see signs or glimpses that God's kingdom is already present in the world? What makes it seem not yet present?

9

From Here to Eternity

The best-selling non-fiction book of the 1970s was *The Late Great Planet Earth*, by Hal Lindsey.[1] After its publication, many Christians treated the book of Revelation as if it were written for the 20th century. Lindsey interpreted the armies of Gog in Revelation 20 as a prophetic reference to the Soviet Union. The 200 million cavalry troops in Revelation 9 were said to be from Communist China. The ten-horned beast in Revelation 13 was identified with the European Common Market, and the images in Revelation 6 (the sun turning black and the sky rolling up like a scroll) were said to be the effects of a worldwide nuclear holocaust. Lindsey also suggested that the mark of the beast in Revelation 13 referred to a universal electronic account number that will govern all business transactions.

Time has changed many of these interpretations. The Soviet Union imploded leaving scattered independent republics in its ruins. The European Common Market now has 27 members and has trouble enough controlling itself, let alone the world. Hal Lindsey's original book has virtually disappeared from store shelves.

But it has been replaced by others. The *Left Behind* series by Tim LaHaye and Jerry Jenkins has sold 62 million copies. The 9th volume in the series, Desecration, became the best selling novel of the year in 2001 (with many of its sales coming after September 11th). The 12th volume, *Glorious*

Appearing, sold 2 million copies before its March, 2006 publication. As of November, 2006, it was still tied for number 2 on the New York Times best-seller list.[2]

The last book of the Bible is a publisher's dream. But what is it really about, and how does it fit into the Bible's plot?

End Times or Past Times

Hal Lindsey was not the first to interpret the book of Revelation as referring to his own time. Until the 4th century most Christian interpreters viewed Revelation as a symbolic portrayal of the fall of Jerusalem in 70 A. D. The beast of Revelation 13 was understood to be the Roman Emperor. But when the Roman Emperor Constantine became a Christian, that interpretation changed.

In the middle ages the interpretation changed again. A 12th century monk named Joachim Flora, a loyalist of the Roman Catholic Church, declared that the beast of Revelation 13 was the Moslem religion and the death wound on its head was the crusades. Later the Pope became embroiled in a power struggle with the Holy Roman Emperor Frederick II. The Pope declared that Frederick was the beast arising out of the sea with blasphemous names on his head. Frederick replied by calling the Pope "The Antichrist," an interpretation later picked up by Protestants during the Reformation.[3]

None of these interpretations would have made sense to the people in the first century for whom the book of Revelation was originally written. Whatever else you say about the book of Revelation, it was originally a letter to seven specific churches in first century Asia Minor, and they were meant to understand it.

In this sense, Revelation is different than apocalyptic sections in the book of Daniel. After detailed visions of future kingdoms portrayed as beasts and horns, Daniel is told in the last chapter, "But you, Daniel, keep the words secret and the book sealed until the time of the end. Many shall be running back and forth, and evil shall increase" (Daniel 12:4). This is repeated five verses later: "Go your way, Daniel, for the words are to remain secret and sealed until the time of the end" (Daniel 12:9).

These visions of the book of Daniel were not meant to be understood in Daniel's own time. The four beasts in Daniel, chapter 7 represent four successive empires that would rise during and after the time of Daniel. The first beast, a winged lion, undoubtedly represented the Babylonians. Statues of winged lions were a popular feature of ancient Babylon. The next three beasts probably refer to the Medes, Persians, and Greeks respectively. The horns would have reminded ancient Jews of the Seleucids, heirs of the Greek Empire who ruled the land of Israel in the 2nd century B. C. E. Their coins often showed rulers wearing a helmet with horns. The little horn probably referred to Antiochus Epiphanes, who reigned from 168-164 B. C. E.[4]

If Daniel was one of the Jews taken captive by the Babylonians around 587 B. C. E., then the people to whom he originally wrote would have had no conception of the Greek Empire or the Seleucids who would rule four centuries later. The visions in the later half of Daniel would have had no meaning for them. Hence Daniel is told to seal them up for a later time.

But the book of Revelation is different. In the last chapter of Revelation the angel tells John, "Do not seal up the words of the prophecy of this book, for the time is near" (Revelation 22:10). For a book that borrows much of its style and many of its images from the book of Daniel, this is a striking difference. Revelation was not meant only for people 20 centuries later. It was meant to be understandable and relevant for people in John's own time. So we must ask: What would these images and symbols mean to Christians in first century Asia?

Unfortunately this question is easier to ask than to answer. In some ways the book of Revelation is like a political cartoon. Late in 2006 I saw a political cartoon showing a tall man with a long nose and jutting chin talking to a shorter man with large pointed ears. The tall man was wearing a coat with the initials "LBJ." The shorter man was wearing the letter "W." The taller man said to the shorter, "Send in more troops." The shorter man said, "But things don't seem to be going too well." The taller man said, "Send in more troops, and say something about a light at the end of the tunnel. People love that."[5]

Can you imagine explaining this cartoon to someone in rural Guatemala? Or to someone living in the United States 200 years from now? What are the two men talking about? Where are they sending troops, and why must they send more? What do the enigmatic letters LBJ mean? Or the cryptic "W"?

To most people living in 2006 the cartoon is readily understandable. LBJ refers to former President Lyndon Baines Johnson. "W" refers to President George W. Bush. The advice to send in more troops is a caricature of President Johnson's response to setbacks in Vietnam, a pattern that President Bush seems prepared to imitate in Iraq. If you know all these details, you understand the irony and even the humor in this cartoon. But imagine how strange and incomprehensible the whole thing would appear to someone from a different culture or a different time in history.

That is our problem with the book of Revelation. To us the symbols sound like the ranting of someone on hallucinogens. But the words and images meant something to those people in first century Asia Minor. They did not need to have the cartoon explained to them. They got the joke. But like the farmer in Guatemala or the person living 200 years from now, we need help to understand it.

Decoding the Symbols

Sometimes Revelation itself gives us clues as to the meaning of certain descriptions or symbols. For example, in Revelation 1:20 we are told that the seven stars held in the hand of the Son of Man and the seven lampstands surrounding him stand for the seven churches. The image reminds us that Jesus holds these churches in his hand and their light is always before him. In chapter 6 as the first four seals on a scroll are broken, four different colored horses emerge. Their significance is explained in the actions of their riders: Conquest, War, Famine, and Death. In chapter 17 we meet a drunken prostitute on a seven-headed beast. This is a totally mystifying image until suddenly in verse 9 we are given a clue: "This calls for a mind that has wisdom: the seven heads are seven mountains on which the woman is seated." Which ancient city was known as the city on seven hills? Rome! This clue is confirmed in verse 5 when we read that the prostitute has a name written on her forehead: "Babylon." We know from other places in the New Testament that Babylon was a name that Jews applied to Rome, because the Roman occupation reminded them of the oppression experienced by Israel under the Babylonians (see I Peter 5:13).[6] I can picture first century Christians laughing at the picture of Rome as a drunken harlot—a true political cartoon!

In other cases, symbols that seem strange to us would have been easily recognizable to many first century Christians, especially Jewish Christians, because they come from the Old Testament:

- The vision of the throne and four living creatures: Revelation 4 and Ezekiel 1
- The sealed scroll: Revelation 5:1-3 and Isaiah 29:11
- The lamb: Revelation 5:6 and Isaiah 53:7
- Stars disappearing and the sky rolling up like a scroll: Revelation 6:13-14 and Isaiah 34:4
- The locusts: Revelation 9:3-9 and Joel 2:1-11
- Eating a scroll: Revelation 10:8-11 and Ezekiel 2:8-3:4
- The beast: Revelation 13:1-3 and Daniel 7:2-7 (In Revelation the four beasts of Daniel are rolled into one.)
- The tree of life: Revelation 22:1-2 and Genesis 2:9 and 3:22-24

Space will not permit me to interpret every symbol in the book of Revelation. (I doubt I could even if I had the space.) A good commentary or study Bible with extended footnotes can help. But look for the possibility that Revelation may interpret the symbols for you. Also look for footnotes or cross references to the Old Testament. Revelation frequently uses images from the Old Testament to show how the entire plot of the Bible is here gathered into a climax. I will say more about this in a moment.

Now a word about numbers in the book of Revelation. Numbers in Revelation are frequently symbolic, as shown by the frequency of the numbers 7 and 12. Notice how often Revelation uses the number 12 and multiples of 12:

- 24 elders (Revelation 4:4)
- 12 stars in a crown (Revelation 12:1)
- 144,000 sealed servants of God (12x12,000; Revelation 7:4-8)
- 12 gates around the new Jerusalem (Revelation 21:12-13)
- 12 foundations for the new Jerusalem (Revelation 21:14)

In the last two cases we do not need to guess what the number symbolizes. We are told that the 12 gates are inscribed with the names of the 12 tribes of Israel and the 12 foundations bear the names of the twelve apostles of Jesus. This gives us a clue about the significance of the 24 elders. They represent the Old Testament people of God and the New Testament people of God, gathered together around God's throne. This is a symbolic portrayal of what Paul described in Romans 11:25-32.

Some religious groups have taken the numbers in Revelation literally. Jehovah Witnesses claim that a special group of only 144,000 will reign with Christ in heaven. But the number 144,000 is symbolic of the inclusion of Israel in God's kingdom. There is no magic cutoff at 144,000, as if heaven had a seating capacity. Revelation 7:9 tells us there was a multitude present that no one could count from every nation, tribe, peoples, and language.

The other key number is 7. The number 7 is ubiquitous in the book of Revelation:

- 7 lampstands and 7 stars (Revelation 1:12, 16)
- 7 churches (Revelation 1:20)
- 7 seals on a scroll (Revelation 5:1)
- 7 horns and eyes (Revelation 5:6)
- 7 angels blowing 7 trumpets (Revelation 8:2)
- 7 headed dragon (Revelation 12:3)
- 7 angels with 7 plagues (Revelation 15:1)

For Christians familiar with the Old Testament, the number 7 would recall the 7 days of creation. Every celebration of the Sabbath was a reminder of the importance of this cycle. On the 7th day God finished the work of creation, so the number 7 implied completion or perfection.[7] Hence 7 churches can stand for all the churches, and a 7 headed dragon can stand for all the oppressive powers that the world has known. Likewise, 7 seals on a scroll represent the whole course of history sealed inside that scroll, and 7 bowls of wrath represent the complete judgment of God on the world's sin.

Time is often pictured in Revelation as half of 7. In Revelation 11:2 the nations are allowed to trample over the holy city for 42 months. This is exactly half of 7 years. In the next verse the two witnesses of God are given authority to prophesy for 1,260 days. If you figure 30 days to a month, this is the same length of time as 42 months—half of 7 years. We see this same time reference again in chapter 12. In verse 6 a woman is given shelter by God from the dragon for 1,260 days, and in verse 14 this time period is described as "a time and times and half a time"—in other words, 3 and ½ years.

If 7 is the number of totality or completion, then half of 7 represents a partial time. The references to 42 months or 1,260 days are not meant to be taken literally. They are symbolic in Revelation for an interim time before the completion of the story.[8]

The Plot in Revelation

One of my favorite movies is a film made in 1993 called Searching for Bobby Fisher. A 7 year-old boy named Josh learns to play chess from street people in New York City. The boy has a natural talent for the game, a talent not seen since Bobby Fisher, the prodigy who won the United States Chess Championship as a teenager. The tension in the movie focuses on how hard the boy's father and coach will push to make him a champion and whether the boy will lose his compassionate heart in the process.

At the end of the movie Josh plays in the championship game of a tournament against another boy who has also been driven by his coach to become the next Bobby Fisher. The parents and coaches are not allowed in the room where the game is played. They must watch on closed circuit television. Late in the game Josh's opponent makes a move, and Josh's coach in the other room says under his breath, "That was a mistake." Then, even though Josh cannot hear him, the coach begins talking as if he is talking to Josh. He says, "You've got him. It's there. Look deep, Josh. It's 12 moves away, but it's there. You've got him."

In the other room Josh is staring at the board. He senses that he has been given an opening but he can't see it. In the other room the coach says under his breath, "Don't move until you see it." Josh stares at the board imagining every possible combination, until suddenly he looks up, and in his eyes you can see that he has got it. He has seen the combination. Then in the most remarkable scene of the movie Josh reaches out to shake hands with his opponent. In the other room his father asks, "What is he doing?" The coach says, "He's offering him a draw." Meanwhile in the game room Josh's opponent asks the same question: "What are you doing?" Josh says, "I'm offering you a draw. Take the draw, and we'll share the championship." His opponent says, "You've got to be kidding. Look at the board. I'm going to win." Josh says, "You've already lost, you just don't know it." But his opponent refuses the handshake, so Josh makes his move. In the process Josh loses his rook, but 11 moves later Josh wins.

This scene gives us a lens through which to view the book of Revelation. In Revelation we see how the game will end. It's twelve moves away, but it is there, if we only have the eyes to see it. The way to final victory is laid out for us, but it will take a significant sacrifice to get there.

In chapters 4-7 the story of Revelation unfolds like scenes in a drama. First we see the throne room of God. As I noted above, Revelation is filled with images and symbols from the Old Testament. Some of the images of Revelation 4 come from Isaiah 6, where Isaiah has a vision of God seated on a lofty throne surrounded by winged seraphs. Other parts of the vision come from Ezekiel 1, where Ezekiel sees a throne

covered by a rainbow and surrounded by four living creatures with wings: one that looked like a lion, one like an ox,
one like a human, and one like an eagle.

Obviously this is a conglomeration of images—much
like you get in a political cartoon. The idea of winged creatures around the throne of God comes from the Old Testament. In the Jewish temple there were carved winged
creatures hovering over the ark of the covenant. There were
also carvings of lions and oxen that decorated different
parts of the temple. Isaiah, Ezekiel, and John all draw their
picture of God's throne in heaven from these images found
in the temple. The difference is that in the kingdom of God
these winged creatures are no longer lifeless carvings. They
are alive. They function like a choir leading the people of
God in worship.

These particular four living creatures may also have a
representative function. They embody wild animals, domestic animals, birds, and humans. In other words, they represent the whole animal kingdom gathered before the throne
of God in worship. As I mentioned earlier, the 24 elders also
have a representative function. They represent the Old Testament people of God (12 tribes) and the New Testament
people of God (12 apostles) gathered together in praise of
their Creator. Around the throne of God in heaven, Israel is
not displaced by the church, it is included. The promises of
God are fulfilled both for Abraham's descendants and for
all the families of the earth. In the process the whole creation rejoices (recall Romans 8:19-21).

Many things in Revelation 4 would have reminded
John's readers of a worship service. The hymns sung in this
chapter are probably hymns that were actually used in their
church services. But everything in these worship services is
more alive and vibrant than anything we have ever experienced. This is a vision of how the whole story will end. It is
twelve moves away, but it is right there if we only see it.

But how will we get there? Revelation 5 introduces a
new symbol: the scroll with seven seals. The scroll represents the course of history leading up to the vision we have
just seen. In other words, the scroll represents the plot![9] But

the scroll is sealed, and no one can open it, meaning that no one can unlock the plot that will get us to the vision of God's kingdom. No wonder John weeps. But then one of the elders says, "Do not weep. See, the Lion of the tribe of Judah, the Root of David, has conquered, so that he can open the scroll and its seven seals" (Revelation 5:5). As we have already seen, these titles describe the Messiah, the promised king who will bring God's righteousness and peace to the whole creation.

I hope you appreciate the drama in the next scene. We have just been told that the Messiah, the promised king, will unseal the scroll. He will unlock the mystery of the ages and reveal the path by which history will arrive at the kingdom of God. Suddenly the house lights dim, the music swells, the curtain opens, the spotlight comes on, and here he is—the hope of the world. Only what appears is not a lion, not even a king, but a lamb—a lamb that looks like it has been slaughtered!

Taken literally, such an image is too grotesque even for a political cartoon. But the first readers of Revelation would have known instantly what it meant. So do we, if we sing the same hymns they did: "Worthy is the Lamb who was slain!…You are worthy to take the scroll and open its seals, for you were slaughtered and by your blood you ransomed for God saints from every tribe and language and people and nation" (Revelation 5:9).

Several patterns in the Bible's plot are caught up in this hymn:

1. God's tendency to choose unexpected people. Who would have expected salvation from a lamb, especially one that was slaughtered?
2. The narrowing of God's focus in order later to expand it. God chooses one nation (Israel), one family within that nation (David), one person within that family (Jesus), in order to bring blessing to all the families of the earth.
3. Salvation through one rejected by his own people. Just as Joseph was sold into slavery by his brothers and ended up saving them from famine, just as Moses was

rejected by the people of Israel and ended up saving them from genocide, just as David was dismissed as too young and small but ended up saving Israel from the Philistines, so Jesus, the one crucified as a blasphemer, ends up saving us.

Philip Yancey tells about a Jewish friend who led tour groups of Christians on pilgrimages to the Holy Land. As he listened to these tour groups talk about the second coming of Jesus, he was amazed to hear them quoting the same scriptures from the prophets that he had learned in Hebrew school—scriptures about a Messiah who would bring peace and justice to our fractured planet. He remarked to Philip, "Wouldn't it be amazing if we found out we were all waiting for the same person."[10]

The truth is that we are. The difference is that when he comes we will recognize him, because we have met him before...on a cross.

In chapter 6 the story turns dark again. The seals are opened, and instead of instant salvation, we see suffering. I will say more about this in the next section.

But in chapter 7 after opening the 7th seal, we are back in heaven. This time the singing comes not just from 24 elders but from a countless multitude. Their song gathers up the hopes that were sung for centuries in the Old Testament—Revelation 7:16-17:

- They will hunger no more and thirst no more (see Isaiah 49:10)
- The sun will not strike them by day, nor any scorching heat (see Psalm 121:6)
- For the lamb at the center of the throne will be their shepherd (see Psalm 23:1)
- And he will guide them to springs of the water of life (see Psalm 23:2 and Isaiah 49:10)
- And God will wipe away every tear from their eyes (see Isaiah 25:8)

Would this not be a perfect ending for the book of Revelation, and for the Bible as a whole? The seventh seal would be broken and the story would end. But it doesn't.

The Big Let Down

At the beginning of Revelation 8, the seventh seal is broken, and there is silence in heaven. Then seven angels are given seven trumpets to blow, and another cycle of seven begins. It is like watching a long freight train crossing the tracks in front of you. Just when the caboose comes into view, the train stops and starts backing up.

This happens not once but several times in the book of Revelation. In chapters 8-9 the seven angels blow their seven trumpets. A new series of disasters befall the world, and at the end of chapter 9, after the sixth trumpet blows, we expect God to intervene and stop the suffering. But God doesn't. Instead God commands John to take a scroll and eat it (Revelation 10:8-11), just as God had commanded the prophet Ezekiel (Ezekiel 2:8-3:4). In both cases eating the scroll symbolizes God's commission to proclaim God's word to people.

We are right back where we were at the end of the gospels and at the beginning of the book of Acts. After his resurrection the disciples asked Jesus, "Lord, is this the time when you will restore the kingdom to Israel?" And Jesus replied, "It is not for you to know the times or periods that the Father has set by his own authority. But you will receive power when the Holy Spirit has come upon you; and you will be my witnesses ..." (Acts 1:6-8). Revelation 11 tells the story of two witnesses sent by God who are rejected and killed, just like some of the apostles in the book of Acts.

You may have heard the term "the Rapture." The Rapture refers to the idea that Christians will be beamed up out of the world, so to speak, before things get really bad. This is the central premise for the *Left Behind* series by Tim LaHaye and Jerry Jenkins.

But there is no reference in the book of Revelation to the Rapture. The scripture passage commonly used to justify the Rapture is I Thessalonians 4:16-17:

> For the Lord himself with a cry of command, with the archangel's call and with the sound of God's trumpet, will descend from heaven, and the dead in Christ will rise first. Then we who are alive, who are

left, will be caught up in the clouds together with them to meet the Lord in the air; and so we will be with the Lord forever.

This does not describe an event in the middle of history. This describes the resurrection and the final triumph of God. There is no indication that the history of a fallen world will continue after this event.

The only thing in Revelation that makes people think a Rapture has occurred is the periodic visions of God's people in heaven (Revelation 7:1-17, 14:1-5, and 19:1-8). But these passages are "flash-aheads" to the final outcome of the story. They are like the coach in *Searching for Bobby Fisher* who sees how the game will end and hopes his student sees it. They are not portraits of those who have been "raptured" out of the world while they were still alive. Many in these visions are described as having died for their faith (Revelation 6:9-11). It is true that the two witnesses are taken up to heaven, but only after they die (Revelation 11:12). Their resurrection, like Jesus' resurrection, anticipates the final victory of God. The only person in Revelation who is snatched up to heaven is the child of the woman in Revelation 12. And that child is a symbolic portrayal of Jesus! When Revelation 7:14 says of the white robed multitude in heaven: "These are they who have come out of the great ordeal," it does not mean they were spared the ordeal. It means they made it through the ordeal and held on to their faith.

Which brings us back to this question: Why does Revelation let us down? Just as the 7th seal is broken and we think that God's kingdom will come at last, a new cycle of seven trumpets begins (Revelation 8:1-2). At the end of chapter 9, we anxiously await the blowing of the 7th trumpet. But the action stops while John and two others are told to go out and do more preaching. Finally, the 7th trumpet is blown and loud voices proclaim, "The kingdom of the world has become the kingdom of our Lord and of his Messiah, and he will reign forever and ever" (Revelation 11:15). Great, the end has finally come! Oops, not yet. The action stops to tell us about the defeat of Satan and the arrival of some beasts. This goes on for three chapters. In Revelation 15 we begin yet another cycle of seven: the seven golden bowls of God's wrath. Haven't we had enough wrath already? In chapter 6 we were told that the sky rolled up like a scroll? What else can happen? But as the bowls are poured out more disasters befall the world. When the seventh bowl is poured out, a voice from heaven says, "It is done!" (Revelation 16:17). But it isn't done. The action goes on for four more chapters.

Why is the story of Revelation told this way? Why do we have these constant let downs, just when we think God's kingdom is at hand?

The whole book of Revelation is intended to teach us patient endurance. It you look back at the first three chapters, you will see this theme running through many of the letters to the seven churches. In a preface to the seven letters John says, "I, John, your brother who share with you in Jesus Christ the persecution and the kingdom and the patient endurance, was on the island called Patmos because of the word of God and the testimony of Jesus" (Revelation 1:9). Notice the three things John shares with the churches to which he is writing:

1. Persecution. John has not been "raptured" out of the world. He is not exempt from the suffering people experience in the world. As a Christian his suffering may even be worse, and the same is true for the Christians to whom he is writing.
2. The kingdom. Yes, John and the people in the churches to whom he writes are suffering. But they share a hope in the coming of God's kingdom, and the whole book of Revelation points forward to that hope.
3. Patient endurance. In the meantime, John and the Christians to whom he writes must hang on to Christ and patiently endure.

Notice all the references to patient endurance and similar phrases in the rest of the book:

- "I know your works, your toil and your patient endurance" (Revelation 2:2).
- "Be faithful unto death and I will give you the crown of life" (Revelation 2:10).

- "I know your works—your love, faith, service, and patient endurance" (Revelation 2:19).
- "Because you have kept my word of patient endurance, I will keep you from the hour of trial that is coming on the whole world to test the inhabitants of the earth" (Revelation 3:10). Note that this verse does not promise Christians exemption from suffering. It promises that God will preserve them so that they do not fail the test.
- "Here is a call for the endurance and faith of the saints" (Revelation 13:10).
- "Here is a call for the endurance of the saints, those who keep the commandments of God and hold fast to the faith of Jesus" (Revelation 14:12).

The book of Revelation is written to help Christians hold on to their faith in Christ and their love for others in a time of severe stress. They are encouraged by visions of how it will all end. But they are also warned repeatedly that the end is not yet. Using the analogy of D-day and V-day, the victory has been assured, but there is still work to be done, suffering to endure, and sacrifices to be made.

Sin on Steroids

One of the recurring plot patterns in the Bible is the ripple effect of sin. The closer we get to the final triumph of God, the more extreme that ripple gets.

In the four horsemen of the apocalypse, Revelation 6:1-8, there is a certain logical progression. The first horseman is a conqueror. Much of the world's suffering begins with human greed and injustice. This leads to the second horseman: war. War then leads to famine, which is symbolized by the third rider holding a pair of scales and saying, "A quart of wheat for a day's pay." That is a high price for a few slices of bread. War produces shortage. Finally famine leads to disease and death—the fourth horseman. Revelation 6 is yet another example of sin radiating out and consuming more and more people in its path.

It is true that these consequences of sin are released by Jesus when he breaks the seals on the scroll. But the implication is that God has been restraining sin. Up to this point the scroll has been sealed! Judgment comes when God finally releases us to have our way with the world.

We see another example of the ripple effect of sin in Revelation 9. The image of a locust plague is drawn from the prophet Joel. But John has added some details that help identify its meaning. He says the locusts were like horses equipped for battle. Their scales were like iron breastplates. The noise of their wings was like the noise of many chariots going into battle. The locust plague is a symbol for the destruction wrought by a human army.

The disasters and plagues pictured in Revelation are not arbitrary punishments thrown at us by an angry, vindictive God. They are the outgrowth of human sin, writ large. At the beginning of chapter 9 we discover that God has been restraining the locust army. They have been locked away in a pit. So far God has actually preserved the world from annihilating itself. Judgment comes when God lets human beings have their way.

After the first Gulf War, *Time* magazine carried this graphic description of Kuwait:

> Dante would have felt right at home in Kuwait, a desert paradise that has suddenly been transformed into an environmental inferno. Across the land hundreds of orange fireballs roar like dragons, blasting sulfurous clouds high into the air. Soot falls like gritty snowflakes, streaking windshields and staining clothes. From the overcast skies drips a greasy black rain, while sheets of gooey oil slap against a polluted shore. Burned out hulks of twisted metal litter a landscape pockmarked by bomb craters, land mines and shallow graves scraped in the sand.[11]

Revelation 8 and 9 could have been a description of Kuwait or Iraq or any number of other places in the world. Paul was not kidding when he said, "For the creation waits with eager longing for the revealing of the children of God."

In Revelation 16 we have another set of seven disasters: seven bowls of God's wrath. These disasters are reminiscent of the plagues in Egypt. Water turns to blood. Frogs emerge. People are afflicted with painful sores. The land is plunged into darkness. The ripple effects of cruelty and injustice that we saw in Egypt are now visited upon the entire earth. What will happen to God's beloved creation?

The Battle of Armageddon

In Revelation 16 when the angel pours out the sixth bowl of God's wrath, John says, "And I saw three foul spirits like frogs coming from the mouth of the dragon, from the mouth of the beast, and from the mouth of the false prophet." The dragon is Satan. The beast and the false prophet are Satan's henchmen, who deceive people into believing that only military might and the power of an empire can save the world. As part of this deception they gather the armies of the world for a climactic battle at a place called Harmagedon, usually spelled Armageddon.

The battle does not actually take place until chapter 19, and when it does, it is a very strange battle. The forces of Satan and the beast are met by a rider on a white horse. The rider is clearly Jesus: "On his robe and on his thigh he has a name inscribed, 'King of kings and Lord of lords'" (Revelation 19:16). But this rider on the white horse does not seem like a typical battlefield hero. Verse 13 says, "He is clothed in a robe dipped in blood." It is not unusual for a warrior in battle to have blood-spattered clothes. But the book of Revelation never uses the word blood in reference to Jesus' enemies. Occasionally it uses the word blood to refer to the ripple effect of sin in nature, like when the moon turns to blood, water turns to blood, or blood mixes with hail and rain on the earth (Revelation 6:12, 8:7, 8:9, 11:6, 14:20, and 16:3-4). But in Revelation the word blood is never used in reference to the blood of Jesus' enemies. Instead it refers to Jesus' own blood or the blood of his followers (see Revelation 1:5, 5:9, 7:14, 17:6, 18:24, and 19:2). Jesus arrives on the field of battle wearing a robe spattered with the blood—not the blood of his enemies but his own blood and possibly the blood of his followers.

Revelation 19:15 says, "From his mouth comes a sharp

sword with which to strike down the nations ...." There is nothing strange about a liberator carrying a sword, but what kind of sword comes out of a person's mouth? A symbolic one! The sword out of his mouth means that his power is in his word. This is confirmed by the name he is given at the end of verse 13: "The Word of God."

Amazingly this strange warrior wins the victory. All the powers of evil in this world are defeated and thrown into the lake of fire. Christianity is not a weak or passive faith. Jesus did not come to help us accommodate to a world of evil and suffering. He came to transform the world—to put an end to idolatry, tyranny, exploitation, violence, greed, lust, and war—all of the things that wreak havoc on God's children and God's creation. But the victory is not achieved by building a stronger military or by writing tougher laws or hiring more police. The victory is won by Christians proclaiming their message: that Jesus is Lord and that we are saved by trusting his power over any other.

When it comes to the battle of Armageddon, Martin Luther had it right:

> Did we in our own strength confide, our striving would
>   be losing;
> Were not the right Man on our side, the Man of God's own
>   choosing.
> Dost ask who that may be? Christ Jesus, it is He,
> Lord Sabaoth his name, from age to age the same,
> And he must win the battle.
> And though his world, with devils filled, should threaten
>   to undo us,
> We will not fear, for God hath willed his truth to triumph
>   through us.
> The prince of darkness grim, we tremble not for him;
> His rage we can endure, for lo! his doom is sure,
> One little word shall fell him. ("A Mighty Fortress Is Our
>   God")

The Redemption of Creation

In Revelation 20 we have another distressing letdown. After the great battle of Armageddon, Satan is bound and thrown into a pit which is locked and sealed for a thousand years. Verses 4-5 tell us,

> Then I saw thrones, and those seated on them were given authority to judge. I also saw the souls of those who had been beheaded for their testimony to Jesus and for the word of God. They had not worshiped the beast or its image and had not received its mark on their foreheads or their hands. They came to life and reigned with Christ a thousand years. (The rest of the dead did not come to life until the thousand years were ended.)

These verses describe the millennium—the special thousand year reign of Christ. Fierce arguments have been waged among Christians over where the millennium falls in the plot. Does the millennium begin with Jesus' resurrection and continue until he comes again? Or is the millennium something that happens in the future just before the final resurrection? Will life in this world get steadily worse until Jesus returns and establishes the millennium (pre-millennialism)? Or will the millennium begin when people turn to Christ and work together to build a just society after which Jesus will come (post-millennialism)?

Frankly, I think these are the wrong questions. To me the question is not when the millennium will come. The question is why it lasts only 1000 years. At the beginning of the millennium Satan is bound and locked in a pit. Why not throw away the key? Why does God let Satan out again? At the same time we are told that those executed for the sake of Christ are raised from the dead and reign with Christ for a thousand years. Why only a thousand years? Why doesn't the millennium last forever?

Apparently something is missing. Even in the millennium when Satan is bound and Christians who have died for their faith are reigning with Christ in heaven—even then something is still unfinished in God's agenda. The unfinished business is the redemption of creation. Yes, some Christian martyrs have been raised from the dead to reign with Christ, but the rest of the dead are still dead. Satan may be bound, but the rest of creation still struggles under the effects of sin and suffering.

This becomes clear when Satan is let out again (Revelation 20:7-10). Once again Satan deceives the nations and gathers its armies for war. Despite the millennium nothing has changed. The rest of the world is just as messed up as it ever was. That is why the millennium is not the end of the story. God is not finished until the whole creation is set free from its bondage to sin and destruction.

Which brings us to the end of the story in Revelation 21-22. In the book of Revelation there is no description of the Rapture—living Christians suddenly taken up to heaven. But there is a kind of Rapture in reverse: the new Jerusalem comes from heaven to earth.[12]

> Then I saw a new heaven and a new earth; for the first heaven and the first earth had passed away, and the sea was no more. And I saw the holy city, the new Jerusalem, coming down out of heaven from God prepared as a bride adorned for her husband. And I heard a loud voice from the throne saying, "See, the home of God is among mortals. He will dwell with them; they will be his peoples, and God himself will be with them; he will wipe every tear from their eyes. Death will be no more; mourning and crying and pain will be no more, for the first things have passed away" (Revelation 21:1-4).

All the cycles of seven in the book of Revelation have prepared us for a new creation, and here it is. So many hopes and promises of the Bible are caught up in these last two chapters:

1. The eternal throne in Jerusalem that God promised to David and his descendants is realized. By the time Revelation was written, Jerusalem had been destroyed as an earthly city. But God's covenant with David is fulfilled through the reign of Jesus in a new eternal Jerusalem.
2. The city has 12 gates inscribed with the names of the

12 tribes of Israel (Revelation 21:12). The promise of blessing to Abraham's descendants is fulfilled.

3. The city also has 12 foundations named for the twelve apostles (Revelation 21:14). The followers of Jesus are included in the promises to Abraham.

4. "The nations will walk by its light, and the kings of the earth will bring their glory into it. Its gates will never be shut by day—and there will be no night there. People will bring into it the glory and the honor of the nations" (Revelation 21:24). Here is fulfilled the hope of blessing for all the families of the earth, a hope that was never forgotten by the Old Testament prophets (see Isaiah 60:3 and 11).

But the most dramatic image is saved for the last chapter. If you recall, after Adam and Eve ate the forbidden fruit, God drove them out of the Garden of Eden so that they would not eat of the tree of life and live forever. The tree of life was not the forbidden tree. Presumably God might have let them eat of that tree and not suffer death, if they had not tried to become their own gods. Now in the last chapter of the Bible the tree of life is back.

> Then the angel showed me the river of life, bright as crystal, flowing from the throne of God and of the Lamb through the city. On either side of the river, is the tree of life with its twelve kinds of fruit, producing leaves for each month; and the leaves of the tree are for the healing of the nations (Revelation 22:1-2).

The creation finally becomes the good place it was meant to be all along.

There is a warning here. Revelation 22:3 says, "Nothing accursed will be found there anymore." This echoes a warning at the end of chapter 21: "But nothing unclean will enter it, nor anyone who practices abomination or falsehood, but only those who are written in the Lamb's book of life" (Revelation 21:27).

If you wonder how you get your name written in the book of life, the answer is given earlier in the book of Revelation. Revelation 13:8 and 17:8 tell us that names are written in the book of life from the foundation of the world. In other words, it is not based on your accomplishments or your righteousness or your character. It is put there by grace—by Jesus' sacrifice for you before you had done anything to deserve it.

But you have to be willing to let Jesus change you. In the kingdom of heaven there is no room for greed, but what you get in return is fulfillment, which greed yearns for in a misdirected way. In the kingdom of heaven there is no place for lust, but what you get in return is love, which lust yearns for in a misdirected way. In the kingdom of heaven there is no room for pride, but what you get in return is community, which we all yearn for in misdirected ways.

In the 1980s during the height of a civil war in Lebanon, the Rev. Benjamin Weir, a Presbyterian missionary, was abducted by Islamic Jihad and held captive for 16 months. People wondered why he and his wife Carol had stayed in Lebanon during that dangerous time. He explained their reasons in an article written the Christmas before his abduction:

> Our hopes focus on peace. The land of Lebanon has been marred, scarred, and charred with all the weapons of war imaginable to humankind. We are witnesses, here in Beirut, to homes destroyed and people brutalized in untold numbers....Our own efforts at rebuilding and renewing seem small and necessarily partial, but we are thankful that God has given us the opportunity to have a part in healing and rebuilding. We are part of the church's efforts to reestablish worship services, to assist persons moving back to villages, to encourage youth leadership, to give support to those whose hope lies in the future.
>
> From our home to yours, we send this, our prayer for peace. The kingdom of God is a kingdom without weapons, without oppressive powers, without torture, without hunger—without exploitation of

individuals and peoples, without prejudice, without an irresponsible use of what God has given us. It is a kingdom full of life, of faith, justice, peace, love—mutual understanding and reconciliation, of real possibilities for every human being. That is what we look toward, and we have no right as Christians to settle for anything less.[13]

The Bible's plot is headed toward a new creation. God is determined to reverse the ripple effect of sin and restore blessing to all the families of the earth. Like the descendants of Abraham, you are invited to become part of that plot, a participant in God's unfolding work.

Suggested Readings for Chapter 9

Revelation, chapters 1-22. Use this chapter to help you get oriented, then use an annotated Bible or a commentary to help you understand specific symbols and references.

Questions for Reflection

1. Where do you see history going? Is life in this world getting better, worse, or staying the same?
2. What situations in your life require "patient endurance"? Which of those situations require patient endurance because of your faith?
3. How can the power of sin and its ripple effect be defeated by words?
4. Why does the Apostles' Creed talk about the "resurrection of the body"? Why is it not enough that when we die our souls go to be with God?

10

Joining the Plot

There was an unusual movie made in the year 2000 called *Memento*. Guy Pearce plays a man named Leonard whose brain was injured during an attack by an intruder who murdered his wife. The injury destroyed Leonard's ability to form new memories. He could still remember things about his life before the injury, like his name, but he could not remember what happened yesterday or the day before. He takes a Polaroid picture of his car so he can remember which car is his. He also takes pictures of the people he meets and writes down their names so he can remember them the next day.

So that the audience will experience Leonard's life in the same way he experiences it, the whole story is shown backwards. The first scene of the movie shows us the last episode of the story. Then the movie shifts to a prior episode. Then the movie shows us the day before that, and so on. The effect is that each new scene of the movie starts out with a situation we do not understand, because we have not seen what happened before. Leonard wakes up in a motel room, and he does not know where he is or how he got there, and neither do we. He meets someone who obviously knows him, but we do not know who the person is, and neither does Leonard. Since he does not remember the people he met the day before, Leonard develops no history of relationship with them. He does not know what to believe or whom to trust. In one of the saddest moments of the movie, a woman whom he thought he could trust tells him that she has been lying to him. Then she laughs because he won't remember what she said. When she leaves, Leonard scrambles to write a note to himself not to trust her. But before he can find a piece of paper or a pen, he is interrupted, and later he forgets what he was going to write.

This movie is a parable of many people's relationship to the Bible and to God. Because so many sermons and Bible studies focus on individual verses or stories from the Bible, our faith has no long-term memory. We see how God acts in specific situations in the Bible, and from this we draw conclusions about how we think God might act in our situation. But we are missing the background—the flow of the plot that led to God's action in that particular case. As a result, we have a faulty understanding of how God will act in our particular situation or how God wants us to act. We suffer from spiritual amnesia.

The Bible is a comprehensive set of notes reminding us of the plot in which we are involved. Understanding how it unfolds will help us understand how we should respond to new situations. It will also give us a sense of who we are and where we fit in the story. As Leonard discovered, memory is the key to identity and direction. Remembering and understanding the story of which we are a part is the key to knowing who we are and where we are going.

Locating Ourselves in the Plot

In Deuteronomy, chapter 26, there are instructions to the people of Israel for their fall stewardship campaign. As they present their offerings in the temple they are instructed to recite a story—Deuteronomy 26:5-9. In these verses we have a short summary of the Bible's plot from Genesis 12 through the end of Joshua:

- "A wandering Aramean was my ancestor." This refers to the story of Abraham, Isaac, and Jacob, who came from the country of Aram and wandered as nomads in the land God promised to give them.

- "He went down into Egypt and lived there as an alien, few in number." Here is the story of Joseph, one of Jacob's sons, who was sold as a slave to the Egyptians by his brothers but who saved his brothers during a famine by providing food for them in Egypt.
- "And there he became a great nation, mighty and populous." God's promise of making Abraham's descendants a great nation began to be fulfilled.
- "When the Egyptians treated us harshly and afflicted us, by imposing hard labor on us, we cried to the Lord, the God of our ancestors; the Lord heard our voice and saw our affliction, our toil, and our oppression. The Lord brought us out of Egypt with a mighty hand and an outstretched arm, with a terrifying display of power, and with signs and wonders." Here we have the story of Moses and the exodus, including how God used plagues and the parting of the Red Sea to deliver the Israelites from slavery in Egypt.
- "And he brought us into this place and gave us this land, a land flowing with milk and honey." This summarizes Israel's journey through the wilderness and entrance into the Promised Land in the time of Joshua.

The striking thing about this recital is the way the speaker puts himself or herself into the plot. "A wandering Aramean was my ancestor." This is not just the story of an ancient group of people long dead. This is my own family history. "The Egyptians treated us harshly and afflicted us. We cried to the Lord, the God of our ancestors.... The Lord brought us out of Egypt with a mighty hand and an outstretched arm."

The people reciting these words were not there in Egypt. The Bible makes that clear. Except for Moses, Joshua, and Caleb, all the Israelites alive at the time of the Exodus died during the journey through the wilderness to the Promised Land. This is a new generation. Moses is speaking to the descendants of those who lived in Egypt. But they are instructed to tell the story as if they were there, as if it happened to them personally.

In a sense it did. They would not be alive, nor exist as a people, if God had not brought their ancestors out of Egypt. If any of them wonder why they must bring some of their hard earned crops as an offering to the Lord, this story reminds them.

Earlier in Deuteronomy, when reminding the people of Israel to keep the Ten Commandments, Moses says, "The Lord our God made a covenant with us at Horeb. Not with our ancestors did the Lord make this covenant, but with us, who are all of us alive today" (Deuteronomy 5:2-3). If the Israelites wonder why they must keep the Ten Commandments, the answer is given in the story of which they have been made a part.

The same is true for Christians. In Romans 11 the apostle Paul describes how Gentiles have been grafted into the family tree of Abraham so that we, too, are inheritors of God's promise to Abraham. This theme is raised in the first chapter of the New Testament when Matthew includes in the genealogy of Jesus some well known Gentile ancestors. It is repeated in the second chapter of the New Testament with the arrival of Gentile wise men who have come to worship "the King of the Jews." It is glimpsed again in the third chapter of the New Testament when John the Baptist says, "Do not presume to say to yourselves, 'We have Abraham as our ancestor'; for God is able from these stones to raise up children to Abraham." And Paul reminds the Galatians, "Just as Abraham 'believed God, and it was reckoned to him as righteousness,' so, you see, those who believe are the descendants of Abraham" (Galatians 3:6-7).

In these ways the New Testament makes it clear that the story of the Old Testament is our story as well. To paraphrase Deuteronomy 5:2-3: "Not only with the Jews did the Lord make a covenant at Horeb, but with us Gentiles living 3,000 years later." We, through Jesus, have been included in the story of Israel.

Putting yourself into the story of the Bible helps explain some of the practices and doctrines of the Christian faith. The story of Adam and Eve eating the forbidden fruit is not limited to Adam and Eve. It is our story as well, which helps explain the doctrine of original sin. We are all participants in the rejection of God that Adam and Eve committed (see Romans 5:12).

In the same way, when Jesus said to the disciples at the last supper, "This is my body, which is given for you" (Luke 22:19), he was not talking only to those first disciples. He was talking to all of us who would believe in him through their message. When we partake of the bread and wine of communion, we acknowledge that his death on the cross was for us, just as much as for those first disciples. Receiving communion makes us participants in the story. Referring to communion, the apostle Paul says, "The cup of blessing that we bless, is it not a sharing in the blood of Christ? The bread that we break, is it not a sharing in the body of Christ? Because there is one bread, we who are many are one body, for we all partake of the one bread" (I Corinthians 10:16-17). Taking communion incorporates us into the story. It makes us recipients of God's grace and participants in Jesus' mission.

The same is true for baptism. The apostle Paul says, "Do you not know that all of us who have been baptized into Christ Jesus were baptized into his death? Therefore we have been buried with him by baptism into death, so that, just as Christ was raised from the dead by the glory of the Father, so we too might walk in newness of life" (Romans 6:3-4). Baptism makes us participants in the story of Jesus. We become inheritors with him of a new life.

In one sense the new life has already begun. We are dead to the old self. We cannot go back to the independent, self-sufficient, and self-centered people we were before. Yet, in another sense, we are not yet fully reborn. The new life of the resurrection is a future event yet to be fully realized. But in baptism we become part of a new story with a new ending.

I mentioned in the last chapter that people at different times in history have seen themselves and their own times reflected in the story of Revelation. Joachim of Flora read the book of Revelation and saw it as a description of his own time in the 12th century. The Reformers read it and applied it to their time in the 16th century. Hal Lindsey read it and saw events of 20th century. Now others are connecting Revelation to events in the 21st century.

I suspect this is not an accident. God gave us the book of Revelation in a form that would allow every generation of Christians to see themselves in the story. The very elasticity of the images and symbols make this possible. The first or second century Christians may have looked at the beast and seen the Roman Empire. But it is not hard to identify other beasts that have arisen since then. Every generation of Christians is meant to see themselves in this story, and the same is true for the entire Bible.

Revising Our Own Life Stories

When the Christian faith is seen as a story with a plot, it gives new meaning to the concept of conversion. Conversion happens when the plot embedded in the Christian story collides with the life story of individuals or groups. In his book *The Promise of Narrative Theology: Recovering the Gospel in the Church,* George Stroup writes,

> The individual's decision to see and live in the world by means of (the Christian) narrative is what Christians call "faith" and the process by which the community's faith and narratives become the individual's is what Christians refer to as "conversion."[1]

As an example, Stroup recalls the story of St. Augustine. In book IV of the *Confessions,* Augustine describes nine years of his life between the ages of 19 and 28. During this time he was a teacher of rhetoric. He had many students eager to learn from him the art of persuasion. His grasp of philosophy astonished his friends, and he entered competitions in reciting dramatic verse. He was also a practitioner of the Manichean religion, believing it to be the best explanation for the problem of evil in the world. If at the age of 28 Augustine had told his life story, he would have described how he became successful and prosperous because of his rigorous intellect and his unflinching commitment to the truth.

But by the age of 43 Augustine had a very different perspective on those years. In the *Confessions* he writes,

> During the space of those nine years, from the nineteenth to the twenty-eighth year of my life, I was led astray myself and led others astray in my turn. We were alike deceivers and deceived in all our different aims and ambitions, both publicly when we expounded our so-called liberal ideas, and in private through our service to what we called religion. In public we were cocksure, in private superstitious, and everywhere void and empty.[2]

This change in the way Augustine tells his life story came as a result of his encounter with the Bible and with several important Christian teachers. When he came to believe the Christian story, it changed the way he saw his own story. He became part of a new story, a plot different than he had previously envisioned for himself.

A more recent example is Charles Colson, the former White House counsel to President Nixon. If Chuck Colson had written his biography in 1972, he would have told the story of a star student in a prep school who became a Marine, then an attorney, and finally the special counsel to the President of the United States. But when he wrote his autobiography, *Born Again,* in 1976, after spending seven months in jail, he told a very different story. The difference resulted from his encounter with the Christian story through a man named Tom Phillips. Phillips reads to him a description of pride from C. S. Lewis' book *Mere Christianity.* Colson writes,

> Just as a man about to die is supposed to see flash before him, sequence by sequence, the high points of his life, so as Tom's voice read on that August evening, key events in my life paraded before me as if projected on a screen. Things I hadn't thought about in years—my graduation speech at prep school—being "good enough" for the Marines— my first marriage into the "right" family—sitting

on the Jaycees' dais while civic leader after civic leader praised me as the outstanding young man of Boston—then to the White House—the clawing and straining for status and position ...

Now, sitting there on the dimly lit porch, my self-centered past was washing over me in waves. It was painful. Agony. Desperately I tried to defend myself. What about my sacrifices for government service, the giving up of a big income, putting my stocks in a blind trust? The truth, I saw in an instant, was that I'd wanted the position in the White House more than I'd wanted money. There was no sacrifice....It was pride—Lewis's "great sin"—that had propelled me through life.[3]

For Chuck Colson, conversion happened when his encounter with the Christian story caused him to see his own life story in a totally new light.

Working from a Different Script

Here is a movie trivia question. What do the following characters have in common: a drunken women's baseball manager, a gay Philadelphia lawyer, a developmentally challenged shrimp boat captain, an army lieutenant in World War II, an astronaut, and an international shipping manager for Federal Express? All of these characters were played by the same actor: Tom Hanks. How does the same actor become a drunken baseball manager in *A League of Their Own*, a gay lawyer in *Philadelphia*, a shrimp boat captain in *Forrest Gump*, an army lieutenant in *Saving Private Ryan*, an astronaut in *Apollo 13*, and a Fed Ex manager in *Cast Away*? The answer is by working from a different script. Changing the script changes the character.

Becoming part of the Bible's plot is an invitation to live in a different script. We saw examples of this in the life of St. Augustine and Charles Colson. An even more dramatic example is the story of Philip Prasad. Philip Prasad was born in India to parents who were Dalits—Untouchables—

the lowest class in India's Hindu culture. He describes his childhood in these words:

> By age of seven, I had mastered the art of behaving like an Untouchable! I was growing up in a bleak, filthy, foul smelling, depressing to this day, Untouchable colony of Kot Mohalla....Schools and education were not in the consciousness of the entire colony. I never heard of anyone talk about getting out of the hellhole and living like other people whose latrines our mothers cleaned to fill our stomachs. There seemed no other life possible for the Untouchables, as we were born in filth, worked in filth, and died in filth. Only later in life would I learn from my father that our mode of existence was sealed in the *The Law of Manu*, the Hindu social code written two millennia ago. The code prescribed our mode of work, our duties, our degrading names, and the place where we should live. The entire Indian society is living according to the script laid out in this book.[4]

Philip Prasad grew up living according to the script laid out for him by his culture. But then Philip's parents became Christians as a result of a Presbyterian missionary who worked about a mile away. They learned a different script. His father realized that he did not have to believe in or obey the caste system and the rules it laid down for the Untouchables. He acquired some books, and with the help of a missionary he mastered both Hindi and Urdu languages. He was then sent to a Presbyterian seminary in India and was ordained to serve a circuit of 60 villages, which he did for 42 years. He also taught his wife, who ran a school for the Untouchable children in a rural village.

Philip himself eventually went to a Christian high school, graduated from a Presbyterian college in India, attended a Presbyterian seminary in Dubuque, Iowa, and returned to India to start village and residential Christian schools and hundreds of churches. He gives numerous examples of how Dalit Christians have learned to live from a different script. One Dalit pastor went to the leaders of his village and said,

"My people no longer clean latrines. We have a new master who expects more from us." The village leaders were upset, but the pastor continued, "The latrine in our village was built by the government, was it not?" The village leaders nodded. "So if we clean this latrine we would be working for the government, would we not?" Again the leaders nodded. "Now all government servants get paid good salaries, do they not?" "Yes," the leaders admitted. The pastor said, "Don't these people in your village who have served you well for centuries deserve a good salary from the government? We will clean your latrines, but in the future we expect to be paid for it like the government workers of other castes."[5]

"We have a new master who expects more from us." That is the script of a chosen people, like the chosen people we have read about so far:

- Abraham, who was called to go out to an unknown land.
- Moses, who dares to tell Pharaoh, "Let my people go that they may worship the Lord."
- David, who takes on Goliath.
- The apostle Paul, who says, "For you were bought with a price; therefore glorify God in your body."

Such people are not intimidated by their lowly status. They recall God's tendency to choose unexpected people and use them in surprising ways to bring God's blessing to the world.

Fitting Ourselves to the Story; Not the Story to Us

In his book, *Mimesis*, Erich Auerbach contrasts the story of the Bible to Homer's epic poem, *The Odyssey*. He writes,

The Scripture stories do not, like Homer's, court our favor, they do not flatter us that they may please us and enchant us—they seek to subject us, and if we refuse we are rebels....Far from seeking, like Homer, merely to make us forget our own reality for a few hours, it seeks to overcome our reality: we are to fit our own life into its world, feel ourselves to be elements in this structure of universal history.[6]

I recently picked up a book called *The Jefferson Bible*. It contains Thomas Jefferson's own edited copy of the Bible. It is fairly thin because he left most of it out. First, he left out the entire Old Testament, because he viewed the Jews with disdain. He said, "Their ideas of (God) and of (God's) attributes were degrading and injurious. Their ethics were not only imperfect, but often irreconcilable with the sound dictates of reason and morality ...."[7] He also left out much of the New Testament. He includes nothing about Jesus' virgin birth or any of the miracles Jesus did. Instead his entire Bible consists of Jesus' parables and sayings, with only a few references to stories of Jesus' life. He tells of Jesus' arrest and crucifixion, but his Bible ends with these words: "Now in the place where he was crucified there was a garden; and in the garden a new sepulcher, wherein never man yet laid. There laid they Jesus: and rolled a great stone to the door of the sepulcher, and departed."[8]

That is the end of Jefferson's Bible. Jesus comes off like a wise, rational, liberal-minded product of the Enlightenment—a kind of ancient Middle Eastern Thomas Jefferson!

The goal of the Bible, however, is not to make the Bible fit our life stories, but to make our lives fit into the Bible's story—to make us part of the Bible's plot. To become followers of Jesus means to become participants in this story:

- To live as heirs of God's promise to Abraham, bringing blessing to all the families of the earth.
- To live as citizens of Jesus' eternal kingdom, where swords are beaten into plowshares and spears into pruning hooks.
- To live as witnesses of the new creation by the power of the Holy Spirit, even as we wait for it.

Understanding the Bible's plot is not just an exercise in literary criticism; it is a spiritual discipline for Christian faithfulness. Understanding the Bible's plot can save us from anti-Semitism—from thinking that the church has replaced Israel and that the Jews can be eliminated. It can also save us from uncritical support of Israel, America, or any other nation that forgets God's ultimate goal: to bring blessing to the world and healing to the creation. When we remember the Bible's plot, we no longer confuse being chosen with being powerful, successful, or rich. The Bible's plot prevents us from blaming God for our problems or despairing that God can yet do anything with us. It reminds us of God's concern for the real world of environment, economics, politics, and family life. But it also prevents us from too closely aligning God's work with any individual, party, or government. Remembering the Bible's plot can give dignity and seriousness to our feeble attempts to serve God in this life, even if the results of those efforts are not seen in our lifetime.

The story is told that one day Christopher Wren, the great British architect, was walking through the building site for St. Paul's Cathedral. He saw a man mixing mortar and asked what he was doing. The man replied, "Sir, I am building a great cathedral."[9]

You may view your life as a lowly mason, mortaring bricks into a wall. But if you see the big picture, you will realize that you are building a great cathedral. You are part of God's centuries long plan to reverse the curse of sin on the creation and bring blessing to all the families of the earth.

In the Bible's plot we are saved by grace. Abraham was chosen before he had done anything to merit that choice. So was David. So are we. But we were not chosen for God's team in order to sit on the bench. Our lives for God may not be perfect. Neither was David's or Abraham's. But they can still make a difference. In the kingdom of God the witness of Israel (the 12 gates) and the witness of the church (the 12 foundations) are built into the structure of the new Jerusalem, and we, even in our weakness and fallibility, can be part of it.

Questions for Reflection

1. In what ways has reading the Bible (and this book) changed the way you view your past?

2. In what ways has reading the Bible (and this book) changed the way you view your future?
3. Where do you see yourself in the Bible's plot? With what characters or time periods do you most identify?
4. How does the Bible's plot change the way you view the Jews? The Arabs? Americans? Any kind of foreigners?

Appendix A:
Order of Bible Stories

Here is the correct order of Bible stories mentioned on the first page of the introduction:

1. Adam and Eve eat the forbidden fruit.
2. Noah builds the ark.
3. Abraham almost sacrifices his son Isaac.
4. Joseph is sold into slavery in Egypt.
5. Moses parts the Red Sea and leads the Israelites out of slavery.
6. Joshua wins the battle of Jericho.
7. David slays Goliath.
8. The Babylonians destroy Jerusalem and take the people of Israel into exile.
9. Daniel survives in the lions' den.
10. Jesus is born in Bethlehem.
11. Jesus is crucified and rises from the dead.
12. The church grows and spreads across the Mediterranean.

Appendix B: The Prophets and Kings of Israel and Judah

(Dates indicate approximate beginning of reign, B. C. E.)

Kings of Judah	Prophets	Kings of Israel
David (1010)	Nathan	David (1010)
Solomon (970)		Solomon (970)
Rehoboam (931)		Jeroboam (931)
Abijah (913)		Nadab (910)
Asa (911)		Baasha (909)
		Elah (886)
		Zimri/Omri (885)
Jehoshaphat (870)	Elijah	Ahab (874)
	Elisha	Ahaziah (853)
Jehoram (848)		Joram (852)
Ahaziah/Queen Athaliah (841)		Jehu (841)
Joash (835)		Jehoahaz (814)
Amaziah (796)	Amos	Jehoash (798)
Uzziah (781)	Hosea	Jeroboam II (793)
		Zechariah (743)
Jotham (740)	Isaiah	Sallum/Menahem (743)
Ahaz (736)	Micah	Pekahiah (738)
Hezekiah (716)		Pekah (737)
		Hoshea (732)
		Fall of Samaria (722)
Manasseh (687)		
Amon (642)	Zephaniah	
Josiah (640)	Jeremiah	
Jehoahaz/Jehoiakim (609)		
Jehoiachin/Zedekiah (598)		
Fall of Jerusalem/Exile (587)	Ezekiel	
	Daniel	
Return from Exile (538)	Haggai	
	Zechariah	
	Prophets whose time period is not given: Joel, Obadiah, Jonah, Nahum, Habakkuk, and Malachi	

Notes

Introduction

[1]William Willimon, "Making a Mark on the World," *Pulpit Resource*, Vol. 35, No. 3 (July-September, 2007):11.

[2]E. M. Forester, *Aspect of the Novel* (New York: Harcourt, Brace, and Company, 1954): 130.

[3]Laurie Kirszner and Stephen Mandell, *Portable Literature: Reading, Reacting, Writing*, Sixth Edition (Boston: Thomson Wadsworth, 2007), 101.

[4]Hans Frei, *The Eclipse of the Biblical Narrative: A Study of Eighteenth and Nineteenth Century Hermeneutics* (New Haven: Yale University Press, 1974).

Chapter 1

[1]Bill Watterson, *The Complete Calvin and Hobbes, Book Two* (Kansas City, MO: Andrews McMeel Publishing, 2005); 199.

[2]"By arranging the motif of rest into the creation week, (Genesis) has given creation the character of an event that moves through time toward its goal. " Claus Westerman, *Genesis 1-11: A Commentary*, translated by John Scullion. (Minneapolis: Augsburg Publishing House, 1974): 90.

[3]"Just as powerful earthly kings, to indicate their claim to dominion, erect an image of themselves in the provinces of their empire when they do not personally appear, so (the human) is placed upon the earth in God's image as God's sovereign emblem. He is really only God's representative, summoned to maintain and enforce God's claim to dominion over the earth." Gerhard von Rad, *Genesis: A Commentary*, translated by John Marks (Philadelphia: The Westminster Press, 1972):60.

[4]Lesslie Newbegin, *Foolishness to the Greeks: The Gospel in Western Culture* (Grand Rapids: William B. Eerdmans, 1986): 81.

[5]"So the serpent holds out less the prospect of an extension of the capacity for knowledge than the independence that enables a man to decide for himself what will help or hinder him.... God had provided what was good for man (2:18!), and had given him complete security. But now man will go beyond this, to decide for himself." Von Rad, *Genesis*: 89.

[6]"Obviously the narrator wants to remove the acceptance of the sacrifice from man and place it completely within God's free will. He refrains from making the decision for Abel and against Cain logically comprehensible ("I will be gracious to whom I will be gracious, and will show mercy on whom I will show mercy," Exodus 33:19). Von Rad, *Genesis*: 104.

[7]See the discussion of this episode in Walter Brueggemann, *Genesis: A Bible Commentary for Teaching and Preaching* (Atlanta: John Knox Press, 1982): 90.

Chapter 2

[1]Claus Westermann, *Genesis 12-36: A Commentary*, translated by John J. Scullion (Minneapolis, Augsburg Publishing House, 1981): 152.

[2]Gerhard von Rad, *Genesis: A Commentary* Revised Edition (Philadelphia: The Westminster Press, 1972): 160.

[3]For an extended discussion of God's gift of land to Israel and the responsibility that

entails for being a blessing to other nations, see W. Eugene March, *Israel and the Politics of Land: A Theological Case Study* (Louisville, KY: Westminster/John Knox Press, 1994).

[4]For a detailed treatment of how Esau, the non-chosen one, shows evidence of being blessed by God, see Frank Spina, *The Faith of the Outsider: Exclusion and Inclusion in the Biblical Story* (Grand Rapids: William B. Eerdmans, 2005): 14-34.

[5]For a more detailed explanation of the story of Tamar, see Spina: 35-51.

Chapter 3

[1]Stan Hughes, "On the Lighter Side: Playground Justice," *Something Better*, February-March, 1993: 5.

[2]In the Anchor Bible, William Propp suggests that Pharaoh's plan is to keep the female slaves so they can be given as wives to Egyptian slaves and produce offspring that will identify themselves as Egyptians rather than Hebrews. He points out that at later times in their history, the people of Israel do the same thing to other nations (see Numbers 31:1-18). William H. C. Propp, *Exodus 1-18—The Anchor Bible: A New Translation with Introduction and Commentary* (New York: Doubleday, 1998): 141.

[3]In his commentary on Exodus, Terrence Fretheim says, "The plagues may thus be viewed as the effect of Pharaoh's anticreational sins upon the cosmic order writ large. ...Their sequencing does have a certain naturalness to it—frogs leaving bloody water, flies drawn to dead piles of frogs, and so forth. But these continuities really serve this purpose: to show that the elements of the natural order are *not* what they were created to be and to do. Their "behaviors" break the bounds of their createdness. It is a picture of creation gone beserk." Terrence Fretheim, *Exodus: A Commentary for Teaching and Preaching*, Louisville: John Knox Press, 1991): 106-110.

[4]The same Hebrew word here translated "revel" is used in Genesis 39:14 to describe the alleged sexual assault on Potiphar's wife.

[5]For a full discussion of Rahab and the nature of her "house," see Spina, pp.53-58.

[6]J. Alberto Soggin calls it less a battle than a liturgy. J. Alberto Soggin, *Joshua: A Commentary* (Philadelphia: Westminster Press, 1972): 86-87.

Chapter 4

[1]For Ruth to uncover Boaz's feet and lie next to him is loaded with sexual innuendo. The word translated "uncover" often occurs in the context of sexual relations (see all the references to uncovering nakedness in Leviticus 18:6-19). In Hebrew, as in English, to "lie" with someone has sexual connotations (Deuteronomy 22:28-29). Robert Hubbard, Jr. *The Book of Ruth* (Grand Rapids, Michigan: William B. Eerdmans Publishing, 1988): 203-204.

[2]Walter Brueggemann, *First and Second Samuel* (Louisville, KY: John Knox Press, 1990): 98-99.

[3]Brueggemann, *First and Second Samuel*: 255-256.

[4]See II Samuel 3:2-5 for a list of David's five oldest sons. The oldest, Amnon, was killed by the third oldest, Absalom, who in turn died in a rebellion against his father David. We do not know what happened to Chileab, the second oldest, but assuming that he is out of the picture, Adonijah is the oldest son left.

[5]Bernhard Anderson, *Understanding the Old Testament* Fourth Edition (Englewood Cliffs, NJ: Prentice Hall, 1986): 265.

[6]Anderson, *Understanding the Old Testament*: 265.

Chapter 5

[1]Some examples are Isaac making peace with Abimelech, the king of the Philistines (Genesis 26), Jacob making peace with his brother Esau, patriarch of the Edomites (Genesis 33), and God instructing Moses to live in peace with the people of Moab (Deuteronomy 2).

[2]James Crenshaw, *Old Testament Wisdom: An Introduction* (Atlanta: John Knox Press, 1981): 116-117.

[3]Harriet Beecher Stowe, *Uncle Tom's Cabin* (New York: Signet Classic, 1998): 422.

[4]In commenting on Job 42:5 Marvin Pope says, "In what sense has Job 'seen' God?...He had hoped for assurance that God was on his side and would vindicate him. This, he insisted, 19:23-27, must come somehow—if not during his life, then later. Now that God has spoken directly to him, Job's demands have been met." Marvin H. Pope, *Job*. The Anchor Bible (New York: Doubleday and Company, 1965): 348.

[5]Bernard Anderson, *Out of the Depths: The Psalms Speak for Us Today* Revised and Expanded Edition (Philadelphia: The Westminster Press, 1983): 30.

[6]"The introduction to the Psalter does not conclude with Psalm 1. It carries over to the second Psalm, as is immediately evident by the absence of a superscription at the beginning of Psalm 2 to mark it off from Psalm 1, as well as by the presence of a concluding "Blessed ..." clause at the end of Psalm 2, which echoes the "Blessed..." clause at the beginning of Psalm 1 and forms a poetic bracket or envelope around both psalms in a way that shows them to be a two part introduction to all that follows." Patrick Miller, *Interpreting the Psalms* (Philadelphia: Fortress Press, 1986): 87. See also Anderson, *Out of the Depths*: 22-23.

[7]There is no unanimous agreement on which psalms should be described as psalms of lament (communal or individual) and which should be described as psalms of thanksgiving or praise (communal or individual). Below is a chart showing how they are categorized by two scholars: Bernard Anderson, *Out of the Depths*, and Claus Westermann *The Psalms: Structure, Context, and Message* (Minneapolis: Augsburg Publishing House, 1980).

Lament and Thanks in the Psalms

	Anderson	Westermann
Laments in Psalms 1-50	24	27
Laments in Psalm 51-100	27	26
Laments in Psalm 101-150	10	4
Thanks/Praise in Psalms 1-50	9	10
Thanks/Praise in Psalms 51-100	8	7
Thanks/Praise in Psalms 101-150	20	25

[8]Crenshaw: 67.

[9]Crenshaw: 74.

[10]The Hebrew word *koheleth*, translated "teacher" or "preacher," has an obscure meaning. It comes from a Hebrew word *kahal* that means assembly. The Greek translation of the word *kahal* is the word *ecclesia*. Hence the Greek version of the Old Testament called this book Ecclesiastes—the leader of an *ecclesia* or assembly. Some English translators thought that sounded like a preacher! Others call him a teacher.

[11]Robert Gordis, *Koheleth—the Man and His World: A Study of Ecclesiastes* (New York: Schocken Books, 1968): 58.

Chapter 6

[1]Frederick B. Speakman, *The Salty Tang* (Westwood, NJ: Fleming H. Revell Company, 1954): 61-62.

[2]Gerhard Von Rad summarizes the new twist in the plot envisioned by the prophets: "(The prophets) regard the coming judgment as sealing the end of Israel's present existence; the security given her by these election traditions is cancelled out because of her guilt. The only thing she can hold on to is a new historical act on the part of Jahweh, the outlines of which the prophets already see, and to which they point with kindled emotions. The prophetic message differs from all previous Israelite theology, which was based on past saving history, in that the prophets looked for the decisive factor in Israel's whole existence—her life or her death—in some future event." Gerhard von Rad, *Old Testament Theology, Volume II: The Theology of Israel's Prophetic Traditions*, translated by D. M. G. Stalker (New York: Harper and Row, 1965): 117. In the rest of the chapter I will try to explain this statement: first by describing how Israel's sin threatened to destroy the covenant and promises God had made (what von Rad calls the "election traditions") and then by describing the radically new basis for Israel's relationship to God envisioned by the prophets.

[3]For other examples see Micah 2:1-2 (economic exploitation), Malachi 2:13-16 (marital unfaithfulness), and Isaiah 42:17 (worship of other gods). Also note Jeremiah 7:1-11and Ezekiel 22:1-12 where all three areas are mentioned together. Many other examples could be cited.

[4]This expression comes from Walter Brueggemann, *The Bible Makes Sense* Revised Edition (Cincinnati, OH: St. Anthony Messenger Press, 2003): 82.

[5]For this interpretation of Jeremiah 30 I am indebted to Walter Brueggemann, *Hopeful Imagination: Prophetic Voices in Exile* (Philadelphia: Fortress Press, 1986): 35-41.

[6]Von Rad. *Old Testament Theology, Volume II*, p. 170.

Chapter 7

[1]For a discussion of some of the sources that make up the Old Testament see Bernhard Anderson, *Understanding the Old Testament* Fourth Edition (Englewood Cliffs, NY: Prentice Hall, Inc., 1986): 19-22.

[2]"History shows, therefore, that the early church opted for a plurality of gospels within limits and that it set considerable store on preserving intact the distinctiveness of each one. What this means theologically is that the early church placed great value on having at its disposal a number of Gospels which it could regard as authoritative and which, because of the distinctiveness of each, could bear multifaceted witness to the essentially multifaceted revelation of God in Jesus Christ." Jack Dean Kingsbury, "The Gospel in Four Editions" in *Interpreting the Gospels*, edited by James Luther Mays (Philadelphia: Fortress Press, 1981): 27.

[3]See an extended discussion of the meaning of the phrase "I am" in Raymond E. Brown, *The Gospel According to John I-XII* (Garden City, NY: Doubleday and Company, 1966): 533-538.

[4]Ben and Carol Weir, *Hostage Bound, Hostage Free* (Philadelphia: The Westminster Press, 1987): 106.

[5]This is the meaning of the time reference in John 19:14. Raymond E. Brown, *The Gospel According to John XIII-XXI* (Garden City, NY: Doubleday and Company, 1966): 883.

[6]Richard Nixon, *In the Arena: A Memoir of Victory, Defeat, and Renewal* (New York: Simon and Schuster, 1990): 89.

[7]C. S. Lewis, *Miracles* (San Francisco: Harper Collins, 2001): 263.

[8]Joachim Jeremias, *Jesus' Promise to the Nations* (Philadelphia: Fortress Press, 1982): 21.

[9]"That there are other sheep who belong to the fold introduces the Gentile mission." Brown, *The Gospel According to John I-XII*: 396.

Chapter 8

[1]From "The Northern Suburbs: Haggerston and Hackney," *Old and New London: Volume 5* (1978): 505-524. URL: http://www.brithish-history.ac.uk/report.aspx?compid=4254

[2]Ernst Haenchen notes that the names of the seven are "Greek without exception." Ernst Haenchen, *The Acts of the Apostles* (Philadelphia: the Westminster Press, 1971): 267.

[3]J. Christiaan Beker notes that the tone of Romans is very different from Galatians, mainly because of differences in their situations. "In Rome he is dealing with a mixed church, not a purely Gentile church as in Galatia." J. Christiaan Beker, *Paul the Apostle: The Triumph of God in Life and Thought* (Philadelphia: Fortress Press, 1980): 70.

[4]"The church of the Gentiles is an extension of the promises of God to Israel and not Israel's displacement." Beker, *Paul*: 332.

[5]"Moreover, unless God's promises to Israel can be trusted, how can they trust His faithfulness and promise in Christ?" Beker, *Paul*: 336.

[6]Gordon Fee, *The First Epistle to the Corinthians* (Grand Rapids, MI: William B. Eerdmans Publishing, 1987): 563-564. In this context the issue is not whether the Corinthians appreciate the real presence of Christ in communion but whether they appreciate each other as members of the body of Christ. Paul anticipates this issue and this particular use of the term "body" in I Corinthians 10:17—"Because there is one bread, we who are many are one body, for we all partake of the one bread."

[7]"In terms of their theology, then, a resurrection of the dead (i.e., a resurrection of dead bodies) is both disgusting (because the body is inimical to salvation) and unnecessary (because our spiritual union with Christ is the redemption of our true self)." Beker, *Paul*: 166.

[8]Beker, *Paul*: 314.

[9]"It is because the Colossian false teachers raise doubts about Christ having overcome the spirit world and seek to ingratiate themselves with these powers by cultic and ascetic measure—which efforts have impressed a segment of the community—that Paul stresses the cosmic role of Christ and the overcoming of the spiritual powers by him." Werner Georg Kummel, *Introduction to the New Testament*, revised edition, translated by Howard Clark Kee (Nashville: Abingdon Press, 1975): 340.

[10]Fee, *The First Epistle to the Corinthians*: 208-213. To hand the man over to Satan means to let him experience life in a world dominated by Satan instead of by Christ. The destruction of the flesh refers not to physical death but to destruction of fleshly desires aimed at sin (see

Galatians 5:24). The goal is not to kill the man but to bring him back to salvation in Christ.

[11]"The present period of the Church is the time between the decisive battle, which has already occurred, and the 'Victory Day.'" Oscar Cullman, *Christ and Time: the Primitive Christian Conception of Time and History*, translated by Floyd V. Filson (Philadelphia: The Westminster Press, 1950): 145.

[12]Gordon Fee defends a translation similar to this against the New Revised Standard Version. Fee, *The First Epistle to the Corinthians*: 316-318.

Chapter 9

[1]Hal Lindsey, *The Late Great Planet Earth* (Grand Rapids, Michigan: Zondervan Publishing, 1970). "Hal Lindsey's *The Late Great Planet Earth*, published in 1970, became the best-selling non-fiction book of its decade." *Time*, July 1, 2002.

[2]*Newsweek*, November 27, 2006.

[3]For a more complete review of the history of interpreting Revelation, see Isbon T. Beckwith, *The Apocalypse of John: Studies in Introduction* (New York: The MacMillan Co., 1919): 318-334.

[4]John J. Collins, *Daniel: A Commentary of the Book of Daniel* (Minneapolis: Fortress Press, 1993): 297-299.

[5]Scott Stantis, *The Spokesman-Review*, December 26, 2006.

[6]"The ancient Mesopotamian city of Babylon had become the political and religious capital of a world empire, renowned for its luxury and moral corruption. Above all it was the great enemy of the people of God. For the early church the city of Rome was a contemporary Babylon." Robert Mounce, *The Book of Revelation* (Grand Rapids, MI: William B. Eerdmans, 1977): 273.

[7]Bruce Metzger, *Breaking the Code: Understanding the Book of Revelation* (Nashville: Abingdon Press, 1993): 13.

[8]"Its primary reference is to the period of the Jewish suffering under the Syrian despot Antiochous Epiphanes in 167-164 BC. It became a conventional symbol for a limited period of time during which evil would be allowed free rein." Mounce, *Revelation*: 221.

[9]After reviewing the problems with other interpretations, G. B. Caird suggests that "the content of the scroll is God's redemptive plan, foreshadowed in the Old Testament, by which he means to assert his sovereignty over a sinful world and so to achieve the purpose of creation." G. B. Caird, *A Commentary on the Revelation of St. John the Divine* (Peabody, MA: Hendrickson Publishers, 1966): 72.

[10]Philip Yancey, *The Bible Jesus Read* (Grand Rapids, MI: Zondervan Publishing, 1999): 213.

[11]*Time*, March 18, 1991.

[12]I am indebted to Barbara Rossing for this image. Barbara Rossing, *The Rapture Exposed* (Boulder, CO: Westview Press, 2004): 147.

[13]Article by Benjamin Weir, *Mission Yearbook of Prayer and Study* (Louisville, KY: Presbyterian Publishing House, 1984).

Chapter 10

[1]George W. Stroup, *The Promise of Narrative Theology: Recovering the Gospel in the Church* (Eugene, OR: Wipf and Stock Publishers, 1981): 174-175.

[2]*Saint Augustine Confessions* (New York: Penguin Books, 1978):71.

[3]Charles W. Colson, *Born Again* (New York: Bantam Books, 1977): 124-125.

[4]*Witnessing Ministries of Christ Annual Performance Report, July 1998-June 1999* (Fresno, CA: Witnessing Ministries of Christ, 1999).

[5]*Witnessing Ministries of Christ Annual Performance Report July 1999 – June 2000* (Fresno, CA: Witnessing Ministries of Christ, 2000).

[6]Erich Auerbach, *Mimesis: The Representation of Reality in Western Literature*, translated by Willard R. Task, Fiftieth Anniversary Edition (Princeton, NJ: Princeton University Press, 2003): 15.

[7]Thomas Jefferson, *The Jefferson Bible: the Life and Morals of Jesus of Nazareth* (Mineola, NY: Dover Publications, Inc., 2006): 9.

[8]Jefferson: 92.

[9]Told by Anthony Campolo, *The Success Fantasy* (Wheaton, Illinois: Victor Books, 1985): 81.

Index of Ten Plot Patterns
in the Bible

1. Promise, threat, and deliverance: *16, 24, 36, 44, 60f, 77f, 83, 92f, 104, 112ff, 157, 167, 193f*

2. The ripple effect of sin: *15ff, 19, 32, 39, 42, 68, 72, 108f, 122f, 147, 157, 165, 188ff*

3. God's tendency to choose unexpected people: *17, 25, 26, 41, 63, 124, 133, 183, 206, 208*

4. The narrowing of God's focus in order later to expand it: *17, 25, 32, 66f, 123f, 128f, 183*

5. A covenant relationship between God and people where both are bound by certain commitments: *18, 26f, 47f, 67, 91, 105f, 115, 143, 162*

6. The sovereignty of God displayed through ironic use of human actions: *31, 36f, 40, 43, 64, 83, 116, 144, 156, 167*

7. Concern for the real world of environment, economics, politics, and family life: *25, 37, 47, 60, 108, 133, 146f, 155, 166f, 208*

8. Foreshadowing of later twists in the plot: *10, 20, 26, 31, 35, 42, 48, 63, 107, 114, 117, 122, 125, 132*

9. Living for a promise not fulfilled in one's lifetime: *30, 50f, 125, 172, 208*

10. The fulfillment of God's promises through a person rejected by God's people: *36, 41, 49, 50f, 64, 124, 137f, 157, 183f,*

Index of Scripture References

LaVergne, TN USA
23 February 2010
174052LV00004B/49/P